BRITISH LIBRARY HISTORY: BIBLIOGRAPHY 1977–1980

edited b

Denis F. Keeling

Compiled by

| Mrs A.H. Brodie | R.E. Huws | D.F. Keeling |
| K.A. Manley | | P. Reynolds |

of the
Library History Group of the Library Association

Library Association London 1983

© 1983 The Library Association. Library History Group of the Library Association, 7 Ridgmount Street, London WC1E 7AE and printed and bound in Great Britain by Bookmag, Inverness.

British Library Cataloguing in Publication Data

British library history, 1977–1980.
  1. Libraries——Great Britain——History——Bibliography.
  I. Keeling, Denis F.   II. Library Association.
  Library History Group
  016.21'00941   Z791.A1

ISBN 0 85365 805 6

CONTENTS

PERIODICAL TITLES ABBREVIATIONS

Aslib Proc.   Aslib Proceedings
Asst Libn   Assistant Librarian
Bod.Lib.Rec.   Bodleian Library Record
Bk Coll.   Book Collector
Bkseller   Bookseller
Br.Lib.J.   British Library Journal
Bull.ABTAPL   Bulletin of the Association of British Theological and Philosophical Libraries
Bull.John Rylands Univ.Lib. of Manchester   Bulletin of the John Rylands University Library of Manchester
Herald of Lib.Sci.   Herald of Library Science
J.Docum.   Journal of Documentation
J.Librarianship   Journal of Librarianship
J.Lib.Hist.   Journal of Library History
J.Welsh Bibl.Soc.   Journal of the Welsh Bibliographical Society
Lib.Assn.Medical Section Bulletin   Library Association Medical Section Bulletin
Lib.Assn. Rare Books Group Newsletter   Library Association Rare Books Group Newsletter
Lib.Assn.Rec.   Library Association Record
Lib.Hist.   Library History
Lib.Hist.Rev.   Library History Review
Lib.Q.   Library Quarterly
Lib.Rev.   Library Review
New Lib.World   New Library World
Pap. Bibl.Soc.Am.   Papers of the Bibliographical Society of America
Private Lib.   Private Library
S.L.A. News   Scottish Library Association News
T.L.S.   Times Literary Supplement
Trans. Cambridge Bibl.Soc.   Transactions of the Cambridge Bibliographical Society

INTRODUCTION

In the introduction to the previous *Supplement* I raised the matter of the availability of sources for the library historian of the future. During the last two years this has received the attention of the Library History Group, and has been the subject of an article in the July 1980 Library Association *Record* by Paul Sturges (3159) of Loughborough University Department of Library and Information Studies. In it he summarizes the results of a questionnaire on the provision British public libraries are currently making for the preservation and care of their own administrative records.

I also drew attention to the need for some form of minimum standard for the writing of librarians' obituaries. This was also considered by the Committee of the Library History Group, and on their behalf I prepared some guidance notes which were printed in the May 1981 Library Association *Record*.

This *Supplement* contains 826 entries, compared with 766 in the 1973–1976 *Supplement* and 746 in the volume covering 1969–1972. This is partly accounted for by a 55% increase in the number of entries relating to librarians, and this in turn is largely accounted for by a 30% increase in obituaries. Whether this can be explained in actuarial terms or not I do not know, but this volume would seem to record the passing of a whole generation of librarians born in the Edwardian era. Particularly sad from our point of view was the death of the library historian Raymond Irwin, the Group's first Chairman, and of the centenarian Frederick Charles Morgan. The latter had undertaken one library role or another for 81 years, until he almost personified library history.

Also included in this section are three biographical theses i.e. Bostle's on George Edward Roebuck (2443), Hendry's on Septimus Pitt (2440) and Godbolt's thesis on Sir John MacAlister (2405), in addition to J.G. Ollé's biography of Savage (2445). The centenary of the death of Panizzi was celebrated by an exhibition at the British Library and ten articles and other publications recorded in this *Supplement*. One is also pleased to note J.G. Ollé's centenary tribute to Arundell Esdaile (2375).

There is also an increase in the number of items on librarianship, which is partly accounted for by articles written in celebration of the Library Association's centenary. These include J.G. Ollé's *The Library Association and the American Library Association: their first fifty years* (2510), Dr. Munford's *The American Library Association and the Library Association: retrospect, problems, and prospects* (2508) and Richard Busby and Keith Manley's *E.W.B. Nicholson, H.R. Tedder and The Library Association* (2502). In addition, a whole issue of *Herald of Library Science* volume 16 no.4 1977 is largely devoted to the centenary.

There are several useful contributions on the history of library cooperation, including Jones's thesis *Inter-library loans: retrospect and prospect* (2482), S.P.L.

Filon's *The National Central Library—a historical review* (2485) and three somewhat overlapping articles by W.H. Brown (2486–8) on the development of library cooperation in Scotland.

Of general studies of British library history one of the most interesting is J.B. Hood's thesis on *The origin and development of the newsroom and reading room from 1650 to date* (2529). There is also the usual batch of theses on the history of library facilities in particular localities, this time Leigh, Lancashire, Newcastle-upon-Tyne, Galashiels and Selkirkshire, Carmarthenshire and County Down, together with interesting articles on Beccles and Easter Ross.

In the field of academic libraries there are two theses on college libraries, namely R.V. Fox's *The development of technological university libraries from the libraries of the colleges of advanced technology* (2536) and *The evolution of libraries in colleges for the education and training of teachers* by S.T. Lucas (2564). Two further theses deal with school libraries, J.M. Potter's *Old school libraries of Lancashire* (2587) and H.A. Farnworth's *History of the school libraries of the London School Board 1870–1904* (2588). Significant contributions to the study of university library history include an international review edited by James Thompson, several of which articles are recorded. Studies of individual libraries include Gaskell's on Trinity College, Cambridge (2612), Durkan's on Glasgow (2621), Hall's thesis on Liverpool (2628), Hunt's chapter on New College, Oxford (2659) and Fuggles's thesis on St. John's College, Oxford (2660). Then there are A.C. Crook's two volumes which provide almost a brick by brick account of the buildings of St. John's College, Cambridge (2609–10).

There are several useful items on parochial libraries. D.E. Gerard has contributed a general article to volume 21 of the *Encyclopedia of library and information science* (2688). Two articles by David Williams refer to the growing awareness of their importance, and to losses, survivals and restorations. The significance of parochial libraries as collections in their own right, rather than as assemblages of odd volumes, and steps taken in Yorkshire to secure their future, is discussed in C.B.L. Barr's *Parish libraries in a region: the case of Yorkshire* (2706). Recent research into the parochial libraries of Suffolk and steps taken to preserve them have borne fruit in *Suffolk parochial libraries: a catalogue*, edited by A.E. Birkby and published by Mansell for the St. Edmundsbury and Ipswich Diocesan Parochial Libraries Committee (2704). R. Wilson has written a short history of St. Margaret's Church Library, King's Lynn (2697) and J.P. Ferguson a detailed study of the parochial libraries founded on the Isle of Man in the early 18th century by Bishop Wilson, who was strongly influenced by the work of Thomas Bray (2701). Lastly, Paul Morgan has tackled a neglected aspect of ecclesiastical library history, and one for which meagre sources survive, in *Nineteenth-century church lending libraries in England* (2690).

The need for a general history of working class libraries mentioned in the previous *Supplement* has been partly met by Nicholson's thesis *Working class readers and libraries: a social history 1800–1850* (2716). Two interesting studies of library provision for working class radicals are J.J. Rowley's *Drink and the* public house in Nottingham, 1830–1860 (2724) and John Noyce's *Radicalism, literacy and a pint of coffee: working people's coffee houses in London 1830–c.1836* (2722). Five articles deal with the history and restoration of the miners' library at Wenlockhead, together with a guide book.

For some reason the percentage of entries relating to public libraries continues to fall, but the overall quality remains high. There is the second edition of Professor Kelly's *History of public libraries in Great Britain* (2941) and his illustrated history intended for a wider readership (2940). There are four further contributions by Alec Ellis to the state of public libraries in the early part of this century (2930–3). R.J.B. Morris's *Parliament and the public libraries* (1948), based on the author's 1974 thesis, provides a survey of relevant legislative activity in England and Wales from 1850 to 1976. C.M. Turner's *The changing social and administrative position of the public library in England and Wales as revealed by legislative activity* (2958) identifies the main legislators and campaigners, examines their aims, motives and tactics, and shows how they were embodied in the legislation. Another analysis of the political forces surrounding public library legislation, but concentrating mainly on the 20th century, is John Pemberton's *Politics and public libraries in England and Wales* (2953). A scathing critique of the origins and development of the public library service is presented in Paul Sykes's *The public library in perspective* (2956). Theses have been written on the history of public libraries in Angus (2964), Blackburn (2968), Glamorgan (2979), Worcestershire (3012) and Worksop (3013); also Bethnal Green (2991) and Paddington (2993). A centenary history of the Mitchell Library, Glasgow was published in 1977 (2981).

By far the largest section is devoted to private libraries. Most of the items are not consciously studies in library history at all. The library interest is subsidiary, the primary concern being biography or social or architectural history. Among the major contributions are a number of monumental catalogues of individual collections. These include the first volume of the *Catalogue of the Pepys Library at Magdalene College, Cambridge* (2882), that of Isaac Newton (2873), the second edition of Sir Geoffrey Keynes's catalogue of the library of Edward Gibbon (2833), Shirley Pargeter's *Catalogue of the library at Tatton Park* (2817) and the sumptuous catalogue of the James A. de Rothschild collection of illuminated manuscripts at Waddesden Manor (2896).

Several recent books have been written by art historians on English country houses. One by Mark Girouard *Life in the English country house: a social and architectural history* (2763) became a best seller. In it he traces the development of library accommodation from the 16th century closet off the bedchamber to the communal library cum living room, reflecting its development from being the personal equipment of the owner of the house to the common property of the family and guests. Dent's article *The private library of the landed classes* (2760) considers its role in informal education in the 18th century. The primary agencies of the informal education of the gentry are seen as the private library, the family, private tutors, travel and circles of association.

Several important studies of the interior decoration and furnishing of country houses are of interest to the library historian. A general account is M.I. Wilson's *The English country house and its furnishings* (2782). Peter Thornton's *Seventeenth-century interior decoration in England, France and Holland* (2780) traces the evolution of book shelving and other items of library furniture in the three countries. A detailed study of an individual 17th century house is provided in the same author's *The furnishing and decoration of Ham House* (2865), published by the Furniture History Society. Libraries, studies and library-drawing rooms are included in John Cornforth's *English interiors 1790–1848; the quest for comfort* (2759), which reproduces contemporary watercolours, many in colour. For the furnishing of the late-19th century domestic library we are indebted to the publication of an English translation of Hermann Muthesius's Edwardian classic *Das Englische Haus* (2775).

Our knowledge of library furniture is also increased by such specialized studies as Eames's *Furniture in England, France and the Netherlands from the twelfth to the fifteenth century* (2531), published by the Furniture History Society, Christopher Gilbert's definitive monograph on Chippendale (2762), Billcliffe's *Charles Rennie Mackintosh: the complete furniture, furniture drawings and interior designs* (2755). Specifically dealing with library furniture are Clive Wainwright's *The furnishing of the Royal Library Windsor* (2923), an article on library furniture in the *Antique Collector* (2769) and an article in the *Connoisseur* on bookcases (2781).

As hinted earlier, libraries by their nature, cannot be more than a minor theme in social and intellectual history. Some of the most intriguing contributions to library history are also the most incidental, e.g. the reference in the recent biography of Elizabeth Fry (3063) to the part played by the reformer and her husband Joseph in providing libraries for all of the coast guard stations in Great Britain. There is much of human interest value, e.g. Mirsky's biography of Sir Aurel Stein (2740) with its fascinating account of his discovery of the library of Buddhist texts in the caves of the Thousand Buddhas on the edge of the Gobi Desert. Also enthralling is T.H. Hall's *Search for Harry Price* (2890) and Wesencraft's articles on *The Harry Price Library* (2891), especially the anecdote telling how Price managed to spirit 160 conjuring books past the customs officers. Particularly recommended in this respect are the two appreciations of the bibliophilic miser and eccentric Solomon Pottesman, who died in 1978. His life was devoted to the search for 'inkies' (incunables), and his most valuable treasures were hoarded in various safe deposits and vaults dotted about London. T.D. Rogers's extracts from Sir Frederic Madden's diaries (2411) throw light upon Madden's personality. It is understandable how the death of several of his children and his financial worries contributed to his embittered nature. As corpses were discovered in country house libraries in detective stories of the 1920s, it was perhaps inevitable that sooner or later sex would crop up in a library setting. In *Passion's child: the extraordinary life of Jane Digby* (2412), Madden was at Holkham in 1827 cataloguing the Long Library when his professional activities were interrupted by the arrival of Coke's daughter, Jane Digby, Lady Ellenborough... Regrettably, even this breakthrough in library history studies is unlikely to boost the sales of the *Bibliography*. Neither will *The shooting affair at Cambridge University Library* (2615), which turns out to be something of a non-event. Which brings me to the phenomenon of 'almost library history'. K.M.E. Murray's *Caught in the web of words: James A.H. Murray and the 'Oxford English Dictionary'* (2741) records Murray's attempt in 1864 and again in 1866–7 to obtain a post in the British Museum Library—without success.

It is hoped that this *Bibliography* will not be used solely for purposeful searches. The user is invited to relax and browse. It is perhaps appropriate that the term 'serendipity' was coined by that most distinguished book collector Horace Walpole.

LIBRARIANS

G E N E R A L

2336   ALA world encyclopedia of library and information services. Chicago,
       American Lib. Assn, 1980. xxii, 601p. illus, tables, ports, bibliog.
           This has a marked American and international bias, but contains some
           general historical articles and a number of brief biographical entries
           of relevance to British library history.

(2398) A. Clarke. Few and far between: women librarians in the nineteenth
        century.

2337   E. A. Clough. A decade of famous names.
       Lib.Assn Rec. 82 (1) 1980, 24-5.
           Further reminiscences of the author's contemporaries during his years
           on the Library Association Council.

2338   E. A. Clough. Gratitude for superb "professional politicians".
       Lib.Assn Rec. 81 (6) 1979, 279, 283.
           Recollection of the Library Association Council and its members,
           c.1947.

2339   W. A. Munford. Past leaders.
       In: The Library Association Centenary Conference: proceedings. Lib.
       Assn, 1977, 12-15.
           Dr. Munford has selected five of the Library Association's Honorary
           Secretaries beginning with MacAlister and ending with McColvin, and
           considers the debt we owe to each. Included are quotations from some
           of their writings.

I N D I V I D U A L

       Hubert APPLEYARD, 1909-1979
2340   [Obituary]
       Lib.Assn Rec. 82 (1) 1980, 31 (J. M. Dace)
           Hubert Appleyard was City Librarian and Curator of Lichfield from
           1946 until his retirement in 1974, when Lichfield was one of the most
           thriving small library systems in the country.

Frank William Stuart BAGULEY, 1929-1980

2341 [Obituaries]

Lib.Assn Rec. 82 (6) 1980, 281 (R. R. Lawson)

Lib.Assn Rec. 82 (8) 1980, 381 (G. Smith)

Coming to Hampshire in 1957, Frank Baguley was Assistant County
Librarian from 1974 to 1980.

Ernest A. BAKER, 1869-1941

2342 W. A. Munford. A librarian eccentric.

New Lib. World 79 (938) 1978, 145-6.

Before leaving librarianship for literary and publishing posts,
Dr. Baker was Librarian of the Midland Railway Institute at Derby,
1893-1904; Chief Librarian of Wallasey, 1904-1906 and Borough
Librarian of Woolwich, 1906-1912. Dr. Munford's vignette concentrates on the unorthodox way in which he secured the Director's
post of the School of Librarianship created at University College,
London, following the First World War, and on his literary endeavours
and enthusiasm for caving.

Jean BALLANTYNE, 1903-1976

2343 [Obituary]

Lib.Assn Rec. 79 (1) 1977, 50 (J. A. Miller)

Miss Ballantyne was appointed Borough Librarian of Crosby,
Lancashire, in 1937, and retained this post until 1961. She was at
a disadvantage owing to the need to provide a library service from
inadequate accommodation.

John Anderson BARKER, 1911-1977

2344 [Obituary]

Lib.Assn Rec. 79 (3) 1977, 164 (D.G.F. Walker)

An outline of Barker's career and interests. He was the first Deputy
Librarian of Leicester University, 1961-1973.

Hugh Desmond BARRY, 1917-1977

(2505) Hugh Barry: above all modest.

Herbert William BELMORE, 1893-1978

2345 [Obituary]

German Life and Letters 32 (2) 1979, 186 (L. Forster)

Mr. Belmore was born in South Africa, but spent most of his life in

Europe, settling finally in England in 1939. From 1943 to 1959 he served as Deputy Librarian of University College, Southampton, later the University of Southampton.

Winifred Mary BENNETTS, 1902-1979

2346 [Obituaries]

Lib.Assn Rec. 81 (5) 1979, 259 (M. M. Willis; J. E. Farmer)

Mrs. Bennetts (née Gayton) was a notable member of that group of pioneering women who were dominant in the early years of the county library movement. Her achievements as County Librarian of Cornwall from 1927 to her retirement in 1976 are noted.

Sidney George BERRIMAN, 1911-1980

2347 [Obituaries]

Lib.Assn Rec. 82 (5) 1980, 243 (P. D. Gee)

Lib.Assn Rec. 82 (7) 1980, 327 (A. M. Dimbleby; E. J. Humphreys)

After working for Essex County Libraries from 1935 to 1952, George Berriman was County Librarian of Middlesex from then until 1965, and was Director of Libraries and Museums, Cheshire, 1965-1972.

Richard Irvine BEST, 1872-1959

2348 T. de Vere White. Richard Irvine Best and his Irish literary contemporaries.

Irish University Review 7 (2) 1977, 168-83.

Best was Director of the National Library of Ireland, 1924-1940. He then became Senior Professor in the School of Celtic Studies in the newly created Institute of Advanced Studies. In 1956 he became Chairman of the Irish Manuscripts Commission. The article consists largely of anecdotes of his early associations with Moore, Joyce and Synge.

Theodore Deodatus Nathaniel BESTERMAN, 1904-1976

2349 E. J. Carter. Theodore Besterman: a personal memoir.

J. Docum. 33 (1) 1977, 79-87.

While not attempting a scholarly evaluation or detailed description of Besterman's career, this extensive memoir by a friend includes Besterman's connections with Aslib and Unesco; his research and publications, especially in connection with Voltaire studies; and includes some mention of his collection of books and pictures.

2350   [Obituary]

Lib.Assn Rec. 79 (1) 1977, 49 (F. C. Francis)

Emphasises Besterman's contribution to bibliography, and especially his "World Bibliography of Bibliographies."

Charles Wilfred BLACK, 1909-1978

2351   [Obituaries]

Lib.Assn Rec. 80 (9) 1978, 478 (W.A.G. Alison)

SLA News 1 (146) 1978, 131-2 (W.A.G. Alison)

C. W. Black was appointed Superintendent of District Libraries with Glasgow City Libraries in 1938. He was appointed Depute City Librarian in 1952 and City Librarian in 1958. He retired in 1974. During this period he was responsible for the post-war development of the service following a decade of restrictions on expenditure, opening seven new libraries, modernising four pre-war libraries and obtaining approval to extend the Mitchell Library on the adjoining St. Andrew's Hall site.

Samuel Clement BRADFORD, 1878-1948

2352   M. Gosset. S. C. Bradford, Keeper of the Science Museum Library 1925-1937: recollections of a colleague whose memory may be at fault.

J. Docum. 33 (3) 1977, 173-6.

Bradford's two main ambitions were to have the Science Museum Library accepted as the National Science Library, and to have UDC adopted universally. Both causes he promoted with energy and enthusiasm.

2353   D. J. Urquhart. S. C. Bradford.

J. Docum. 33 (3) 1977, 177-9.

After an initially unfavourable impression of Bradford and his method of working, the author came to appreciate his efforts towards the establishment of a National Science Library.

Henry BRADSHAW, 1831-1886

2354   R. Myers. George Isaac Frederick Tupper, facsimilist, 'whose ability in this description of work is beyond praise' (1820?-1911).

Trans. Cambridge Bibl. Soc. 7 (2) 1978, 113-34.

Although this article concerns the printer Tupper, there are frequent references to his friend Henry Bradshaw, University Librarian of Cambridge.

John BROGAN, 1940-1979

2355 [Obituaries]

Lib.Assn Rec. 81 (3) 1979, 153; 81 (4) 1979, 210

SLA News 1 (149) 1979, 240-1 (J.W.)

Jack Brogan began his career with Lanark County Libraries. In 1969 he went to Clydebank where he worked first as Chief Assistant and then as Depute. In 1971 he moved to Greenock as Depute, returning to Clydebank 18 months later as Chief Librarian.

James Duff BROWN, 1862-1914

2356 I. V. Malhan. James Duff Brown and his contributions.

Herald of Lib.Sci. 17 (1) 1978, 53-8.

A brief summary of his contribution to librarianship.

Edward Frank BROWNING, 1914-1978

2357 [Obituary]

Lib.Assn Rec. 80 (12) 1978, 650 (E. Stone)

Lecturer-in-charge of the School of Librarianship, Isleworth (subsequently Ealing), 1949-74.

Thomas Edward CALLANDER, 1909-1978

2358 [Obituaries]

Lib.Assn Rec. 80 (10) 1978, 527 (E. Clough)

Lib.Assn Rec. 80 (11) 1978, 585 (K. M. Newbury; A. O. Meakin)

Tom Callander was successively Chief Librarian of Coulsdon and Purley, Lambeth and Croydon. He retired in 1969. He was editor of the Library Assistant in the early 1930s, and his involvement in Library Association affairs culminated in his being elected President for 1968.

Frank CAMPBELL, 1863-1905

2359 G. Spinney. Frank Campbell 1863-1905.

Government Publications Review 4 (1) 1977, 21-9

Campbell joined the staff of the British Museum Library in 1884 and retired because of ill health in 1900. Although he received no recognition or encouragement from his superiors, he made considerable contributions in the field of government publications, national and international bibliography.

Eric CEADEL, 1921-1979

2360   [Obituary]
        Lib.Assn Rec. 82 (2) 1980, 87 (D. W. Dewhirst)
        Eric Ceadel was Librarian of Cambridge University Library from 1967
        to 1979.

        Desmond John CLARKE, 1907-1979

2361   [Obituary]
        An Leabharlann 8 (2) 1979, 39-40
        Clarke was Chief Librarian of the Royal Dublin Society until 1974, and
        was a Foundation Fellow and President of the Library Association of
        Ireland.

        Eric Allen CLOUGH, 1914-1979

2362   [Obituaries]
        Lib.Assn Rec. 82 (1) 1980, 27 (E. Dudley)
        Lib.Assn Rec. 82 (2) 1980, 87 (P. Havard-Williams; D. R. Bartlett)
        Chief Assistant Librarian of Hull, 1946-1948; Deputy of Brighton,
        1948-1951; Deputy of Bristol 1951-1963, and City Librarian of South-
        ampton from 1963 to 1974. From 1975 to 1979 Eric Clough was Research
        Fellow, School of Librarianship, Polytechnic of North London. His
        contribution to Library Association activities and publications is
        also discussed.

        Herbert COBLANS, 1909-1977

2363   E. J. Carter. Herbert Coblans: a biography.
        J. Docum. 34 (4) 1978, 259-78. port., bibliog.
        Coblans joined the staff of Aslib in 1964 and became editor of the
        Journal of Documentation in 1966. This biography and appreciation
        draws on the recollections of his professional colleagues. It is
        followed by an extensive bibliography of his writings.

2364   R. A. Fairthorne. Herbert Coblans, 1909-1977: a personal tribute.
        J. Docum. 33 (2) 1977, 103-5.
        A tribute which seeks to reflect the personality of Coblans as seen
        by the writer, rather than to chronicle his life and career. His role
        as managing editor of the Journal of Documentation is given pro-
        minence.

2365   [Obituary]
        Lib.Assn Rec. 79 (4) 1977, 228 (D. J. Foskett)
        Gives most weight to Coblan's overseas service.

6

James Watson COCKBURN, 1908-1980

2366 [Obituaries]

Lib.Assn Rec. 82 (8) 1980, 382 (C. S. Minto)

SLA News 1 (158) 1980, 120-1 (C. S. Minto)

James Cockburn joined the staff of Edinburgh Public Libraries in 1926.
He was appointed Deputy City Librarian in 1953, and became City Librarian and Curator on the retirement of C. S. Minto.

Florence Elsie COOK, 1905-1980

2367 [Obituary]

Lib.Assn Rec. 82 (8) 1980, 381 (L. Paulin)

Flora Cook was Deputy County Librarian of Kent from 1932 to 1938,
County Librarian of Cumberland from 1938 to 1945 and County Librarian
of Lancashire from 1945 to 1965.

Henry Octavius COXE, 1811-1881

(2648) K. A. Manley. A copyright problem for H. O. Coxe.

James Arthur DEARDEN, 1924-1976

2368 [Obituaries]

Bk Coll. 26 (2) 1977, 256, 258 (D. A. Harrop)

Lib.Assn Rec. 79 (3) 1977, 165 (D. A. Harrop)

After serving in the John Rylands Library and the Manchester Public
Library System, Dearden was appointed Librarian of Reading Technical
College in 1959. He held a similar post at Southampton, before being
appointed Senior Lecturer in Bibliography at the College of Librarianship, Wales in 1966. His principal interest was in type design.

Arscott Sabine Harvey DICKINSON, 1893-1979

2369 [Obituary]

Lib.Assn Rec. 81 (11) 1979, 555 (J. K. Antill)

Mr. Dickinson served as Librarian of the States of Jersey Public Library from 1934 until his retirement in 1959. He and his wife opted
to remain in Jersey at the outbreak of war, and suffered internment in
Germany from 1942-1945.

Alexander DOW, 1902-1977

2370 [Obituaries]

Lib.Assn Rec. 79 (3) 1977, 165 (W. B. Paton)

SLA News 1 (137) 1977, 208-10

After holding public library posts in Glasgow and Bolton, Dow was appointed Burgh Librarian of Coatbridge in 1935, where he remained until his retirement in 1968. He was active in professional affairs in Scotland.

Robert Forrester DREWERY, 1907-1978

2371 [Obituaries]
Lib.Assn Rec. 80 (11) 1978, 586 (J. T. Gillett)
Lib.Assn Rec. 81 (1) 1979, 11 (G. Thompson)
Bert Drewery spent his whole career in the service of Kingston-upon-Hull Public Libraries, the period 1950 to 1972 as Chief Librarian.

Alun Roderick EDWARDS, 1920-

2372 A. C. Davies. Alun R. Edwards: atgofion personal.
Llais Llyfrau Hydref 1980, 4.
Alun Creunant Davies, Director of the Welsh Books Council, records his personal reminiscences of Edwards's pioneering schemes which paved the way for the eventual founding of the Council in 1964.

2373 A. R. Edwards. Yr hedyn mwstard: atgofion Alun R. Edwards. Llandysul, Gwasg Gomer, 1980. 197p. illus, ports.
Autobiographical volume by one of the more influential Welsh public librarians. Mr. Edwards held the post of County Librarian of Cardiganshire from 1950 to 1974, and following local government re-organisation he was appointed the first County Librarian of Dyfed, a post which he occupied until his retirement in 1980. Among many aspects of his career discussed in this work are his contribution to the development of the library service in Cardiganshire, the Welsh Books Council and the College of Librarianship, Wales. His work as a member of the Bourdillon Committee (1962) and his minority report on the basic standards of provision necessary for Welsh language books is detailed in chapter 11 (pp.103-17).

Florence ELLISON, 1910-1978

2374 [Obituaries]
Lib.Assn Rec. 80 (8) 1978, 385 (R. Davidge; P. Miles)
Librarian of Royal Holloway College, 1946-70.

Arundell James Kennedy ESDAILE, 1880-1956

2375 J. G. Ollé. Arundell Esdaile: a centenary tribute.
J. Librarianship 12 (4) 1980, 217-28.

Esdaile, a 'scholar - librarian' of the best sort, spent his professional career at the British Museum, where he became Secretary. He was dominant in Library Association affairs between the wars and edited the Library Association Record after a period of committee rule. The author has included many witty and apt quotations from Esdaile's writings.

George Lancelotte EVANS, 1919-1979

2376 [Obituary]

Lib.Assn Rec. 82 (1) 1980, 27, 29 (M. Broome)
George Evans was Librarian and Curator of Hitchin from 1950 to 1951, then occupied various senior posts in Hertfordshire County Libraries before his death in 1979. He made a particularly important contribution to Hertfordshire museum and local history services.

George Ellis FLACK, 1893-1978

2377 [Obituary]

Lib.Assn Rec. 80 (5) 1978, 259 (R. S. Smith)
Librarian of University College, Nottingham (subsequently University of Nottingham) 1931-58.

Harold Gould FLETCHER, 1906-1978

2378 [Obituaries]

Lib.Assn Rec. 81 (2) 1979, 92-3 (J. R. Wood; H. C. Wise)
Deputy Borough Librarian, Cheltenham, 1927-29; Librarian and Curator successively of Stalybridge, Stafford and Leamington Spa. He was appointed Borough Librarian and Curator, Cheltenham in 1950.

Frank GARDNER, 1908-1980

2379 [Obituaries]

Lib.Assn Rec. 82 (9) 1980, 447 (R. P. Hawkes)
Lib.Assn Rec. 82 (12) 1980, 613 (L. White)
Covers his achievements as Borough Librarian of Luton from 1938 to 1971, together with his wider contribution to librarianship.

George GLAZIER, 1902-1978

2380 [Obituary]

Lib.Assn Rec. 80 (11) 1978, 586-7 (C. Muris)
George Glazier was County Librarian of Bedfordshire, 1925-67.

Sir Edmund William GOSSE, 1849-1929

2381   A. Olden.   Among tyrants: Gosse at the British Museum.
       Lib.Rev.   Vol 26 Summer 1978, 95-9.
       Edmund Gosse started work in the cataloguing department of the
       British Museum in 1867, at the age of 17, and left for a translator's
       post at the Board of Trade in 1875.   The article tells of cold, badly-
       lit rooms, ignorant and tyrannical librarians and indolent assistants
       and supervisors.

       James GREEN, 1918-1979

2382   [Obituaries]
       Lib.Assn Rec.   82 (1) 1980, 29
       Lib.Assn Rec.   82 (4) 1980, 204 (F. Sainsbury)
       Jimmy Green was Borough Librarian of East Ham from 1960, and of New-
       ham following amalgamation in 1965, until his death.

       Christopher Wharton HANSON, 1902-1979

2383   [Obituary]
       J. Docum.   35 (3) 1979, 163 (G. Woledge)
       One of the fields in which Hanson found fulfilment was scientific
       information.   From 1945-1959 he was Information Officer of the
       British Scientific Instrument Research Association.   From 1959 until
       his retirement in 1967 he was the first head of the Aslib Research
       Department.

       Cyril HARGREAVES, 1911-1977

2384   [Obituary]
       Lib.Assn Rec.   79 (5) 1977, 280 (A. E. Baker)
       As Deputy (1945-55) and later Borough Librarian (1955-73) of Bedford,
       Hargreaves introduced a number of improvements.

       Edward Rhys HARRIES, 1897-1979

2385   [Obituary]
       Lib.Assn Rec.   81 (11) 1979, 555 (G. Davies)
       Mr. Harries was County Librarian of Flintshire from the foundation of
       the County Library Service in 1925 until his retirement in 1964.

       Robert HARRISON, 1820-1897

2386   S. Gillam.   "Genial temper and ready and agreeable speech".
       Lib.Assn Rec.   79 (5) 1977, 247-9.

Harrison's early career is outlined prior to his appointment as Librarian of the London Library (1857-1893). His work there is described in detail. It was in the London Library that work preparatory to the establishment of the Library Association was undertaken, in which Harrison took part.

Daniel Denton HASLAM, 1916-1978

2387 [Obituary]
Lib.Assn Rec. 80 (10) 1978, 526 (K. C. Harrison)
Deputy Secretary of the Library Association, 1948-76.

Mary HAWORTH, 1915-1978

2388 [Obituary]
Lib.Assn Rec. 80 (11) 1978, 587 (J. S. Burden)
Deputy Borough Librarian, Kettering, 1952-74.

Thomas HEARNE, 1678-1735

2389 J. M. Levine. Dr. Woodward's shield: history, science, and satire in Augustan England. Univ. of California Press, 1977. x, 362 p. front., plates, ports.
Chapter 10 is concerned with the antiquary Thomas Hearne, and refers to his work of re-organisation at the Bodleian Library. Unfortunately, there is only the briefest mention of Dr. Woodward's library of over 4,000 volumes, most of them dealing with ancient Rome.

Reginald Harrison HILL, 1894-1976

2390 [Obituary]
Bod.Lib.Rec. 9 (6) 1978, 311-3
R. H. Hill worked in the Bodleian Library, 1908-44, latterly as Secretary to the Librarian; Librarian of the National Central Library, 1945-58.

Leslie Williams HORSFALL, 1905-1980

2391 [Obituary]
Lib.Assn Rec. 82 (12) 1980, 613 (R. Clark)
Leslie Horsfall was Borough Librarian of Kidderminster from 1939 to 1969.

E. Wyndham HULME, 1859-1954

2392 J. M. Lee. E. Wyndham Hulme: a reconsideration.

In: The variety of librarianship: essays in honour of John Wallace
Metcalfe, edited by W. Boyd Rayward. Sydney, Lib.Assn of Australia,
1976, 101-13.

> Examines Hulme's contribution to the study of cataloguing and classi-
> fication, in particular, his concept of literary warrant. His work
> is set in its historical context and his unwarranted neglect is
> accounted for.

Richard William HUNT, 1908-1979

2393 A. C. De La Mare and B. C. Barker-Benfield, editors.
Manuscripts at Oxford: an exhibition in memory of Richard William Hunt
(1908-1979), Keeper of Western Manuscripts at the Bodleian Library Oxford, 1945-1975, on themes selected and described by some of his friends.
Oxford, Bodleian Library, 1980. x, 155p. front., illus, facsims, ports.

> The introduction and several of the contributors refer to Hunt's
> achievements in the field of mediaeval manuscripts. A supplementary
> bibliography of his published writings is appended. Mediaeval lib-
> raries are also mentioned.

2394 [Obituary]
Bod.Lib.Rec. 10 (3) 1980, 143-5

> Dr. Hunt was Keeper of Western Manuscripts in the Bodleian Library
> from 1945 to 1975, and a mediaeval scholar of international repute.

Frederick George Baxendale HUTCHINGS, 1902-1978

2395 A guarded, pleasant life: an interview with F.G.B. Hutchings.
New Lib.World 78 (919) 1977, 14-17.

> This article has been condensed from a recorded interview with David
> Gerard. Hutchings talks about the public library scene since he
> joined the staff of the Mitchell Library, Glasgow in 1922, recalling
> some of the librarians under whom he served.

2396 [Obituaries]
Lib.Assn Rec. 80 (7) 1978, 365, 367 (W.B.P.)
Lib.Assn Rec. 81 (1) 1979 11 (R. B. Stokes)

> Borough Librarian, Rugby, 1932-38; Deputy City Librarian, Sheffield,
> 1938-43; Deputy City Librarian, Leeds, 1943-46; City Librarian, Leeds,
> 1946-63. President of the Library Association, 1967.

Raymond IRWIN, 1902-1977

2397 [Obituary]
Lib.Assn Rec. 79 (5) 1977, 279-80 (R. Staveley)

Irwin was County Librarian of Northampton and subsequently Lancashire
before his appointment as Director of the School of Librarianship,
University College, London in 1945. He retired in 1968. He will be
remembered particularly for his urbane and scholarly studies on
various aspects of the history of libraries.

Minnie Stewart Rhodes JAMES, 1865-1903

2398   A. Clarke. Few and far between: women librarians in the nineteenth
century.
In: One hundred years: a collection to celebrate the Library Association Centenary, by members of the library staff at CLW. Aberystwyth,
College of Librarianship Wales, 1977, 25-40.

> The first part of the article deals with the incidence of female
> employees in various kinds of 19th century libraries, and such matters
> as salaries, professional opportunities and involvement in profes-
> sional affairs. The second part follows the career of Miss Minnie
> Stewart Rhodes James, Librarian of the People's Palace in the Mile
> End Road, and discusses her contribution to librarianship, particu-
> larly in the field of the training of library assistants. A biblio-
> graphy of her published works is appended.

Christina KEOGH, 189 -1963

2399   T. Hall. Christina Keogh: pioneer - the Irish Central Library for
Students and the foundation of the Library Council.
An Leabharlann 9 (4) 1980, 123, 125-7, 129. bibliog.

> Miss Keogh was the first Librarian of the Irish Central Library for
> Students and served in that capacity from 1923 to 1960. When the
> Library Council was set up in 1948 she was appointed Secretary, and
> was indefatigable in furthering the library movement in Ireland
> throughout her career.

Derrick William KING, 1908-1980

2400   [Obituary]
Lib.Assn Rec. 82 (9) 1980, 447

> Derrick King was Librarian of the War Office from 1954 to 1973.

George Henry LAWRENCE, 1920-1977

2401   [Obituary]
Lib.Assn Rec. 79 (10) 1977, 611 (D. Harrison)

> Lawrence was Chief Librarian of Sevenoaks (1965-1974) and Librarian

of the Sevenoaks Division of the County Library (1974-1977).

Thomas John LEAN, 1841-1910

(3010) G. Williams. Swansea: three chiefs in five decades.

Joseph LIGHTBOWN, 1913-1980

2402 [Obituaries]
Lib.Assn Rec. 82 (9) 1980, 449 (N. Higham; K. W. Humphreys)
Joe Lightbown came to Bristol University in 1952 and was Deputy from
1961 to 1978.

Reginald Northwood LOCK, 1913-1976

2403 [Obituary]
Lib.Assn Rec. 79 (5) 1977, 280 (S. Fox)
Lock was first Head of the School of Librarianship at Birmingham Col-
lege of Commerce, 1950-1971.

George Watson LONGMUIR, 1910-1979

2404 [Obituary]
SLA News 1 (149) 1979, 241 (W. McK. M.)
George Longmuir was County Librarian of the Shetlands, 1947-1976.

Sir John Young Walker MacALISTER, 1856-1925

2405 L. S. Godbolt. Sir John Young Walker MacAlister: (1856-1925): a
biography. Lib.Assn, 1975. xi, 547p. front., plates, facsims, ports,
bibliog. [Thesis approved for Fellowship of the Library Association.
Typescript]
This biography traces MacAlister's family background, education and
his early professional life as Sub-Librarian of the Liverpool Library,
1878-1880 and Librarian of the Leeds Library, 1880-1887. Four chapters are devoted to his influence within the Library Association, of
which he was Joint Honorary Secretary, 1887-1892 and Honorary Secretary, 1893-1898. In addition there is coverage of his founding and
editing of The Library and the part he played in the foundation of
the School of Librarianship at University College, London in 1919.
The remainder covers his contribution to the medical profession, in
particular, his librarianship of the Royal Society of Medicine, 1887-
1925.

Neil Russell McCORKINDALE, 1921-1977

2406 [Obituaries]

Lib.Assn Rec. 80 (3) 1978, 140 (P. Grant)

SLA News 1 (143) 1978, 17-18 (P. Grant)

Neil McCorkindale started his career in Greenock Public Library in 1939. He spent three years in Stoke Newington, seventeen years as Burgh Librarian of Galashiels, six years as County Librarian of Aberdeenshire and two years as Chief Librarian of the North East of Scotland Library Service. He was active in the affairs of the Scottish Library Association.

Francis Noel McDONALD, 1910-1980

2407 [Obituaries]

Lib.Assn Rec. 82 (2) 1980, 85 (K. C. Harrison; E. O. Reed)

Frank McDonald was Borough Librarian of Paddington from 1956 until amalgamation in 1965, when he became Deputy City Librarian of Westminster. He retired in 1975.

Mary McLEAN (née Duncan), 1903-1976

2408 [Obituary]

SLA News 1 (137) 1977, 208.

Mrs. McLean joined Dumfriesshire Public Libraries in 1925 as a junior assistant. On the outbreak of war she was appointed as interim librarian, an office which was officially made permanent in the post-war period. She planned the reorganisation of the Ewart Library in Dumfries and pioneered the county's branch and mobile library provision.

Robert Duncan MACLEOD, 1886-1973

2409 M. Weir. Macleod of the Review: an appreciation.

Lib.Rev. Vol.27 Spring 1978, 14-18.

Reminiscences of R. D. Macleod, with special reference to his founding and editing the Library Review, but also mentioning his early career in public libraries, his work for the C.U.K.T. and W and R Holmes, and his other publications.

Sir Frederic MADDEN, 1801-1873

2410 R. W. and G. P. Ackerman. Sir Frederic Madden: a biographical sketch and bibliography. Garland, 1979. xvi, 97p.

Rev. Lib.Hist. 5 (3) 1980, 89-90 (K. A. Manley)

The bibliography forms the major part. The biographical essay seeks to set his writings within the context of his life and times, with little attempt at an assessment of his librarianship.

(2426) M. Borrie. Panizzi and Madden.

2411   T. D. Rogers, editor. Sir Frederic Madden at Cambridge: extracts from Madden's diaries 1831, 1838, 1841-2, 1846, 1859 and 1863. Cambridge Bibliographical Society, 1980. xiv, 94p. front., plates, facsims, ports. Rev. T.L.S. March 5, 1981, 258 (A. Bell)

Madden's visits to Cambridge were for the collation of texts for volumes he was editing. There are many comments (many of them caustic) on manuscripts to be found in various colleges, and on the colleges themselves and their staffs. There are also bitter comments on the British Museum Trustees' practice of purchasing manuscripts. The diaries also shed light on Madden's personality, especially the references to the death of several of his children in infancy and his financial worries.

2412   M. F. Schmidt. Passion's child: the extraordinary life of Jane Digby. Hamish Hamilton, 1977. xvii, 268p. front., plates, ports, bibliog.

In the Spring of 1827 Frederic Madden was at Holkham cataloguing the Long Library when Coke's granddaughter Jane Digby, Lady Ellenborough arrived there. His journal records the progress of their fleeting affair.

Stanley Walter MARTIN, 1904-1978

2413   [Obituary]

Lib.Assn Rec. 81 (4) 1979, 210 (K. R. McColvin)

Stanley Martin came to Lambeth as a Senior Assistant in 1927. He was appointed Deputy Librarian in 1947 and was Chief Librarian from 1951 until his retirement in 1969.

William McBarron MARTIN, 1917-1980

2414   [Obituaries]

Lib.Assn Rec. 82 (5) 1980, 243.

SLA News 1 (156) 1980, 59 (B. D. Osborne)

William Martin was Burgh Librarian of Dumbarton (taking charge of Dumbarton District Libraries after amalgamation) from 1949 until his retirement in 1979.

Kennard Desmond MILLER, 1915-1980

2415 [Obituary]
Lib.Assn Rec. 82 (6) 1980, 281 (N. Emery)
Ken Miller joined the Stoke-on-Trent Public Library Service in 1932.
He was appointed Deputy in 1946 and acted as City Librarian from 1955
to his retirement in 1974.

Frederick Charles MORGAN, 1878-1978

2416 F. C. Morgan's writings: a list published to mark his one hundredth
birthday, 29th June 1978. Hereford, Hereford Cathedral Library, 1978.
12, [3] p.

2417 P. Morgan. Frederick Charles Morgan.
Lib.Hist. 4 (5) 1978, 137-40.
A tribute to F. C. Morgan, Honorary Librarian of Hereford Cathedral
Library, on the occasion of his 100th birthday. A select biblio-
graphy of his publications and contributions to periodicals is
appended.

2418 [Obituaries]
Lib.Assn Rec. 80 (9) 1978, 479 (S. Milligan)
Lib.Assn Rec. 80 (11) 1978, 588 (A. S. Wright)
Frederick Charles Morgan was Librarian, Stratford-upon-Avon, 1903-10;
Malvern, 1910-25; City Librarian, Hereford, 1925-45. He then acted
as Honorary Librarian, Hereford Cathedral Library from 1945 until the
time of his death.

2419 P. Whiteman. Eighty-one years a librarian.
Lib.Assn Rec. 79 (10) 1977, 536-9. ports.
An edited recording of an interview with F. C. Morgan in which he
recalls his career as Librarian of Stratford-upon-Avon, Malvern and,
principally, Hereford, and events in his life since then.

Sir Owen Frederick MORSHEAD, 1893-1977

2420 [Obituary]
The Times June 3, 1977, 14.
After acting as Pepys Librarian at Magdalene College, Cambridge,
Sir Owen was Librarian and Assistant Keeper of the Royal Archives at
Windsor Castle from 1926 to 1958, and was subsequently Librarian
Emeritus.

Charles Edward MUDIE, 1816-1890

2421 T. Hubbard. "I hate you, Mr. Mudie."
Lib.Rev. Vol.27 Autumn 1978, 160-4.
A review article dealing with George Moore's Literature at nurse, or
circulating morals edited by Pierre Coustillas (see no.2253).

Alan Noel Latimer MUNBY, 1913-1974

(2773) A.N.L. Munby. Essays and papers: edited, with an introduction, by
Nicolas Barker.

Thomas William MUSKETT, 1901-1977

2422 [Obituaries]
Lib. Assn Rec. 80 (1) 1978, 44 (G. C. Otter)
Lib. Assn Rec. 80 (2) 1978, 92 (M. Manley-Smith)
County Librarian, East Riding of Yorkshire, 1929-35; Hertfordshire,
1935-42; Borough Librarian, Banbury, 1946 until his retirement.

Edward Williams Byron NICHOLSON, 1849-1912

(2502) R. J. Busby and K. A. Manley. E.W.B. Nicholson, H. R. Tedder and The
Library Association.

(2646) M. Heaney. The Bodleian classification of books.

(2647) K. A. Manley. The Bodleian classification of manuscripts.

(2649) K. A. Manley. E.W.B. Nicholson and the Bodleian Facsimile Series.

Edgar OSBORNE, 1890-1978

2423 [Obituaries]
Lib. Assn Rec. 81 (2) 1979, 92 (K. Mantell)
Lib. Assn Rec. 81 (6) 1979, 307 (F. A. Sharr)
Edgar Osborne was the first County Librarian of Derbyshire, from
1923 until his retirement in 1954. His personal collection of
children's books was given to Toronto Public Library in 1949.

Bernard Ira PALMER, 1910-1979

2424 W. A. Munford. Bernard Palmer: a memorial.
New Lib.World 80 (947) 1979, 89-90.
Bernard Palmer was Education Officer of the Library Association from
1947 to 1974. During that time he integrated the library schools with
the Association's educational programme, guided the Association
through a series of syllabus changes and later prepared the way for

internal examining by the schools themselves.

2425 [Obituaries]
Herald of Lib.Sci. 18 (4) 1979, 362-4 (S. G. Berriman)
Lib.Assn Rec. 81 (4) 1979, 209-10 (L. Paulin); 81 (5) 1979, 258-9
(S. G. Berriman; D. J. Foskett; P. Havard-Williams); 81 (12) 1979, 604
(J. H. Shera)
> Bernard Palmer joined the staff of Acton Public Library in 1927,
> becoming Deputy in 1937. From 1948 to 1974 he was the Library
> Association's Education Officer, and his achievements in the field
> of education for librarianship are here celebrated.

Sir Anthony PANIZZI, 1797-1879
2426 M. Borrie. Panizzi and Madden.
Br. Lib. J. 5 (1) 1979, 18-36. port.
> The hatred between Sir Frederic Madden, Keeper of Manuscripts, and
> Panizzi is a sad episode in British Museum history, but well docu-
> mented. Disagreements lasted until the end, when Panizzi was awarded
> a far higher pension.

2427 British Library. Department of Printed Books. Sir Anthony Panizzi 1797-
1879: an exhibition from 12 April to 15 July 1979. British Library
Board, 1979. [4] p. port., bibliog.
> Not an exhibition catalogue as such, but a summary of Panizzi's life
> and work to accompany the exhibition.

2428 A. C. Brodhurst. A side-light on Panizzi in the letters of Prosper
Mérimée.
Br. Lib. J. 5 (1) 1979, 57-75.
> Mérimée and Panizzi corresponded regularly between 1850 and 1870, but
> only the former's letters survive. They were previously printed in
> 1881 in a much mutilated text.

2429 M.R.D. Foot. Gladstone and Panizzi.
Br. Lib. J. 5 (1) 1979, 48-56.
> Gladstone's and Panizzi's correspondence shows that they were close
> friends. The article dwells on their concern for Italian political
> prisoners and on Panizzi's knighthood.

2430 E. J. Miller. Antonio Panizzi and the British Museum.
Br. Lib. J. 5 (1) 1979, 1-17. port.
> A useful summary of Panizzi's career by his biographer (see no.57),
> emphasising that his appointment was solely on his merits. Describes
> his evidence to the 1836 Commission of Inquiry, and how he became

Keeper of Printed Books. Details his many achievements.

2431 A. Panizzi and S. Smirke. [Letters]
Br. Lib. J. 5 (1) 1979, 47.
Letters by Panizzi and Sydney Smirke, each claiming to have origi-
nated the idea of the domed reading room. They are reprinted from
The Times July 30-31, 1866.

2432 D. V. Reidy. Some hitherto unpublished Panizziana from Italy.
Br. Lib. J. 5 (1) 1979, 36-46, illus.
The Biblioteca Municipale A. Panizzi in Reggio Emilia contains many
of Panizzi's personal and official papers. Alternative sketches and
memoranda for a new reading room are reproduced.

2433 S. Schacht. Antonio Panizzi's librarianship and its representation in
the pioneering library journals.
Libri 29 (4) 1979, 273-310
Libri 30 (3) 1980, 177-231
The first article traces Panizzi's career in the Department of
Printed Books and is based mainly on published materials. In the
second, three early journals, all published on the Continent, have
been examined for articles and reports on Panizzi's work. Each one
in turn is characterised, the principal articles are described in detail, and other sources of information noted more briefly. There are
extensive footnotes and a bibliography.

2434 P. J. Weimerskirch. Antonio Panizzi's acquisitions policies for the
library of the British Museum. Columbia Univ., 1977. 350p. [Thesis
approved for D.L.S. degree. Typescript]
The stock of the British Museum more than doubled between 1837, when
Panizzi became Keeper of Printed Books, and 1856, when he became
Director. The author shows how Panizzi achieved this by his ener-
getic policies, such as lobbying government members for higher grants
and giving priority to buying rare and foreign books.

2435 P. J. Weimerskirch. Sir Anthony Panizzi.
In: Encyclopedia of library and information science. Vol.21. New York,
Dekker, 1977, 309-33. port., bibliog.
A general account of his achievements at the British Museum, with
particular reference to his acquisition policies. The extensive
bibliography includes a number of foreign language items.

William Bryce PATON, 1907–

2436   F. McAdams. A bibliography of W. B. Paton.
In: Of one accord: essays in honour of W. B. Paton, edited by Frank
McAdams. Glasgow, Scottish Lib. Assn, 1977, 110–22.
Lists his contributions to library literature and information about
him.

2437   W. E. Tyler. William Bryce Paton.
In: Of one accord: essays in honour of W. B. Paton, edited by Frank
McAdams. Glasgow, Scottish Lib. Assn, 1977, 1–8. port.
A general survey of his career, beginning in 1925 at the Mitchell
Library, Glasgow, and covering his work at Watford, Airdrie, Greenock,
the Scottish School of Librarianship, and in particular at Lanarkshire, where between 1950 and his retirement in 1972, he built up one
of the foremost library services in the United Kingdom. His contribution to librarianship and to music, the Church and other local
organisations are all covered.

Harold Neville Percival PEPIN, 1899–1978

2438   [Obituary]
Lib.Assn Rec. 81 (2) 1979, 92 (H. Redford)
Beginning in 1913, his professional career was spent in Bournemouth
Public Libraries, from 1955 as Deputy and latterly as Chief, retiring
in 1964.

Alexander John PHILIP, 1879–1955

2439   W. A. Munford. Alex J. Philip.
New Lib.World 80 (944) 1979, 28–30.
Librarian of Gravesend from 1903 to 1946, Philip was also author,
editor and publisher of works on librarianship.

Septimus Albert PITT, 1877–1937

2440   J. D. Hendry. S. A. Pitt: his contribution to libraries and librarianship. University of Strathclyde. Department of Librarianship, 1978.
[2], iv, 197p. front., illus, facsims, map, plans, ports, bibliog.
[Thesis submitted for the degree of M.A. Typescript]
The first chapter deals with Pitt's family background and formative
years at Aberdeen. Chapter 2 records his move to Glasgow, and studies
his contribution to the formation of the Glasgow District Libraries
System. Chapter 3 assesses his role as City Librarian at Coventry
from 1908 until his return to Glasgow in 1915 as City Librarian. The

remainder of the thesis is largely devoted to his work at Glasgow, his promotion of open access in Scotland and his overall contribution to his profession.

Leslie Mervyn REES, 1911-1978

2441 [Obituary]
Lib.Assn Rec. 80 (11) 1978, 588-9 (H. A. Prescott)
Leslie Rees joined the staff of Swansea Public Libraries in 1927. He was appointed Deputy Borough Librarian in 1937 and was Borough Librarian from 1939 until his retirement in 1974.

Thomas RICHARDS, 1878-1962

2442 T. Parry. Thomas Richards 1878-1962.
Trafodion Cymdeithas Hanes Bedyddwyr Cymru 1979, 30-46.
An account of Richards as scholar (he was a prolific writer on historical topics) and Librarian of the University College at Bangor, North Wales (1926-1946). He is shown to have built up the library as a major research library for Welsh studies.

George Edward ROEBUCK, 1877-1953

2443 C.A.R. Bostle. George Edward Roebuck: a critical study of his life and work. Lib.Assn, 1975. 2 vols. [Thesis approved for Fellowship of the Lib.Assn. Typescript.]
A detailed study of his pioneering work at Stepney and at Walthamstow where he arrived in 1907 and stayed until his retirement in 1946, and also of his involvement in the development of his profession. An abstract is given in Lib.Hist. 4 (1) 1976, 13.

Ernest Albert SAVAGE, 1877-1966

2444 W. A. Munford. My friend Savage.
New Lib.World 80 (946) 1979, 67-8.
Personal reminiscences of Dr. Savage, with comments on J. G. Ollé's Ernest A. Savage: librarian extraordinary, 1977.

2445 J. G. Ollé. Ernest A. Savage: librarian extraordinary. Lib.Assn, 1977. xiii, 225p. plates.
Rev. J. Librarianship 10 (2) 1978, 141-4 (G. Jones)
Lib.Assn Rec. 79 (12) 1977, 701 (K. C. Harrison)
Lib.Hist. 4 (6) 1978, 184-5 (W. R. Aitken)
SLA News 1 (42) 1977, 389 (C. S. Minto)
Savage served as an assistant in the public libraries of Croydon in

1890-95 and 1898-1904 and at Watford in 1895-98, before becoming
chief librarian at Bromley, 1904-6, Wallasey, 1906-15, Coventry,
1915-22, and Edinburgh, 1922-42. Always a controversial figure in
Library Association circles due to his forthright views, he served as
Hon. Secretary from 1928 to 1934. Though partially blind, he published many books and articles, including Old English libraries and
A librarian's memories.

2446   J. G. Ollé. Ernest Albert Savage.
In: Encyclopedia of library and information science. Vol.26. New York,
Dekker, 1979, 322-31. bibliog.
    A general biographical essay, covering his early years at Croydon, his
chief librarianship of Wallasey, Coventry, and especially Edinburgh
from 1922 to his retirement in 1942. Also covered are his revitali-
sation of the Library Association and his contribution to public librarianship.

William Charles Berwick SAYERS, 1881-1960
2447   J. G. Ollé. William Charles Berwick Sayers.
In: Encyclopedia of library and information science. Vol.26. New York,
Dekker, 1979, 331-6. bibliog.
    A study of his work at Croydon Public Libraries from 1904 to his re-
tirement in 1947, and his wider contribution to librarianship, especially concerning the Library Assistants' Association and in the
fields of children's librarianship and classification.

Heinz SCHURER, 1910-1979
2448   [Obituary]
Lib.Assn Rec. 81 (6) 1979, 307 (M. Brook).
    A German emigré who eventually became Librarian of the School of
Slavonic and East European Studies of the University of London, 1956-
1972.

Robert SHACKLETON, 1919-
2449   N. Davis. Dr. Robert Shackleton.
Bod.Lib.Rec. 10 (3) 1980, 141-3.
    An appreciation of Bodley's Librarian from 1966 until 1979, formerly
Chairman of the Committee on Libraries of Oxford University.

Noel SHARP, 1905-1978
2450   [Obituary]

<u>Lib.Assn Rec.</u> 81 (2) 1979, 93 (A. H. Chaplin)

A member of the staff in the Department of Printed Books of the
British Museum and Superintendent of the Reading Room, 1952-1959.
He was chief editor of the General Catalogue from 1948 and was active
in the field of the principles of cataloguing. He was Keeper of the
Department, 1959-1966.

Herbert Maurice SHERRY, 1893-1979

2451   [Obituary]

<u>Lib.Assn Rec.</u> 81 (8) 1979, 406 (R. Lawson)

Herbert Sherry was the first County Librarian of Hampshire, from 1925
until his retirement in 1959.

Stanley SNAITH, 1903-1976

2452   K. C. Harrison. Stanley Snaith: a memoir.

<u>New Lib.World</u> 78 (925) 1977, 125-6.

Largely an assessment of Snaith's reputation as a poet and author.

2453   [Obituary]

<u>Lib.Assn Rec.</u> 79 (5) 1977, 280 (F. M. Gardner)

The obituary comments on Snaith's controversial contributions to the
'Library Assistant' beginning in 1930. He was appointed Chief Assistant at Bethnal Green in 1929, eventually becoming Borough Librarian
in 1950. He will be remembered as a bookman and as a writer and poet.
Library administration was not really his metier.

William STEWART, 1909-1977

2454   [Obituaries]

<u>Lib.Assn Rec.</u> 79 (4) 1977, 228, 230 (W. B. Paton)

<u>SLA News</u> 1 (138) 1977, 253-4.

After serving the Mitchell Library, Glasgow for 14 years, Mr. Stewart
was appointed as Burgh Librarian of Hamilton in 1941, a post which
he occupied until his retirement in 1973. He transformed a somewhat
moribund institution into one of the foremost library services in the
country and planned the opening of the Hamilton Museum. He established Britain's first civic film library in 1953 and took an active
part in the Scottish Library Association.

Stanley Cecil SUTTON, 1907-1977

2455   [Obituary]

In: India Office Library and Records: Report for the year 1977.

Foreign and Commonwealth Office, 1979, 1-18. plates, port.

> Stanley Sutton was appointed Sub-Librarian of the India Office Library in 1935, and was Director at the time of his retirement in 1972. The reorientation of the Library following the Independence of India and Pakistan is assessed.

Douglas TAYLOR, 1916-1978

2456 [Obituary]

Lib.Assn Rec. 81 (3) 1979, 153 (D. Williamson)

> Deputy Librarian, Halifax, 1939-74, then, following local government reorganisation, Central Librarian, Calderdale, 1974-78.

Henry Richard TEDDER, 1850-1924

(2502) R. J. Busby and K. A. Manley. E.W.B. Nicholson, H. R. Tedder and The Library Association.

Francis John TESKEY, 1920-1980

2457 [Obituary]

An Leabharlann: The Irish Library 9 (2) 1980, 49-51 (J. Hughes)

> Frank Teskey was Head of the English Department and Librarian of Stranmillis College of Education. Over a period of 30 years he had developed the Library into one of the most outstanding in its field in the U.K.

Anthony THOMPSON, 1911-1979

2458 [Obituary]

Lib.Assn Rec. 82 (1) 1980, 31 (K. C. Harrison)

> Anthony Thompson will be primarily remembered for his work for IFLA, for which he acted as Secretary.

Samuel Edward THOMPSON, 1852-1924

(3010) G. Williams. Swansea: three chiefs in five decades.

Leslie George TOOTELL, 1916-1980

2459 [Obituary]

Lib.Assn Rec. 82 (8) 1980, 381 (K. B. Swallow)

> After working for Sheffield City Libraries since 1946, Leslie Tootell was Librarian of Sheffield College of Technology (later Sheffield Polytechnic) from 1964 to 1978.

William TYNEMOUTH, 1914-1977

2460   [Obituaries]

Lib.Assn Rec. 79 (12) 1977, 716-7 (A. Wallace; E. Clough)

Lib.Assn Rec. 80 (2) 1978, 92 (W. Caldwell)

Tynemouth was Deputy City Librarian of Newcastle upon Tyne from 1947 and City Librarian from 1964 to 1970. He was noted in the field of staff training and planned the new city library of 1968. He was active in professional affairs.

William UPCOTT, 1779-1845

2461   T. D. Rogers. Thomas Symonds to William Upcott.

Bod.Lib.Rec. 10 (3) 1980, 196-9

Upcott was a noted collector and Sub-librarian of the London Institution. This letter of 1834 refers to his resignation from the latter, and also to the delivery of the Douce books to the Bodleian Library.

Sir Charles WILKINS, 1749-1836

2462   M. Lloyd. Sir Charles Wilkins, 1749-1836.

In: India Office Library and Records: Report for the year 1978.

Foreign and Commonwealth Office, 1979, 8-39. illus, facsims, ports.

Sir Charles was the East India Company's first Librarian, from 1801 until his death in 1836. However, much of the article concentrates on his contribution to Sanskrit scholarship and his printing activities in Calcutta in the 1770s.

Cyril Hackett WILKINSON 1888-1960

(2922) R. Sayce. Another Oxford bibliophile: C. H. Wilkinson (1888-1960).

David Glyndwr WILLIAMS, 1912-1978

2463   [Obituaries]

Lib.Assn Rec. 81 (3) 1979, 153 (R. Davies); 81 (4) 1979, 210 (F. Hallworth)

Deputy County Librarian, Glamorgan, 1937-1961; County Librarian, Glamorgan, 1961-1974; County Librarian, Mid Glamorgan, 1974-1976.

LIBRARIANSHIP

G E N E R A L

(2336)   ALA world encyclopedia of library and information services.

2464   W. Ashworth.   Special librarianship in Great Britain and the Library
Association.
Herald of Lib.Sci.   16 (4) 1977, 343-7.
   A brief summary of the progress of special librarianship in Great
   Britain, its influence on librarianship as a whole, and the involve-
   ment of the Library Association.

2465   R. J. Edwards.   In-service training in British libraries: its development
and present practice.   Lib.Assn, 1977.   ix, 232p. bibliog.
   Based on his 1974 Fellowship thesis (see no.1678).   The first three
   chapters trace the history of in-service training from mediaeval times
   to 1904; 1904-1945 and 1945 to date, respectively.   The subject is
   related to such factors as the size of libraries, the degree of dele-
   gation, the employment of female staff and professional education.
   Chapter 4 covers the development of library school field work.

(3153)   S. J. Glogoff.   Cannons' Bibliography of Library Economy and its role in
the development of bibliographic tools in librarianship.

(2527)   K. C. Harrison.   Chronology of libraries and librarianship in the British
Isles, 1800-1977.

(2528)   D.F.W. Hawes.   Reflections on some social, philosophical and educational
influences on British library history 1880-1965.

(3154)   P. A. Hoare.   Library history.

(3155)   D. F. Keeling, editor.   British library history: bibliography 1973-1976.

(2941)   T. Kelly.   A history of public libraries in Great Britain, 1845-1975.

(3156)   Library Association Library.   FLA theses: abstracts of all theses accepted for the Fellowship of the Library Association from 1964.

(2356)   I. V. Malhan.   James Duff Brown and his contributions.

2466   A. Mole.   The development of library management concerns, 1870-1950.
In: Studies in library management.   Vol.6.   The coming of age of library
management 1960-1980, edited by Anthony Vaughan.   Bingley, 1980, 73-110.
   Considers the distinctive body of routines, procedures and profes-

sional tasks which over the period entitled the librarian to the freedom to control his library and to professional status, and attempts to show why library management concerns have emerged in the way they have.

2467　A. C. Montgomery. Professionalism in British librarianship - its growth since 1945. Lib.Assn, 1979. 303p. illus, tables, bibliog. [Thesis submitted for Fellowship of the Library Association. Typescript]

"Features of professionalism are considered in relation to the development in the structure and practice of librarianship in Britain during the period, using historical data and statistics where possible measured against the sociological criteria".

(3158)　J. G. Ollé. Library history.

(2511)　P. W. Plumb, compiler. Libraries by association: the Library Association's first centenary.

(3160)　R. J. Taylor, editor. Library and information studies in the United Kingdom and Ireland, 1950-1974; an index to theses.

2468　J. Thompson. A history of the principles of librarianship. Bingley, 1977, 236p. bibliog.

Rev.　Asst Lib.　71 (12) 1978, 143-4　(G. Williams)
　　　J. Lib.Hist.　13 (3) 1978, 367-9　(M. H. Harris)
　　　Lib.Hist.　4 (5) 1978, 168-9　(J. G. Ollé)
　　　Lib. Q.　48 (4) 1978, 548-9　(S. D. Neill)
　　　Lib.Rev.　Vol.27　Spring 1978, 52-3　(N. A. Webber)
　　　T.L.S.　Dec. 30, 1977, 1532　(D. J. Urquhart)

Endeavours to establish the historical foundations for a modern theory of librarianship. Chapters are devoted to such topics as the purpose of libraries, conservation, access, the role of the librarian, classification, cataloguing and the design of libraries.

Examples from all periods and many parts of the Western world are taken from secondary sources.

(2959)　K. Weibel and others, editors. The role of women in librarianship 1876-1976: the entry, advancement, and struggle for equalisation in one profession.

A R C H I T E C T U R E

(2929)　M. Dewe. H. T. Hare: Edwardian library architect.

(2992)　M. Dewe. Public library buildings in Hammersmith: benefactors and architects.

(2990) A. Service. London 1900.

(2601) R. S. Smith. The history of academic library buildings.

(2562) A. Vaughan. British academic library buildings since 1964: a comparative study.

B I N D I N G

2469   H. M. Nixon. Five centuries of English bookbinding. Scolar Press, 1978. 232, [9] p. facsims, bibliog.

   100 bindings are illustrated and described. The accounts are based on a series of articles appearing in The Book Collector, which aimed to feature only bindings which had not been published previously in book form and to provide new facts about them wherever possible. The book provides much information concerning their provenance, private patronage of bookbinders and the binding practice of particular libraries.

C A T A L O G U I N G

(2838) W. J. Bate. Samuel Johnson.

2470   D. Batty. The sheaf catalog.
   In: Encyclopedia of library and information science. Vol.27. New York, Dekker, 1979. 312-9. bibliog.

   Mentions the occurrence of the sheaf catalogue in England, and innovations in sheaf binder design in the late 19th and early 20th. centuries.

2471   J. Downing. Anniversary and birth: AA 1908 to AACR2.
   Lib.Assn Rec. 81 (2) 1979, 66-7.

   A look at three reviews of the 1908 Anglo-American Code published in 1908-9.

2472   E. J. Hunter and K.G.B. Bakewell. Cataloguing. Bingley, 1979. 197p. map, diagrs.

   Chapter 2 consists largely of chronological charts covering major developments from 1787 to 1981.

2473   A. Jeffreys. Cataloguing and classification: the Anglo-American concorde.
   In: University library history: an international review, edited by James Thompson. Bingley, 1980, 147-69.

   A short and selective account of some of the more salient features in the history of cataloguing and classification in British and Irish university libraries, particularly during the last 150 years.

(2676) W. R. Jones. Franciscan education and monastic libraries: some documents.

(2392) J. M. Lee. E. Wyndham Hulme: a reconsideration.

2474   G. London. The place and role of bibliographic description in general
        and individual catalogues: a historical analysis.
        Libri 30 (4) 1980, 254-84.
        A survey of cataloguing codes in Europe and America, including the
        1841 BM rules, the 1883 LA rules, the 1908 Anglo-American code and
        further British and international developments up to AACR2.

2475   A. Lunn. BNB/BSD 1949-1979: thirty years of bibliographic achievement.
        British Library, Bibliographical Services Division, 1979. 12p.
        Looks at the organisation's aims, services and operations from an
        historical point of view. The entries in this bibliography are
        arranged by date of publication.

2476   R. W. Pfaff. Montague Rhodes James. Scolar Press, 1980. xvii, 461p.
        front., bibliog.
        Chapters 6, 8 and 9 record in some detail the series of catalogues of
        manuscripts James produced mainly during the period 1895-1910. Most
        of his attention was given to the mediaeval manuscripts in Cambridge
        Colleges, and this led to a number of important investigations into
        mediaeval library history. His methodology is described and his
        achievement is assessed. The work concludes with a bibliography of
        his scholarly writings.

2477   W. B. Rayward. The search for subject access to The Catalogue of
        Scientific Papers 1800-1900.
        In: The variety of librarianship: essays in honour of John Wallace
        Metcalfe, edited by W. Boyd Rayward. Sydney, Lib.Assn of Australia,
        1976, 146-70.
        Examines the unsuccessful attempts made by the Royal Society to secure
        subject access to the Catalogue, and in so doing, throws light on
        contemporary library practice in the field of subject cataloguing and
        indexing.

CLASSIFICATION

2478   E. J. Coates. Classification in information retrieval: the twenty years
        following Dorking.
        J. Docum. 34 (4) 1978, 288-99.

An attempt to discover whether there has been any coherent trend in classification activity since the International Study Conference on Classification for Information Retrieval held at Dorking in 1957. There has been a major expansion of practical activity, but no new theoretical breakthrough.

(2646) M. Heaney. The Bodleian classification of books.

(2473) A. Jeffreys. Cataloguing and classification: the Anglo-American concorde.

(2392) J. M. Lee. E. Wyndham Hulme: a reconsideration.

(2647) K. A. Manley. The Bodleian classification of manuscripts.

(2447) J. G. Ollé. William Charles Berwick Sayers.

(2477) W. B. Rayward. The search for subject access to The Catalogue of Scientific Papers 1800-1900.

2479 H. G. Schulte-Albert. Classificatory thinking from Kinner to Wilkins: classification and thesaurus construction, 1645-1668.
Lib. Q. 49 (1) 1979, 42-64.
Discusses and evaluates the contribution of the educator George Dalgarno and John Wilkins, Bishop of Chester, in the field of general conceptual classification, in the context of the interest in mid-17th century Britain in a universal language which would overcome the language barrier. The study also traces the relationship between Wilkins's thesaurus and the modern information-retrieval thesaurus.

C O - O P E R A T I O N

2480 D. Cox. Co-operation among university libraries in the United Kingdom. In: University library history: an international review, edited by James Thompson. Bingley, 1980, 170-86.
Covers various aspects of co-operation since the 1920s.

2481 J. Davey. Looking back and thinking aloud: 20 years in interlending. Interlending Review 8 (2) 1980, 45-8.
A personal account of some of the developments which have occurred in the field of interlending in Great Britain during the last twenty years, with particular reference to the British Library Lending Division.

2482 B. Jones. Inter-library loans: retrospect and prospect. Loughborough, Loughborough Univ. of Technology. Department of Library and Information Studies, 1979. [3], vii, 234p. illus, tables, bibliog. [Thesis sub-

mitted in partial fulfilment of the requirements of M.A. degree. Type-
script].

Chapter 1 provides a summary of the early introduction of voluntary
and unco-ordinated regional schemes and the establishment of the
National Central Library. Chapter 2 assesses the recommendations on
interlending which were included in various reports from 1942 to 1962
in order to determine the extent to which these recommendations
resulted in formal action. Chapter 3 covers the transitional years
from 1962 to 1972.

2483   P. W. Plumb. Development of library co-operation in Great Britain.
<u>Herald of Lib.Sci.</u> 16 (4) 1977, 347-52.

A general outline history from the 14th century to the present day.

IRISH CENTRAL LIBRARY FOR STUDENTS

(2399)   T. Hall. Christina Keogh: pioneer - the Irish Central Library for
Students and the foundation of the Library Council.

NATIONAL CENTRAL LIBRARY

(2828)   British Library. Lending Division. The Edwin Gardiner chess collection.

2484   S.P.L. Filon. The National Central Library: an experiment in library
co-operation. Lib.Assn, 1977. xv, 300p. plates, ports, tables, bibliog.
<u>Rev. Lib.Hist.</u> 4 (4) 1977, 123-4 (W. J. Murison)

<u>Lib. Q.</u> 49 (3) 1979, 332-4 (R. Stokes)

<u>Notes and Queries</u> 25 (3) 1978, 288 (J.H.P. Pafford)

The first nine chapters form a history of the Central Library for
Students, 1916-1930 and of the National Central Library from 1930
until the Dainton Report and the ending of its separate existence.
Much additional historical information (including statistics) is
contained in the following chapters devoted to services and methods,
and in the appendices.

(2390)   [Obituary of Reginald Harrison Hill, 1894-1976]

2485   D. J. Urquhart. The National Central Library - a historical review.
<u>J. Docum.</u> 34 (3) 1978, 230-9.

The N.C.L. originated in the recommendations of the Kenyon Committee
of 1927 from which the author makes frequent quotations. Subsequent
developments are indicated including regional bureaux, voluntary co-
operation and the requirements of scientific literature which led to
the establishment of the N.L.L.S.T. With confused terms of reference
and limited financial support, it is surprising that the N.C.L. was
able to achieve anything.

2486   W. H. Brown. Co-operation in transition.

In: Of one accord: essays in honour of W. B. Paton, edited by Frank McAdams. Glasgow, Scottish Lib.Assn, 1977, 35-43.

    An historical survey of library co-operation in Scotland from the founding of the Scottish Central Library for Students in 1921 to its amalgamation with the National Library of Scotland in 1974.

2487   W. H. Brown. Interlibrary co-operation in Scotland.

British Library Lending Division Review 5 (4) 1977, 134-8.

    The history and development of library co-operation in Scotland is described in some detail.

2488   W. H. Brown. The Scottish Central Library.

In: Encyclopedia of library and information science. Vol.27. New York, Dekker, 1979, 127-31.

    Records the history of the Scottish Central Library for Students, established by the C.U.K.T. in 1921. In 1953 it accepted responsibility for the Scottish Union Catalogue from the Regional Library Bureau of Scotland. In 1974 the functions of the library were transferred to and amalgamated with those of the National Library of Scotland.

EDUCATION

(2465) R. J. Edwards. In-service training in British libraries: its development and present practice.

2489   M. Marshall. 100 years older and wiser?

Lib.Assn Rec. 79 (4) 1977, 195, 197.

    An examination of education and training of children's librarians.

(2424) W. A. Munford. Bernard Palmer: a memorial.

(2425) [Obituaries of Bernard Ira Palmer, 1910-1979]

2490   B. I. Palmer. A century of education for librarianship in Britain.

In: Of one accord: essays in honour of W. B. Paton, edited by Frank McAdams. Glasgow, Scottish Lib.Assn, 1977, 73-89.

    A brief general survey.

2491   B. I. Palmer. A century of progress: education for librarianship in the U.K.

Herald of Lib.Sci. 16 (4) 1977, 365-70.

    A general outline history.

BIRMINGHAM COLLEGE OF COMMERCE, SCHOOL OF LIBRARIANSHIP

(2403)   [Obituary of Reginald Northwood Lock, 1913-1976]

COLLEGE OF LIBRARIANSHIP, WALES

(2373)   A. R. Edwards. Yr hedyn mwstard: atgofion Alun R. Edwards.

(2368)   [Obituaries of James Arthur Dearden, 1924-1976]

EALING COLLEGE OF HIGHER EDUCATION, SCHOOL OF LIBRARIANSHIP

(2357)   [Obituary of Edward Frank Browning, 1914-1978]

LOUGHBOROUGH UNIVERSITY OF TECHNOLOGY, DEPARTMENT OF LIBRARY AND
INFORMATION STUDIES

2492   L. M. Cantor and G. F. Matthews. Loughborough from College to
University: a history of higher education at Loughborough 1909-1966.
Loughborough Univ. of Technology, 1977. 200p. illus.
Rev. Lib.Assn Rec. 79 (5) 1977, 268 (K. Stockham)
> Contains a brief note on how the first full-time courses in librarian-
> ship were inaugurated by Roy Stokes in 1947 and how the County Library
> Service was set up in 1922.

UNIVERSITY COLLEGE LONDON, SCHOOL OF LIBRARY, ARCHIVE AND INFORMATION
STUDIES

(2397)   [Obituary of Raymond Irwin, 1902-1977]

UNIVERSITY OF SHEFFIELD, POSTGRADUATE SCHOOL OF LIBRARIANSHIP AND
INFORMATION SCIENCE

2493   W. L. Saunders. University of Sheffield Postgraduate School of Lib-
rarianship and Information Science.
In: Encyclopedia of library and information science. Vol.27. New York,
Dekker, 1979, 325-32.
> The origins of the school are discussed in some detail, and subse-
> quent developments in its courses more briefly. Informal approaches
> were made by the Library Association in 1960, and the first students
> were admitted in 1964.

L A W

2494   R. Bell. Legal deposit in Britain (part 1).
Law Librarian 8 (1) 1977, 5-8.
> An outline of the history of legal deposit in Britain from Bodley's
> agreement with the Stationers Company in 1610 to the mid-Victorian
> period, largely based on Partridge.

ORGANISATIONS

ASLIB

(2363) E. J. Carter. Herbert Coblans: a biography.

2495 E.M.R. Ditmas. Looking back on Aslib.
   In: Essays on Aslib edited by Peter J. Taylor. Aslib, 1978, 61-6.
   Originally published in Lib.Rev. Winter 1961, 268-70, 272-4.
   Miss Ditmas was appointed Secretary in 1933, and acted as Director
   until the end of 1949, although she says little of the post-war
   period.

2496 R. S. Hutton. The origin and history of Aslib.
   In: Essays on Aslib edited by Peter J. Taylor. Aslib, 1978, 17-31.
   Originally published in J. Docum. 1 (1) 1945, 6-20.
   Following discussion of earlier attempts at the co-ordination of
   information services, there is an account of the first Conference of
   1924, the work of the Standing Committee, the themes of later conferences and the diversification of services, particularly during
   wartime.

2497 L. Moholy. The Aslib Microfilm Service: the story of its wartime
   activities.
   In: Essays on Aslib edited by Peter J. Taylor. Aslib, 1978, 33-47.
   Originally published in J. Docum. 2 (3) 1946, 147-73. The Service
   began to operate in 1942, following a survey of the deficiencies in
   the supply to British libraries of current scientific and technical
   periodicals from enemy and enemy-controlled countries. After the War
   it became the Central Medical Library Bureau of the Royal Society of
   Medicine, assisting the rehabilitation of devastated medical libraries
   in the liberated countries.

(2383) [Obituary of Christopher Wharton Hanson, 1902-1979]

(2365) [Obituary of Herbert Coblans, 1906-1977]

2498 S. Syme. Aslib: the difficult years.
   Lib.Rev. Vol.29 Winter 1980, 256-64. bibliog.
   A general survey from its foundation in 1924 to the early 1970s,
   concentrating on the early years and the period 1928 to 1942, when
   C.U.K.T. funding had ceased and before Government grants commenced.

2499 L. Wilson. Aslib and the development of information management.
   In: Essays on Aslib edited by Peter J. Taylor. Aslib, 1978, 1-15.
   Originally published in British librarianship today edited by W. L.

Saunders. Lib.Assn, 1976, 15-29. Considers three phases in Aslib's growth, from 1924 to the late 1940s, as a classic example of a voluntary association; from 1950 to 1965, a period of growth with industry and business as the principal targets; and subsequent orientation in the direction of a development organisation on behalf of information services generally.

BRITISH AND IRISH ASSOCIATION OF LAW LIBRARIES

2500   E. M. Moys. B.I.A.L.L: landmarks of the first ten years.
Law Librarian 11 (1) 1980, 3-5.
Explains how the Association came into being in 1969, and outlines major developments in its activities.

CARNEGIE UNITED KINGDOM TRUST

(2932) A. Ellis. Rural library services in England and Wales before 1919.

FRIENDS OF THE NATIONAL LIBRARIES

2501   F. Strong. The Friends of the National Libraries.
Archives 13 (60) 1978, 180-9.
The Friends of the National Libraries was launched in 1931, and from the beginning helped not only the British Museum and the National Libraries of Scotland and Wales, but also many other libraries and record offices throughout the country. Some of the activities and concerns of the Friends are described, particularly its increasing involvement with archives.

IFLA

(2458) [Obituary of Anthony Thompson, 1911-1979]

LIBRARY ASSISTANTS' ASSOCIATION

(2447) J. G. Ollé. William Charles Berwick Sayers.

LIBRARY ASSOCIATION

(2464) W. Ashworth. Special librarianship in Great Britain and the Library Association.

2502   R. J. Busby and K. A. Manley. E.W.B. Nicholson, H. R. Tedder and The Library Association.
In: The Library Association. Study School and National Conference, Brighton, 1978. Proceedings, 124-9.
An account of the Conference of 1877, its results, and the first five years of The Library Association's existence, with special reference to the part played in these formative years by Nicholson and Tedder.

(2337) E. A. Clough. A decade of famous names.

(2338) E. A. Clough. Gratitude for superb "professional Politicians".

(2994) J. Cowell. A city's contribution to the LA's first hundred years.

(2405) L. S. Godbolt. Sir John Young Walker MacAlister: (1856-1925): a
        biography.

2503   K. C. Harrison. One hundred years of professionalism: The Library
        Association. 1877-1977.
        Herald of Lib.Sci. 16 (4) 1977, 370-6.
        A brief record of the Association's progress and achievements is
        followed by details of the centenary celebrations.

2504   D. D. Haslam. The Library Association and international relations.
        Herald of Lib.Sci. 16 (4) 1977, 380-90.
        Outlines the growth of the Association's international relations
        activities since the 1950s.

(2528) D.F.W. Hawes. Reflections on some social, philosophical and educational
        influences on British library history 1880-1965.

2505   Hugh Barry: above all, modest.
        Lib.Assn Rec. 79 (11) 1977, 618-9. port.
        Hugh Barry was Secretary of the Library Association from 1959 to 1974.
        He died in 1977. Trained as a barrister, he became in effect the
        Association's first executive secretary. This extended obituary
        records the main achievements of his term of office. These include
        the successful negotiations with University College, London for a new
        headquarters for the Association, the reorganisation of the committee
        structure of the Council, Sections and Groups, and his easing the
        passage of the 1964 Act through both Houses of Parliament.

2506   J. W. Jones. Thoughts on libraries and librarianship. First Inter-
        national Conference of Librarians: inaugural address.
        Herald of Lib.Sci. 16 (4) 1977, 307-35.
        Reproduces the text of John Winter Jones' inaugural address delivered
        at the Conference of Librarians of All Nations held in London in
        October 1977, which led to the formation of the Library Association.

2507   N. Kaula. A century of library movement in Britain: chronology of the
        Library Association, (1877-1977).
        Herald of Lib.Sci. 16 (4) 1977, 298-307.

2508   W. A. Munford. The American Library Association and the Library Associ-
        ation: retrospect, problems, and prospects.

In: Advances in librarianship vol.7 edited by Melvin J. Voigt and
Michael H. Harris. Academic Press, 1977, 145-76.

A largely historical comparison of the two Associations under such
headings as origins, organisation, professional education, publications, etc.

(2424) W. A. Munford. Bernard Palmer: a memorial.

2509 W. A. Munford. Concise thoughts on some Library Association achievements
(1877-1977).
Herald of Lib.Sci. 16 (4) 1977, 376-9.

Dr. Munford quotes from an address given by Sir Gregory Foster, the
then Provost of the University College, London, at a meeting in 1922
in the pioneer school of librarianship. He then considers the
Association's achievements up to and since that date in such fields
as education for librarianship, professional literature and library
co-operation.

(2444) W. A. Munford. My friend Savage.

(2339) W. A. Munford. Past leaders.

(2425) [Obituaries of Bernard Ira Palmer, 1910-1979]

(2387) [Obituary of Daniel Denton Haslam, 1916-1978]

(2375) J. G. Ollé. Arundell Esdaile: a centenary tribute.

(2445) J. G. Ollé. Ernest A. Savage: librarian extraordinary.

(2446) J. G. Ollé. Ernest Albert Savage.

2510 J. G. Ollé. The Library Association and the American Library Association: their first fifty years.
J. Librarianship 9 (4) 1977, 247-60.

Although both associations were founded within a year of each other,
their development soon followed different tracks. Various simi-
larities and differences are shown, e.g. in publications and education, and the author concludes that the L.A. suffered in comparison
to the A.L.A. because of lack of financial resources rather than want
of ideas.

(2951) W. B. Paton. Exciting times - another view of how the L.A. responded
to the wind of change.

(2952) J. E. Pemberton. A century of library politics.

2511 P. W. Plumb, compiler. Libraries by association: the Library Association's first centenary. Lib.Assn, 1977. 48p.

This pamphlet describes itself as 'an attempt to relate pictorially some aspects of librarianship during that century with the Association's influence.'

(2954) R. Pritchard. The Library Association, benefaction and the public library movement.

LIBRARY ASSOCIATION. COUNTY LIBRARIES SECTION

2512 J. C. Kennedy. The Library Association, County Libraries Section: its inception, growth and influence 1920-1960. Lib.Assn, 1975. v, 141p. [Thesis approved for Fellowship of the Library Association. Typescript.]
A detailed study of its constitution, aims, objects and organisation, the latter subject being subdivided into aspects such as officers, membership, sub-committees and finance. Major reports are discussed and summaries are provided of papers read at the County Libraries Section sessions at the Lib.Assn Annual Conferences, 1927-1960. There is also a general summary of county library development.

LIBRARY ASSOCIATION. MEDICAL SECTION

2513 L. T. Morton. The origin and development of the Medical Section. In: The Library Association Centenary Conference: proceedings. Lib. Assn, 1977, 79-80.
Brief mention is made of the Medical Library Association of Great Britain which was formed in 1909 only to expire two years later. The Medical Section of the Library Association began in 1947 as the Medical Sub-section of the University and Research Section, becoming a full Section in 1949. Its activities and achievements during the 30 years of existence are summarised.

LIBRARY ASSOCIATION. REFERENCE, SPECIAL AND INFORMATION SECTION

2514 E. Hargreaves. Over my shoulder ...
In: The Library Association. Reference, Special and Information Section. proceedings of the Silver Jubilee Study Group, Cambridge, April 2nd-5th, 1976; edited by G. Plumb. Lib.Assn. Reference, Special and Information Section, 1977, 5-10.
A backward glance at the Section's 25 years of existence.

LIBRARY ASSOCIATION. UNIVERSITY AND RESEARCH SECTION

(2519) T. H. Bowyer. The founding of the Standing Conference of National and University Libraries (SCONUL).

LIBRARY ASSOCIATION.   YOUTH LIBRARIES GROUP

2515   D. Aubrey.   Enthusiasm has defeated apathy.
        <u>Lib.Assn Rec.</u> 79 (4) 1977, 191-2.
            Early attempts in the 1930s and 1940s to form a professional group for
            children's librarians are outlined. The Youth Libraries Group, formed
            in 1947, has been concerned with the conservation of early children's
            books and with professional standards in the children's library
            service.

OXFORD UNIVERSITY SOCIETY OF BIBLIOPHILES

2516   Oxford University Society of Bibliophiles. The Warden's meeting: a
        tribute to John Sparrow. Oxford, The Society, 1977. [9], 131p. front.,
        facsims.
            The Society was founded in 1951, and met at John Sparrow's lodgings
            in All Souls. Most of the contributors write about a notable book in
            their possession. Much is revealed about the nature of the Society
            and its activities. A check-list of Sparrow's writings is appended.

PRIVATE LIBRARIES ASSOCIATION

2517   R. Cave. Private Libraries Association.
        In: Encyclopedia of library and information science. Vol.24. New York,
        Dekker, 1978, 192-3.
            The Association was founded as a society of private book collectors
            in 1956. Based in London, it has an international membership. The
            article provides a brief record of its development and its publishing
            programme.

ROXBURGHE CLUB

2518   J. Turner. The Roxburghe Club.
        <u>Antiquarian Book Monthly Review</u> 6 (8) 1979, 318-9, 321, 323-5. facsim.,
        ports, bibliog.
            A brief account of John 3rd Duke of Roxburghe, the sale of his books
            by auction in 1812, and the foundation and history of the Club, con-
            centrating mainly on the personalities involved.

SCONUL

2519   T. H. Bowyer. The founding of the Standing Conference of National and
        University Libraries (SCONUL).
        In: University library history: an international review, edited by
        James Thompson. Bingley, 1980, 208-28.
            Explains the reasons for dissatisfaction among members of the

University and Research Section membership with the Library Association's handling of university and research library matters in the late 1940s, and records the events leading to the inaugural meeting of SCONUL held on 21st September, 1950.

SCOTTISH LIBRARY ASSOCIATION

2520   W. R. Aitken.   The Scottish Library Association.
In: Encyclopedia of library and information science.   Vol.27.   New York, Dekker, 1979, 131-6.   bibliog.
Largely devoted to its 22 years as an independent association, from its foundation in 1908 to its becoming a branch of The Library Association in 1931.

STRATHCLYDE LIBRARIANS' CLUB

2521   J. Brogan.   The Strathclyde Librarians' Club.
In: Encyclopedia of library and information science.   Vol.29.   New York, Dekker, 1980, 175-6.
The Club was founded in Glasgow in 1927 on the suggestion of R. D. MacLeod.   Its objectives are to stimulate the ideals of librarianship and to encourage social and cultural activities and whatever tends to widen the association of librarianship.   Its growth, concerns and activities are outlined.

P U B L I S H I N G

(2363)   E. J. Carter.   Herbert Coblans: a biography.

(2364)   R. A. Fairthorne.   Herbert Coblans, 1909-1977: a personal tribute.

(2365)   [Obituary of Herbert Coblans, 1906-1977]

(2453)   [Obituary of Stanley Snaith, 1903-1976]

2522   N. Roberts.   Ten years of library journals in Great Britain, 1969-79.
J. Librarianship 11 (3) 1979, 163-82.
Documents the growth of professional periodicals, often with pointed comments on their worth.

2523   Ten years of Journal of Librarianship, 1969-79.
J. Librarianship 11 (1) 1979, 1-3.
A brief account of how the journal came into being.

(2409)   M. Weir.   Macleod of the Review: an appreciation.

LIBRARIES

(2336) ALA world encyclopedia of library and information services.

2524 E. D. Johnson and M. H. Harris. History of libraries in the western
world. 3rd ed. Metuchen, N. J., Scarecrow Press, 1977. vi, 354p.
bibliog.
Rev. Lib.Assn Rec. 79 (8) 1977, 434 (J. Allred)
Comprehensive review of western library history. Brief accounts of
British mediaeval and national libraries, but little on public libraries. See nos. 145 and 953 for previous editions.

2525 A. D. Rider. A story of books and libraries. Metuchen, N. J., Scare-
crow Press, 1976. x, 173. bibliog.
Rev. Lib.Assn Rec. 79 (5) 1977, 265. (J. Knott)
Designed as a textbook for social science and humanities courses at
American high schools, and including suggestions for project work.
It provides an outline world history of book production and lib-
raries, concentrating on the classical and mediaeval periods and the
history of major collections e.g. the Bodleian and the British Museum.

(2468) J. Thompson. A history of the principles of librarianship.

B R I T I S H   I S L E S

(2465) R. J. Edwards. In-service training in British libraries: its development
and present practice.

2526 F. C. Francis. Independent libraries in England: a survey of selected
institutional, proprietary and endowed libraries, October 1973 - December
1975. Report presented to the Council on Library Resources, Washington.
Nether Winchendon, Aylesbury, Bucks, The Author, 1977. [5], 143p.
bibliog.
Rev. Lib.Rev. Vol.27 Winter 1978, 237-8 (P. Morgan)
This is a re-issue, with corrections and revisions, of the report
first issued in a limited typescript edition in 1976. The object was
to investigate the plight of a number of libraries owned by private
institutions, and to suggest how their problems could be solved.
Observations concerning the evolution and changing status of such
libraries appear in the main body of the report. An appendix provides

notes (including historical details) on the fifty libraries surveyed.

2527 K. C. Harrison. Chronology of libraries and librarianship in the British Isles, 1800-1977.
Herald of Lib.Sci. 16 (4) 1977, 289-98.

2528 D.F.W. Hawes. Reflections on some social, philosophical and educational influences on British library history 1880-1965. University College, London. School of Library, Archive and Information Studies, 1978. [4], x, 185p. table, bibliog. [Thesis presented in partial fulfilment of the requirements for an MA degree. Typescript]
The study is divided into three periods, 1880-1919, 1920-1944 and 1945-1965. Within each period relevant political, economic, social, scientific, religious and other factors are examined. This is fol- lowed by a survey of contemporary theories of librarianship, libraries as bibliographic systems and developments within the Library Associa- tion.

(3154) P. A. Hoare. Library history.

2529 J. B. Hood. The origin and development of the newsroom and reading room from 1650 to date, with some consideration of their role in the social history of the period. Lib.Assn, 1978. [1], iv, 404p. bibliog.
[Thesis submitted for Fellowship of the Library Association. Typescript]
Seeks to establish the origin of the newsroom and reading room and record their development and subsequent demise, within the various movements outside of the public library movement. Chapters are devoted to coffee houses (including Victorian coffee houses and temperance institutions) clubs, subscription libraries, athenaeums, mechanics' institutes, working men's clubs, co-operative societies, and reading rooms within the political and religious movements of the 19th and 20th centuries.

(3155) D. F. Keeling, editor. British library history: bibliography 1973-1976.

(4940) T. Kelly. Books for the people: an illustrated history of the British public library.

2530 N. R. Ker. Medieval manuscripts in British libraries. 2: Abbotsford - Keele. Oxford, Clarendon Press, 1977. xliii, 999p.
Rev. Lib.Hist. 4 (4) 1977, 119-20 (E. Yeo)
Rev. T.L.S. May 12, 1978, 535 (W. O'Sullivan)
For vol.1 see no.1723. Arrangement is by town and then by institution. Bibliographical notes on individual manuscripts include details of provenance. Brief notes are also provided on the historical back-

43

ground of some of the collections.

(3156) Library Association Library. FLA theses: abstracts of all theses accepted for the Fellowship of the Library Association from 1964.

(3157) Library history in archives: West Midlands.

(4689) H. M. Nixon. Five centuries of English bookbinding.

(3158) J. G. Ollé. Library history.

(2511) P. W. Plumb, compiler. Libraries by association: the Library Association's first centenary.

(3160) P. J. Taylor, editor. Library and information studies in the United Kingdom and Ireland, 1950-1974: an index to theses.

MIDDLE AGES

(3135) M. T. Clanchy. From memory to written record: England 1066-1307.

(2393) A. C. De La Mare and B. C. Barker-Benfield, editors. Manuscripts at Oxford: an exhibition in memory of Richard William Hunt (1908-1979).

2531 P. Eames. Furniture in England, France and the Netherlands from the twelfth to the fifteenth century. Furniture History Society, 1977. xxiv, 303p. plates, bibliog.
There is description and analysis of armoires and chests designed to contain books and muniments. Most of the examples are from cathedrals, churches and colleges. Several are illustrated.

(3152) J. Gibbs, compiler. A bibliography of the published writings of N. R. Ker.

(2677) F. S. Merryweather. Bibliomania in the Middle Ages.

(2476) R. W. Pfaff. Montague Rhodes James.

NINETEENTH CENTURY

2532 H. Davies. Using 'public' libraries in Victorian England. In: One hundred years: a collection to celebrate the Library Association Centenary, by members of the library staff at CLW. Aberystwyth, College of Librarianship Wales, 1977, 47-68.
Considers the pattern of community library provision, including that provided by voluntary effort and commercial enterprise as well as by public libraries, and discusses the services they provided, including such matters as opening hours, subscriptions, bookstocks, catalogues and book issue methods.

IRELAND

2533 C. Cochrane. Good news from a troubled province.
Lib.Assn Rec. 81 (12) 1979, 583-5. illus.
> Primarily a survey of developments during the 1970s, but also in-
> cludes a small amount of earlier history.

SCOTLAND

2534 W.A.G. Alison. Libraries in Scotland.
In: Encyclopedia of library and information science. Vol.27. New York,
Dekker, 1979, 86-97. table, bibliog.
> A general survey, including historical notes.

ANGUS

(2964) N. Craven. The development of public libraries in Angus, 1870-1975.

BECCLES, Suffolk

2535 M. Ellwood. Library provision in a small market town, 1700-1929.
Lib.Hist. 5 (2) 1979, 48-54.
> A study of library provision in Beccles before the opening of the
> County branch library in 1929. A parochial library was formed in
> 1707. A book club flourished in the 1770s and its rules are des-
> cribed in some detail. A subscription library named the Public
> Library and Scientific Institution existed from 1835 until the First
> World War. Circulating libraries and subscription newsrooms of the
> 19th and early 20th centuries are also mentioned.

BLACKBURN

(2968) J. L. Heyes. Libraries in Blackburn: a history of the major library
institutions from 1787 to 1974.

BOLTON

(2970) T. Dunne. Bolton Public Libraries, 1853-1978: one hundred and twenty-
five years in retrospect.

BRISTOL

2536 W. Barrett. The history and antiquities of the city of Bristol.
Gloucester, Sutton, 1980. 704p. plates.
> Facsimile reprint of 1st ed., Bristol, Pine, 1789. There are details
> of the City Library, particularly of the house given in 1615 to house
> it, and its rebuilding in 1739, the Bristol Library Society and the
> libraries of the Grammar School and All Saints Church.

CARMARTHENSHIRE

2537   D. F. Griffiths. History of 'public libraries' in Carmarthenshire.
       Library Association, 1980. [9], v, 426p. tables, bibliog. [Thesis sub-
       mitted for Fellowship of the Library Association. Typescript].
           Covers diocesan and parochial libraries, literary and scientific
       institutions, mechanics' institutes, village reading rooms and lib-
       raries, miners' institutes, and the Llanelli Borough Library and
       Carmarthenshire County Library to 1974. Particular attention is paid
       to developments which occurred in Llanelli and its environs. The
       thesis underlines the great disparity which existed between rural
       and industrial Carmarthenshire in terms of library development.
       Several library catalogues are reproduced in appendices.

       CHESTER

2538   A history of the county of Chester, edited by B. E. Harris. Vol.3.
       Oxford U.P., for the Institute of Historical Research, 1980. xvi, 276p.
       front., illus, plates, maps. (Victoria history of the counties of Eng-
       land).
           Includes brief details of the Mechanics' Institute and the Cathedral
       and Abbey libraries in Chester.

(3086) E. G. Williams. The Chester Society of Natural Science founded by
       Charles Kingsley in 1871.

       COLCHESTER

2539   A.F.J. Brown. Colchester 1815-1914. Chelmsford, Essex County Council,
       1980. 206p. plates.
           There are references to the Castle Book Society (f. 1752), the Sub-
       scription Library of 1803, other subscription libraries, the
       Mechanics' Institute, Literary Institute and Public Library.

       DONCASTER

2540   A. Thrall. The history of adult education in 19th century Doncaster.
       Doncaster, Museums and Arts Service, 1977. [2], 101p. illus. facsim.,
       bibliog.
           Much of the main text and appendices is devoted to library provision,
       in particular, to the Public Library opened in 1869, the Subscription
       Library of 1821, the Mechanics' and Apprentices' Library founded in
       1826, later becoming the Doncaster Mechanics' Institute, the Great
       Northern Railway Mechanics' Institute established in 1853, and the
       Lyceum in 1836.

2541   J.R.R. Adams. A history of libraries in County Down from the earliest
period to the year 1900. Lib.Assn, 1977. [1], 268p. plates, facsims,
bibliog. [Thesis approved for Fellowship of the Library Association.
Typescript].

Part 1 covers the period up to the end of the 18th century, in
particular, the monastic libraries and the growth of community library facilities during the 18th century. Part 2 covers the 19th century, and includes chapters on reading societies, circulating libraries, middle class newsrooms, library provision for the working
class, religious and temperance libraries, etc. There is also mention of uniquely Irish library movements such as the Repeal reading
rooms. Most libraries were very small: the only type which could
bear comparison with the best in other parts of Britain was the private library. Several sets of library rules and regulations are
reproduced in appendices.

DUBLIN

2542   D. Guinness. Georgian Dublin. Batsford, 1979. 235p. illus, plates,
plans.

Contains little historical information about libraries, but a number
of excellent illustrations of library interiors and plans, in
particular, of Archbishop Marsh's Library.

2543   G. N. Wright. An historical guide to the City of Dublin. Dublin, Four
Courts Press: Irish Academic Press, 1980. [2], xxxv, 260 [4]p. plates.
Facsimile reprint of 2nd ed., London, Baldwin, Cradock and Joy, 1825.
There are notes on the chief libraries giving details of their situ-
ation, buildings, furnishings, management, accessibility and out-
standing collections and treasures.

EASTER ROSS, Ross and Cromarty

2544   I.R.M. Mowat. Literacy, libraries and literature in 18th and 19th century Easter Ross.
Lib.Hist. 5 (1) 1979, 1-10.

The cultural background of this predominantly Gaelic speaking Highland
community is outlined, followed by an account of library provision,
including private, parochial, Kirkwood, school and subscription libraries. The writer concludes that while the provision of community
libraries was generally inadequate both in numbers and stock, such
libraries as existed benefitted mainly the English-speaking middle

class which was able to supplement its reading from private collections. The lower class Gaelic monoglots were largely deprived of the reading experience, being provided with neither libraries nor alternative means of obtaining literature, which was, in any case, severely limited in output and subject matter.

EDINBURGH

(3057) G. H. Ballantyne. The Signet Library Edinburgh and its librarians, 1722-1972.

GALASHIELS

(2552) A. Carter. The history and development of the library services of Galashiels and Selkirkshire.

GLAMORGAN

(2979) S. Scott. Public library development in Glamorgan 1920 to 1974: an area study with particular reference to Glamorgan County Library.

HORSHAM

2545 A. Windrum. Horsham: an historical survey. Phillimore, 1978. xi, 212p. front., illus, plates, facsims, port., map, bibliog.
There is brief mention of a number of 19th century libraries, including parish libraries, two library societies, the Horsham Literary and Scientific Institute, a Book and Tract Society Library and a Book Society run by the Unitarians from 1830 to 1940.

KING'S LYNN

2546 H. J. Hillen. History of the Borough of King's Lynn, with a new introduction by Raymond Wilson. East Ardsley, Wakefield, E.P. Publishing, 1978. 2 vols. fronts, illus, plates, maps, plans.
Facsimile reprint of 1st ed., Norwich, The Author, 1907. Historical information concerning the library of St. Margaret's Church (f. 1631) and St. Nicholas's Chapel (f. 1617) is given. The Subscription Library (f. 1797) and the Stanley Library founded in 1854, a subscription library endowed by Lord Stanley and by the Corporation, were for some time housed together with a newsroom, museum and concert hall at the Athenaeum opened in 1854. The Carnegie Library was opened in 1905.

LEEDS

2547 D. Fraser, editor. A history of modern Leeds. Manchester, Manchester U.P., 1980. xiv, 479p. illus, maps, tables, ports.

Several contributors mention literacy and libraries, particularly libraries as an aspect of middle-class culture. The main institutions of the 18th and 19th centuries e.g. the Leeds Library and the Philosophical and Literary Society are discussed. Several institutions catered for merchants, especially the Commercial News Room and Leeds Exchange, which opened in 1806. It contained a large newsroom with maps, gazetteers, directories, national and provincial newspapers and commercial periodicals. Adjoining it, a suite of rooms was provided, where merchants could transact business in private.

LEIGH, Lancs

2548 N. Ackers. The history of Leigh Library and its antecedents. Lib.Assn, 1977. viii, 234p. illus, bibliog. [Thesis approved for Fellowship of the Library Association. Typescript].

Following chapters devoted to the history of the town and of various 19th century libraries, two chapters are devoted to the Leigh Literary Society, with emphasis on its promotion of adult education and its role in the adoption of the Public Libraries Acts. Chapters 5-8 cover the development of Leigh Public Library from its formation in 1894 to 1974.

LONDON. BETHNAL GREEN

(2991) M. M. Chrimes. Libraries in Bethnal Green 1850-1922.

MIDDLESBROUGH

(3133) F. Bell. Reading habits in Middlesbrough.

MIDDLESEX

2549 A history of Middlesex, edited by T.F.T. Baker. Vol.6. Oxford U.P., for the Institute of Historical Research, 1980. xx, 228p. front., illus, plates, maps. (Victoria history of the counties of England).

Includes references to 19th century reading rooms, and public, parish, and circulating libraries in Friern Barnet, Hornsey, Highgate, Muswell Hill, Crouch End and Finchley, as well as to the Highgate Literary and Scientific Institution.

NEWCASTLE UPON TYNE

2550 J. Knott. A history of the libraries of Newcastle upon Tyne to 1900. Newcastle upon Tyne, Univ. of Newcastle upon Tyne, 1975. [3], 331p. bibliog. [Thesis submitted for Master of Letters degree. Typescript].

Traces the development of libraries in the town from the mid-18th century to the end of the 19th century. Separate chapters are devoted

to the library of St. Nicholas' Church, circulating libraries (with a
chronological checklist of such libraries given in appendix 2) the
Literary and Philosophical Society, newsrooms, Mechanics' Institute
and the Public Library. Included as an example of a library of Dis-
sent is the Vestry Library of the Hanover Square Unitarian Chapel,
which possesses a borrowers' register for the period 1787-1809.

OXFORD

2551 A history of the county of Oxford, edited by A. Crossley. Vol.4. Oxford
U.P., for the Institute of Historical Research, 1979. xx, 506p. front.,
illus, plates, maps. (Victoria history of the counties of England).
Covers the city of Oxford and includes references to the library of
Short's coffee-house (1668), various 18th and 19th centuries sub-
scription and circulating libraries and reading rooms, the Public
Library, and the Oxford Institute Library (f. 1884).

SELKIRKSHIRE

2552 A. Carter. The history and development of the library services of
Galashiels and Selkirkshire, including the social and economic factors
influencing that development. Univ. of Strathclyde, Department of
Librarianship, 1975. iv, 380p. front., illus, maps, plan, tables,
facsims, bibliog. [Thesis submitted for M.A. degree. Typescript].
Traces the development of community libraries in the County of
Selkirkshire from 1772 to the present day, including parish and
Sabbath school libraries, subscription and circulating libraries,
mechanics' institutes and public libraries.

STAFFORD

2553 A history of the county of Stafford, edited by M. W. Greenslade and
D. A. Johnson. Vol.6. Oxford U.P., for the Institute of Historical
Research, 1979. xx, 294p. front., illus, plates, maps. (Victoria
history of the counties of England).
Includes the borough of Stafford, and contains references to a town
library of the 17th century, circulating libraries and book clubs of
the 18th and 19th centuries, the Stafford Philosophical Society,
mechanics' institute, public library and the William Salt Library.

SUSSEX

2554 A history of the county of Sussex, edited by T. P. Hudson. Vol.6 part 1.
Oxford U.P., for the Institute of Historical Research, 1980. xx, 307p.
front., illus, plates, maps. (Victoria history of the counties of
England).

Covers Bramber rape, and includes references to reading rooms and
public libraries of the 19th and 20th centuries in Broadwater, Clapham, Findon, Heene, Lancing, Shoreham, Sompting, West Tarring and
Washington. Also mentioned is Steyning, with a subscription library,
reading room, mechanics' institute and voluntary lending library.
Libraries in Worthing included subscription libraries, various
institutes, public libraries, and a public house which provided
reading facilities.

2555 J. Lowerson and J. Myerscough. Time to spare in Victorian England.
Hassocks, Sussex, Harvester Press, 1977. [8], 151p. plates, facsims,
bibliog.

A number of Sussex libraries are mentioned, including that of the
Battle Mechanics' Institution (f. 1825), a couple of working men's
clubs in Brighton, one of which advertised the 'largest bagatelle
board' in the town, and various public libraries and country reading
rooms.

WARRINGTON

2556 W. B. Stephens. Adult education and society in an industrial town:
Warrington 1800-1900. Exeter, Univ. of Exeter, 1980. v, 158p. tables.
Much information is provided about the Mechanics' Institute (f. 1825)
and the Public Library (f. 1848). Libraries of scientific societies
and a church institute are also mentioned.

WIGHT, Isle of

(3011) M. Howley and I. Orton. Seventy-five years: the first county library.
A history of the Isle of Wight County Library 1904-1979.

WILTSHIRE

2557 A history of Wiltshire, edited by D. A. Crowley. Vol.11. Oxford U.P.,
for the Institute of Historical Research, 1980. xx, 284p. front.,
illus, plates, maps. (Victoria history of the counties of England).
Brief references to late 19th and early 20th century libraries and
reading rooms in No Man's Land, Redlynch and Wroughton.

WOOTTON BASSETT, Wilts

2558 P. J. Gingell. The history of Wootton Bassett. Wootton Bassett,
Wootton Bassett Historical Society, 1977. [5] 154, [4]. illus, plates,
map. ports.

The Mutual Improvement Society founded in 1886 possessed a library.
The library of the National School was transferred to the Town Hall

in 1890 and became known as the Town Library. The latter subscription library continued until 1935, when it was recognised that
it could no longer compete with the recently established public library service.

WORCESTERSHIRE

(3012) M. F. Nauta. A history of Worcestershire County Library 1923-1974.

YORK

2559 J. H. Moran. Education and learning in the city of York 1300-1560.
York, Univ. of York, Borthwick Institute of Historical Research, 1979.
[5], 49p.
Includes an analysis of book bequests from testamentary evidence,
mention of a number of major book collectors, mainly ecclesiastics,
and details of the library of the Minster, the Augustinian Friary and
St. Mary's Abbey.

YORKSHIRE

2560 A history of the county of York, East Riding, edited by K. J. Allison.
Vol.4. Oxford U.P., for the Institute of Historical Research, 1979.
xvi, 187p. front., illus, plates, maps. (Victoria history of the
counties of England).
Covers the Hunsley Beacon area. No public libraries are mentioned,
but there are references to reading rooms of the 19th and 20th centuries at Cherry Burton, Everthorpe, Cottingham, South Dalton,
Elloughton, Etton, North Newbald, Rowley and Skidby, and to a 19th
century parochial lending library at South Cave.

2561 J. Smurthwaite. A collection of Yorkshire library catalogues.
Lib.Hist. 4 (4) 1977, 112-4.
A list of library catalogues, including Sunday school libraries,
mainly from the Sheffield area. They formed part of the library of
William Thomas Freemantle, the Sheffield antiquary, which is now
housed in the Brotherton Library, Leeds.

2562   A. Vaughan. British academic library buildings since 1964: a comparative study.
J. Librarianship 12 (3) 1980, 179-98.
A list and descriptions of 53 major buildings.

C O L L E G E

2563   R. V. Fox. The development of technological university libraries from the libraries of the colleges of advanced technology. City Univ., 1978. vii, 301p. plans, tables. [Thesis submitted for the degree of M. Phil. Typescript].

An historical introduction traces the development of colleges of advanced technology from the mechanics' institutes of the early 19th century. This is followed by brief histories of each college. The planning and development of the polytechnic libraries is seen as a crucial part of the move towards university level work.

2564   S. T. Lucas. The evolution of libraries in colleges for the education and training of teachers, from the beginnings to the publication of the College of Education Libraries Research Project Report (1973). Loughborough, Loughborough Univ. of Technology Department of Library and Information Studies, 1975. xii, 319p. plans, bibliog. [Thesis submitted in part fulfilment of the requirements for the award of M.A. degree. Typescript].

The first chapter covers the 19th century, from the monitorial system, and the establishment of residential training institutions in the 1840s. Chapters 2 and 3 cover the period 1900-1939 and 1940-1973 respectively. Other chapters investigate the role of professional bodies, the contribution made by H. M. Inspectorate and the emergence of tutor-librarianship.

2565   G.C.K. Smith-Burnett. The development of the college library. In: The College library: a collection of essays edited by George Jefferson and G.C.K. Smith-Burnett. Bingley, 1978, 17-59.

The first section covers the development of library facilities in colleges of technology and further education in England and Wales, in particular, the period since the foundation of the Colleges of Technology and Further Education Sub-section of the Library

Association's University and Research Section in 1954. This is followed by sections covering polytechnics, colleges of education and colleges controlled by Scottish local education authorities.

GLASGOW. ANDERSONIAN INSTITUTION

2566 Shui Yim Tse. Radical Clydeside: the Andersonian, 1796-1964. **Lib.Rev.** 26 (3) 1977, 178-83.

Traces the development of the Andersonian Library from the foundation of the Andersonian Institution under the bequest of the Radical John Anderson, Professor of Natural History in the University of Glasgow. In 1886 Anderson's College was combined with other institutions to form the Glasgow and West of Scotland Technical College, later renamed the Royal College of Science and Technology. Real progress was made after the Andersonian Library appointed its first full-time librarian in 1905. In 1964 the College achieved university status.

GLASGOW. SCHOOL OF ART

(2755) R. Billcliffe. Charles Rennie Mackintosh.

HERTFORDSHIRE

(2572) J. A. Edwards. The changing role of libraries in colleges of further education in Worcestershire.

ISLEWORTH, Middlesex

2567 D. Jones. A history of Maria Grey College and its relationship with the University of London Area Training Organisation.
In: University of London. Institute of Education Library. Education Libraries Bulletin, Supplement 21, 1978. Books, libraries and teachers; towards a history of the London Institute of Education Area Library Service. Essays presented to Olive Stokes, edited by Margaret Couch, 29-34. bibliog.

Bishopsgate College for the training of women teachers, was founded at Bishopsgate in 1878. When it moved to Fitzroy St. W.1. it became known as Maria Grey College. New premises were built at Brondesbury in 1892, and the move to Isleworth began in 1949. There is a brief account of the library established at Brondesbury and its expansion at Isleworth. Since 1976 the College has formed part of the West London Institute of Higher Education.

LONDON COLLEGE OF ST. MARK AND ST. JOHN, Chelsea

2568 B. C. Bloomfield. The Library of the College of S. Mark and S. John.
In: University of London. Institute of Education Library. Education

Libraries Bulletin, Supplement 21, 1978. Books, libraries and teachers: towards a history of the London Institute of Education Area Library Service. Essays presented to Olive Stokes, edited by Margaret Couch, 35-47. plate, bibliog.

St. John's College, Battersea and St. Mark's College, Chelsea were both founded in 1840 as teachers' training colleges. The development of their scanty library facilities is recorded. The colleges merged on the Chelsea site in 1923. By 1937 there were about 4,000 volumes. The Octagon was adapted as a library in 1956, in which year the first full-time librarian was appointed. Progress was rapid from that time until 1973, when the College moved to Plymouth.

LONDON. NORTHAMPTON POLYTECHNIC INSTITUTE

2569 S. J. Teague. The City University: a history. The University, 1980. ix, 270p. front., plates, ports.

The Northampton Polytechnic Institute, London, was founded in 1896, achieved College of Advanced Technology status in 1957, and became the City University in 1966. There is a considerable amount of information about the Skinners' Library, particularly concerning the efforts made since the late 1950s to improve what had been one of the most inadequate college libraries of its kind, in the country.

LONDON. ROYAL COLLEGE OF MUSIC.

2570 Miss Banner's library.
Royal College of Music Magazine Vol.74 February 1978, 9-11.

A brief history of library facilities at the College from its foundation in 1883 until Miss Barbara Banner was appointed Librarian in 1940. She retired in 1977, and this article includes a tribute to her achievements. A reference and antiquarian collection was in existence at an early date. There were various attempts during this century at providing lending services, but with little success until Miss Banner's time.

READING

(2368) [Obituaries of James Arthur Dearden, 1924-1976]

SHEFFIELD

(2459) [Obituary of Leslie George Tootell, 1916-1980]

SOUTHAMPTON

(2368) [Obituaries of James Arthur Dearden, 1924-1976]

STRANMILLIS

(2457) [Obituary of Francis John Teskey, 1920-1980]

TOTTENHAM

2571 E. Edmondston. A Tottenham centenary.
In: University of London. Institute of Education Library. Education
Libraries Bulletin, Supplement 21, 1978. Books, libraries and teachers:
towards a history of the London Institute of Education Area Library
Service. Essays presented to Olive Stokes, edited by Margaret Couch,
24-8.

St. Katharine's College, Tottenham was founded in 1878 as a teachers
training college. It was renamed All Saints on its merger with
Berridge House, Hampstead. There is a short account of the library
since 1948, when a number of small collections of books housed in
various departments were formed into a united library.

WORCESTERSHIRE

2572 J. A. Edwards. The changing role of libraries in colleges of further
education in Worcestershire. Lib.Assn, 1978. [4], 232p. [Thesis
approved for Fellowship of the Lib.Assn. Typescript].

Examines the changing role of libraries in colleges of further
education in Worcestershire in relation to national developments,
and practice in the county of Hertfordshire in particular. Covers
the origins of the various Worcestershire college libraries and their
development to date, discussing the changing role of the staff and
changing staffing patterns.

T H E O L O G I C A L   C O L L E G E

BRISTOL

2573 N. S. Moon. Education for ministry: Bristol Baptist College, 1679-1979.
Bristol, Bristol Baptist College, 1979. x, 150p. front., plates,
facsim., ports.

A library was formed in the late 18th century and was augmented by
major bequests, particularly that of Andrew Gifford (1700-1784), a
former tutor. Some of the most important Bibles, mediaeval manuscripts and early printed books in the Gifford Collection are listed
in Appendix B. About 3000 non-theological books were sold in the late
1950s to finance building works.

2574 Sotheby and Co. Catalogue of Western Manuscripts (including 'The
Property of the Bristol Baptist College', lot 49). Sotheby, 14 December,
1977. n.p.

> Although only one item, this manuscript of the Wycliffite Bible de-
> serves recording on several grounds. It contains the extremely rare
> first version of the first full translation of the Bible into English
> and the presence of verbal glosses are important for philological and
> chronological reasons. Bequeathed to the College by Andrew Gifford
> (1700-1784), earlier owners included the topographers William
> Harrison (1534-1593) and William Lambard (1536-1601) and the book
> collector James West (1704-1772).

EDINBURGH

2575 Sotheby and Co. Catalogue of rare ... Scottish books ... [including]
the property of The Free Church College, Edinburgh. Edinburgh, 27 September, 1979. 258 lots. 24p.

> Religious works are prominent but there is much historical, literary
> and general matter, periodical literature, and, interestingly, Lyell's
> Principles of geology 4 vols (1835).

LONDON. HEYTHROP COLLEGE

2576 M. J. Walsh. Heythrop College Library.
Libraries Bulletin, Univ. of London 1 (10) 1977, 14-17.

> The origins of the library are traced back to 1606, when a Jesuit
> seminary was founded in Louvain. It moved to Liège in 1626, where it
> remained until its transfer to Stoneyhurst in Lancashire in 1794. It
> moved again to Heythrop in Oxfordshire in 1926 and to London in 1970.
> The College now forms part of the University of London. The col-
> lection is now estimated at c.200,000 volumes, a very large proportion
> being pre-1801 imprints.

LONDON. NEW COLLEGE

2577 G. F. Nuttall. New College, London, and its library: two lectures.
Friends of Dr. Williams's Library, 1977. 61p.

> The first lecture traces the history of the Dissenting Academies at
> Homerton, Hoxton and Northampton, whose libraries were brought to-
> gether when the Homerton and Highbury and Coward Colleges united in
> 1850 to form New College. Particular attention is paid to the per-
> sonalities involved. The second lecture discusses the collections in
> some detail, including the personal library of Philip Doddridge, the
> collection of 1900 funeral sermons and the collection of 500 items on

life after death formed by the 19th century minister Edward White. A great many items are cited and their provenance indicated. In all, parts of the libraries of 12 Congregationalist Academies are represented.

2578   Sotheby and Co. Catalogue of printed books (including 'The Property of New College, London', pp.19-27, lots 91-130). London, Sotheby, 1 January, 1977.

The more important titles in this collection are several early Bibles and New Testaments. One of these, Bible, _Greek_ (Frankfort, 1697), bears the inscription: 'This is the identical book with which Dr. Johnson knock'd down Osborne the Bookseller & bought by me at Harleian Sale. J. Miles'.

NORTHAMPTON

2579   M. Deacon. Philip Doddridge of Northampton, 1702-51. Northampton, Northamptonshire Libraries, 1980. 212p. front., illus, plates, plan, facsims, ports, bibliog.

The rules of the library of Doddridge's Dissenting Academy in Sheep Street, Northampton, are listed in appendix 9.

S C H O O L

2580   A. Ellis. Books and the child.
In: The Library Association Centenary Conference: proceedings. Lib.Assn, 1977, 54-7.

Refers briefly to the decline in reading standards in secondary schools in the 1870s, and to school library provision in the 1870s and 1880s.

2581   M. Seaborne and R. Lowe. The English school: its architecture and organisation. Vol.2: 1870-1970. Routledge, 1977. xix, 240p. plates, plans, bibliog.

A large number of school libraries receive the briefest of mention.

BLOXHAM

2582   B. S. Smith. A history of Bloxham School. Bloxham School and the Old Bloxhamist Society, 1978. ix, 206p. front., illus, maps, ports, bibliog.

All Saints' School was founded in 1853 by Rev. John William Hewett who gave the school his personal library. There were 2000 volumes by the time the Egerton Memorial Library was built in 1894. There is also mention of the Liddon Library being used by the prefects for formal beatings!

BRADFORD

2583   F. C. Pritchard. The story of Woodhouse Grove School. Bradford, The
        School, 1978. xiv, 411p. front., illus, plates, plans, ports, bibliog.
            The school, situated four miles from Bradford, was opened in 1812 as
            a Methodist boarding school. Early spasmodic attempts at library
            provision are well described. Special accommodation was secured in
            1862 and improved accommodation followed in 1955 and 1974.

        DOWN

(2712) J.R.R. Adams. Library provision for children in County Down prior to
        1850.

        ETON

2584   P. Quarrie. The Library of Eton College.
        Factotum 1 (5) 1979, 19-23. facsim.
            The Library's cataloguer draws attention to some unusual 18th century
            items and to the large collection of peculiarly Etonian material.

        GUILDFORD

2585   D. M. Sturley. The Royal Grammar School Guildford. Guildford, The
        School, 1980. xvi, 173p. front., plates, maps, plans, ports, bibliog.
            A large part of the library of John Parkhurst, Bishop of Norwich
            (1512-1575) was bequeathed to the town of Guildford, and housed at
            the School. Its history, including subsequent donations, accom-
            modation and catalogues, is recorded in chapter 8. A major in-
            vestigation and restoration took place in the 1890s, including the
            repair of the chains, and a major long-term restoration programme is
            currently proceeding. The Mallison Library, the School's modern
            library, is also referred to.

        JERSEY

2586   D. J. Cottrill. Victoria College Jersey, 1852-1972. Phillimore, 1977.
        [7] 123p. plates.
            Contains several brief passages concerning the library, in particular,
            boys' presentations, benefactions, refurbishing and general expansion
            during the 1890s and 1900s, its revitalising during 1925-9 and the new
            building of 1972.

        LANCASHIRE

2587   J. M. Potter. Old school libraries of Lancashire: a continued history,
        1885-1978. Loughborough, Loughborough Univ. of Technology. Department

of Library and Information Studies, 1979. 201p. illus, map, tables. [Thesis submitted in partial fulfilment of MA degree. Typescript].

Continues Richard Copley Christie's "The Old Church and School Libraries of Lancashire" published in 1885 by the Chetham Society. A chapter is devoted to each of the twelve grammar schools, summarising Christie's findings, adding further information which has since come to light, and recording the library's development to date. The concluding chapter compares the history of the school libraries and assesses some of the factors which have affected the survival of the old libraries and the development of the present ones.

LONDON

2588   H. A. Farnworth. A history of the school libraries of the London School Board 1870-1904. Loughborough, Loughborough Univ. of Technology, Department of Library and Information Studies, 1977. 76p. illus. [Thesis submitted in partial fulfilment of the requirements of MLS degree. Typescript].

Chapters are devoted to London School Board libraries 1870-1904, bookstocks, and public library development and the London School Board.

2589   C. W. Scott-Giles and B. V. Slater. The history of Emanuel School, 1594-1964. The Old Emanuel Association, 1977. 258p. front., illus, plates, map, ports.

The School was founded as Emanuel Hospital in Westminster in 1594, and was removed to Wandsworth in 1883. There is brief mention of the lending library formed in 1857, the subscription library which existed in the 1890s, the library built in 1907 and the reorganisation of 1922 and 1956.

RATHFARNHAM, near Dublin

2590   G. K. White. A history of St. Columba's College, 1843-1974. Old Columban Society, 1980. ix, 200p. plates.

The College was founded in 1843 as an Anglican public school, and moved to its present site seven miles from Dublin in 1849. A library was formed in 1840s, and for many years was financed by boys' subscriptions and gifts. Many books were destroyed in the fire of 1896, and a new library was opened in 1919. The writer was librarian from 1936 to 1973.

TENBURY WELLS, Worcs

2591   Sotheby and Co. Catalogue of the ... Toulouse-Philidor Collection of manuscript and printed music. Sotheby, 26 June, 1978. 87p. front., plates.

A remarkable collection of 17th century music, almost wholly by French composers, published or transcribed in France, and formed by a son of Louis XIV, Louis Alexandre de Bourbon, Comte de Toulouse (1678-1751). The court copyist of music, and thus copyist of the present collection was André Danican Philidor l'aîné (1647-1730). The collection was acquired for the College by the Revd. Sir Frederick Ouseley (1825-1889) the major Victorian collector of music and founder of St. Michael's College, which granted choral scholarships. Ouseley, ironically, was not fully aware of the provenance of the collection.

TENBY

2592   W. Harrison. Greenhill School Tenby 1896-1964: an educational and social history. Cardiff, Univ. of Wales Press, 1979. xiv, 386p. plates, maps, diagrs, ports, bibliog.

Details of the library appear on pages 160-1 and 270. Separate small collections were formed initially in 1897, one for the boys and one for the girls. Its subsequent growth and the provision of special accommodation is briefly outlined.

WINCHESTER

2593   J.M.G. Blakiston. Sir Thomas Phillipps and Winchester College. Bk Coll. 28 (2) 1979, 210-35. plates, facsims.

In 1853 Phillipps arranged that on his death part of his collection should pass to Winchester College. The conditions of this gift and the negotiations between Phillipps and the College are described. Phillipps was not satisfied with the response of the College, and apart from a few donations during his life-time, none of his books came to Winchester.

2594   P. Yeats-Edwards. The Warden and Fellows' Library at Winchester College. Factotum 1 (6) Oct.1979, 22-6.

A brief historical survey covering early donors, purchasing policy, accommodation etc., drawing attention to some of the rarer books.

U N I V E R S I T Y

(2480) D. Cox. Co-operation among university libraries in the United Kingdom.

(2563) R. V. Fox. The development of technological university libraries from the libraries of the colleges of advanced technology.

2595   K. W. Humphreys. Special collections in university libraries (excluding copyright libraries) and in public libraries.
In: The Library Association Centenary Conference: proceedings. Lib. Assn, 1977, 27-30.

Various types of special collections e.g. gifts and bequests, deposited libraries, and categories of material e.g. early printed books, manuscripts, etc. are considered, and numerous examples from various periods are given.

(2473) A. Jeffreys. Cataloguing and classification: the Anglo-American concorde.

2596   R. O. MacKenna. University library organisation.
In: University library history: an international review, edited by James Thompson. Bingley, 1980, 92-108.

Developments in post-war library organisation are considered, in the context of the three main phases of university development, i.e. the post-1944 Education Act era, the rapid expansion following the Robbins Report of 1963 and the painful return to more normal conditions in the 1970s, and the shift from concentration on book processing to concentration on reader service.

2597   F. W. Ratcliffe. The growth of university library collections in the United Kingdom.
In: University library history: an international review, edited by James Thompson. Bingley, 1980, 5-32. tables.

In the context of the Parry and Atkinson Reports, the growth of book collections at Oxbridge, London and the more recently founded universities between 1949/50 and 1977/78 is compared. In addition, the growth of the University of Manchester collections since their foundation in 1851 is outlined.

2598   N. Roberts. Aspects of British university librarianship, 1877-1977.
College and Research Libraries 38 (6) 1977, 460-76.

Developments during the last century are divided into three major periods, 1877-1919, 1920-1945 and 1946-1977, covering library services, staffing, management attitudes, buildings and automation. The role of the University Grants Committee in library development is stressed.

2599   N. Roberts. Financing of university libraries in the United Kingdom.
In: University library history: an international review, edited by James Thompson. Bingley, 1980, 109-27. tables.

Covers the period from the mid-19th century to the present day, with emphasis on the period since 1913. Includes general financial information e.g. the extent of Treasury grants in the early period, and library expenditure as a proportion of total university expenditure. There is also a breakdown of library expenditure.

2600 J. M. Smethurst. University library staffing in the United Kingdom.
In: University library history: an international review, edited by James Thompson. Bingley, 1980, 56-76.
Covers the last 50 years, discussing advances in staffing numbers, status, salaries, etc.

2601 R. S. Smith. The history of academic library buildings.
In: University library history: an international review, edited by James Thompson. Bingley, 1980, 128-46. bibliog.
A brief survey of the development of British and other university library buildings from the 13th century to the present time.

2602 J. F. Stirling. Academic libraries in transition: 1960-1980.
In: Studies in library management. Vol.6. The coming of age of library management 1960-1980, edited by Anthony Vaughan. Bingley, 1980, 13-29.
Contrasts the growth era of the 1960s with its experimentation and developments in organisation, technology and services, with the problems besetting university libraries in the 1970s as a result of increasing financial restrictions.

2603 M. Wise. "Jupiter's nod": notes on some nineteenth century academic libraries.
In: One hundred years: a collection to celebrate the Library Association Centenary, by members of the library staff at CLW, Aberystwyth, College of Librarianship Wales, 1977, 69-77. bibliog.
Illustrates the growth of British university libraries in the 19th century and comments on various aspects of their services and problems involving their provision.

ABERDEEN

2604 University of Aberdeen Library. A short-title catalogue of books printed on the Continent of Europe, 1501-1600, in Aberdeen University Library. Oxford U.P., for the Univ. of Aberdeen, 1979. xii, 313p.
Bk Coll. 29 (4) 1980, 600-3 (D. E. Rhodes)
Accompanying the catalogue are indexes of provenance, listing special collections, individual owners and institutional owners. Calvinist theology and medicine are particularly well represented.

2605   R. Brinkley. The Powell, Swinburne and Camden Hotten collections of the
Library of the University College of Wales, Aberystwyth.
L.A. Rare Bks Group Newsletter 1 (12) 1978, 8-12.

> These collections comprise mainly 19th century literature collected
> by, or relating to, the poet Swinburne and his friends, George E. J.
> Powell (1842-82) and John Camden Hotten (d.1873).

2606   T. G. Lloyd. The College Library 1872-1976. Aberystwyth, Univ. College
of Wales, 1977. 15p. illus.

> A history of the Library from its origins to the opening of the Arts
> Library on the new College site. Analyses changing emphasis under
> successive personalities. A Welsh language edition of this booklet
> appeared at the same time, entitled Llyfrgell y Coleg.

BANGOR

(2442) T. Parry. Thomas Richards 1878-1962.

BRISTOL

(2402) [Obituaries of Joseph Lightbown, 1913-1980]

CAMBRIDGE

(2641) R.J.A. Finch. The development of libraries in the Universities of
Oxford and Cambridge 1870-1939.

2607   M. R. James. Collections of manuscripts at Cambridge: their history,
sources and contents.
Trans. Cambridge Bibl.Soc. 7 (4) 1980, 395-410.

> In this previously unpublished Sandars lecture of 1903, James describes
> each of the pre-Reformation library collections in Cambridge in turn,
> mentioning the more important books and listing their various cata-
> logues. The author regrets that Cambridge libraries were more de-
> pendent on benefactions than purchases, and refers to the major
> benefactors, such as Archbishop Parker.

(2855) D. J. McKitterick, editor. The library of Sir Thomas Knyvett of Ash-
wellthorpe, c.1539-1618.

(2476) R. W. Pfaff. Montague Rhodes James.

(2411) T. D. Rogers, editor. Sir Frederic Madden at Cambridge.

CAMBRIDGE. CORPUS CHRISTI COLLEGE

(2878) R. I. Page. Christopher Marlowe and the library of Matthew Parker.

CAMBRIDGE. JESUS COLLEGE

2608   A. Gray and F. Brittain. A history of Jesus College, Cambridge.
Revised ed. Heinemann, 1979. xiii, 226p. front., plates, ports.
    The College was founded in 1496. Briefly describes the revival of
the Old Library under the Mastership of Dr. Edmund Bollero from 1663
to 1679, and which continued into the early 18th century. In 1912
the Shield Library was established for the use of undergraduates.

CAMBRIDGE. KING'S COLLEGE

(2799)   A. Ashbee. Instrumental music from the library of John Browne (1608-
1691), Clerk of the Parliaments.

CAMBRIDGE. MAGDALENE COLLEGE

(2882)   Magdalene College, Cambridge. Catalogue of the Pepys Library at Magdalene College, Cambridge.

(2420)   [Obituary of Sir Owen Frederick Morshead, 1893-1977]

(2884)   E. M. Wilson. Samuel Pepys and Spain.

CAMBRIDGE. ST. JOHN'S COLLEGE

2609   A. C. Crook. From the foundation to Gilbert Scott: a history of the
buildings of St. John's College, Cambridge 1511 to 1885. Cambridge, The
College, 1980. viii, 183p. front., illus, plates, plans, maps, bibliog.
    Pages 42-55 record in some detail the building of the library which
was completed in 1628, and the negotiations with the donor, John
Williams, Bishop of Lincoln, which commenced in 1623. Appendix 5
sets out the relevant accounts.

2610   A. C. Crook. Penrose to Cripps: a century of building in the College of
St. John the Evangelist, Cambridge. Cambridge, The College, 1978. x,
235p. front., plates.
    Chapters 11 and 3 provide a painfully detailed record of building
works associated with the library and muniment rooms respectively,
based on primary sources. The period covered is from the 1880s to
the 1970s. In particular, there is an account of the restoration of
the library roof in 1928 after its being attacked by death watch
beetles which extended their activities to the books themselves, the
provision of a reading room in 1938 and improvements in stack accommodation since 1956.

2611   D. J. McKitterick. Two 16th-century catalogues of St. John's College
library.
<u>Trans. Cambridge Bibl.Soc.</u> 7 (2) 1978, 135-55.

An account of the library during the 16th century is followed by the
text of two inventories, dated 1544 and 1557/8; the first lists 92
volumes.

CAMBRIDGE. TRINITY COLLEGE

2612 P. Gaskell. Trinity College Library: the first 150 years. Cambridge
U.P. 1980. xix, 275p. illus, facsims, tables, plans.
T.L.S. Apr.24, 1981, 471. (G. Naylor)
Traces the steps whereby the Library grew from small beginnings in
the mid-16th century into the greatest of the Oxbridge college libraries. The contents of the Library are also described at a time
when Trinity men were central in their contribution to England's
spiritual, intellectual and scientific development. The history is
divided into two periods, from 1546 to 1600 and from 1601, when the
New Library was nearing completion, to 1695, when the Wren Library
was brought into use. Appendix A consists of a catalogue of the Library in 1600. Other appendices cover other 17th century catalogues,
the science books in c.1645, donations, a list of librarians, and
library regulations, 1651.

2613 J. Turner. Graciousness and effectiveness.
Lib.Assn Rec. 79 (9) 1977, 480-1. illus.
A description of the Wren Research Library at Trinity College. Its
present building was designed by Sir Christopher Wren, and houses a
rich collection, some of the most important items of which are described. Books acquired since 1920 are held in another library, the
present state of which is also described.

CAMBRIDGE. UNIVERSITY LIBRARY

2614 A.J.C. Bainton, compiler. 'Comedias sueltas' in Cambridge University
Library: a descriptive catalogue. Cambridge, Cambridge Univ. Library,
1977. xvi, 281p.
Rev. Bk Coll. 26 (4) 1977, 592, 595-6 (D. W. Cruickshank)
Library 33 (4) 1978, 341-3 (V. Dixon)
A complete list of Spanish plays in the University Library published
separately before 1800. Their provenance is explained in the intro-
duction. Most of them were donated in 1905 and 1933.

2615 J. Dreyfus. The shooting affair at Cambridge University Library.
Trans. Cambridge Bibl.Soc. 7 (3) 1979, 391-3.
A 1940 accident.

(2354) R. Myers. George Isaac Frederick Tupper, facsimilist, 'whose ability in this description of work is beyond praise' (1820?-1911).

(2360) [Obituary of Eric Ceadel, 1921-1979]

EDINBURGH

(2909) K. C. Crawford. The Dugald Stewart collection (Edinburgh University Library).

(2837) W. F. Engel. J. O. Halliwell-Phillips and the Edinburgh University Library.

(2862) C. P. Finlayson. Clement Litill and his library: the origins of Edinburgh University Library.

2616 P. D. Hancock. A short history of Edinburgh University Library compiled from various sources. Edinburgh, Edinburgh Univ. Library, 1980. [1], 18p.

The University received its royal charter in 1582, but the genesis of the University Library occurred in 1580 when the Edinburgh advocate Clement Little bequeathed his collection of some 300 legal and theological books to the Town and Kirk of Edinburgh. The growth of the Library and the contribution made by successive librarians up to the present is summarised. The librarians are listed in an appendix.

(2907) M.C.T. Simpson. Books belonging to Adam Smith in Edinburgh University Library: a survey of newly discovered items, with a general discussion.

GLASGOW

2617 J. Baldwin. Glasgow University Library's manuscripts: the non-Hunterian collections.
Bibliotheck 8 (4-6) 1977, 127-55. plates.

The earliest manuscripts in the Library are greek papyri from Egypt. Outside the Hunterian Collection there are 75 mediaeval manuscripts, some of which are described and their provenance traced in this article. Among later manuscripts, the Ferguson Collection of alchemical manuscripts and the papers of the painter Whistler, are noteworthy. The Library also possesses collections relating to the history of science, Scottish history, and music.

2618 H. M. Black. The Stirling Maxwell Collection of emblem books in Glasgow University Library.
Bibliotheck 8 (4-6) 1977, 156-67. plates, port.

This collection came to the Library in 1958, and contains emblem books and works on allied topics. Maxwell's life and collecting interests are described. The bulk of the collection is from the 17th century. Some of the items and bindings are described.

2619   C. H. Brock. The rediscovery of James Douglas.
       Bibliotheck 8 (4-6) 1977, 168-76. plates.
       The papers of James Douglas, the anatomist (1675-1742) are in the Hunterian Library, although how they came to be there is not clear. The systematic examination of the papers started in the early 20th century. They include material on phonetics, medicine and botany. Douglas also made a study of the Latin poet Horace, but his collection of editions was sold after his death.

2620   A. L. Brown. History in the making.
       College Courant 29 (58) 1977, 6-11.
       Glasgow University Library's catalogue of 1691 and the place of historical works in it, is considered in this historical survey of the study of history at the University.

2621   J. Durkan. The early history of Glasgow University Library: 1475-1710.
       Bibliotheck 8 (4-6) 1977, 102-26. plates.
       The first recorded gift to the Library was in 1475. Further donations were made during the 16th and 17th centuries, but during the 17th century purchases appear more regularly in the records. The first librarian was appointed in 1641. The library policies of successive Principals are examined. The stock and physical arrangements at the end of the period are described.

(2867) J. Durkan and J. Kirk. The University of Glasgow, 1451-1577.

        HULL

2622   T. W. Bamford. The University of Hull: the first fifty years. O.U.Press for the Univ. of Hull, 1978. x, 290p. plates, maps, tables, ports.
       A number of passages testify to the lack of library facilities at the time the first students were admitted, the very low level of expenditure on library materials in the 1930s and 1940s after the hurried purchase of the foundation collections, and the marked progress under the Vice-Chancellor Brynmor Jones, 1956-1972.

2623   Brynmor Jones Library. The Brynmor Jones Library, 1929-1979: a short account. Hull, Univ. of Hull, 1979. 36p. plates, ports.
       The Library's development is divided into four periods, each allocated its own chapter. Much attention is paid to the new building, stage one of which was completed in 1959 and stage two in 1969.

2624   L. J. Harris and B. Ll. James. The library of St. David's University
       College, Lampeter.
       Bk Coll. 26 (2) 1977, 195-227. plates.
           At the time the College opened, in 1827, the library possessed 4,000
           books. This was soon considerably increased by donations from its
           founder, Bishop Thomas Burgess and from Thomas Phillips. An out-
           standing feature is the large collection of tracts and pamphlets of
           the period 1638-1787 donated by Thomas Bowdler and collected by
           earlier members of his family. The growth of this collection is
           examined in some detail.

2625   D.T.W. Price. A history of Saint David's University College, Lampeter.
       Vol.1: to 1898. Cardiff, Univ. of Wales Press, 1977. xv, 222p. front.,
       plates, ports, bibliog.
           Chapter 9 deals with the College library, much of the information
           being provided by Brian Ll. James. The foundation collection, con-
           sisting of several substantial donations including the Tract Col-
           lection, was in existence before the College opened in 1827. By 1852
           the library contained over 35,000 volumes, but accessions almost dried
           up during the latter half of the century. Other references to the
           library are scattered throughout the book.

       LEEDS

2626   Brotherton Library. A catalogue of the Icelandic Collection, University
       Library, Leeds. Leeds, The Library, 1978. ix, 166p.
           The basis of the collection is the library of an Icelandic historian
           which was acquired in 1929. Originally consisting of some 5325 books,
           the number has since doubled.

2627   P. S. Morrish. The Brotherton Library, its Judaica and Cecil Roth.
       University of Leeds Review Vol.23 1980, 218-33. facsims.
           Yorkshire College, which later became the University of Leeds, was
           founded in 1874. Within a few years Semitic courses were held, and
           the slow growth of the Hebraic collections are described in this con-
           text. Growth quickened with the opening of the Brotherton Library in
           1936, but the collections were transformed by the acquisition of the
           major portion of the library of Cecil Roth in 1961. Some of Dr.
           Roth's most important manuscripts and printed books are described.

LEICESTER

(2344) [Obituary of John Anderson Barker, 1911-1977]

LIVERPOOL

2628   A. W. Hall. Library provision in the University of Liverpool, 1881-1938: the origins, growth and establishment of a decentralised library system. Univ. of Strathclyde, Department of Librarianship, 1975. [8] vi, 235p. illus, plan, bibliog. [Thesis submitted for M.A. degree. Typescript]
The first four chapters trace the history of the Library in the three periods 1881-1903; 1903-1918; 1918-1938. Chapter 5 analyses the reasons for the evolution of such an intensively decentralised system and the inherent advantages and disadvantages.

LONDON. CITY UNIVERSITY

(2569) S. J. Teague. The City University: a history.

LONDON

2629   B. Naylor. The libraries of London University: a historical sketch. In: University library history: an international review, edited by James Thompson. Bingley, 1980, 229-49. tables.
The University of London received its Royal Charter in 1836, but many of its institutions, e.g. the undergraduate medical schools, were founded long before that date. This forms a general history of the major collections.

2630   R. M. Nicholas. The development of medical libraries within the University of London and associated institutes. Ann Arbor, Michigan. University Microfilms International, 1978. 166p. illus, table, bibliog. Facsimile produced by microfilm-xerography of a dissertation submitted in part requirement for the MA degree in Librarianship at University College, London. School of Library, Archive and Information Studies, 1976. Covers 14 Medical Schools and 12 Institutes of the British Postgraduate Medical Federation. Chapter 1 deals with the origin and development of the Medical School Libraries founded before 1800: chapter 2 deals with those founded after 1800, and chapter 3 deals with the Institute Libraries.

LONDON. CHARING CROSS HOSPITAL MEDICAL SCHOOL

(3066) L. S. Godbolt. At the end of all our work is a patient.

LONDON. HEYTHROP COLLEGE

(2576) M. J. Walsh. Heythrop College Library.

70

LONDON. KING'S COLLEGE

2631   G. Huelin. King's College London, 1828-1978. Univ. of London, King's
        College, 1978. xii, 248p. plates, ports.

        Many passages relate to major acquisitions and to accommodation prob-
        lems during the 20th century, in particular, during the librarianship
        of Robert Hutton.

2632   A. M. Shadrake. The War Studies Library at King's College, London
        University.

        Aslib Proc. 29 (8) 1977, 295-301.

        The library, set up to meet the needs of a lectureship in military
        studies, originated in 1953 with a special grant. Its development to
        1977 is briefly recorded.

LONDON. LONDON SCHOOL OF ECONOMICS AND POLITICAL SCIENCE

2633   J. Harris. William Beveridge: a biography. Oxford, Clarendon Press,
        1977. [8], 488p. front.

        Pages 297-300 are concerned with the controversy surrounding the 1933
        proposal to transfer the library and several of the staff of the
        Frankfurt Institut für Sozialforschung to the London School of
        Economics. The Institute was well-known as a centre of Marxist
        studies and was threatened with confiscation by the German government.
        However, it was eventually offered asylum in Geneva.

(2899) Schmollers' Penguins.

2634   S. and B. Webb. The letters of Sidney and Beatrice Webb, edited by
        Norman Mackenzie. Cambridge U.P., in co-operation with the London School
        of Economics and Political Science, 1978. 3 vols.

        A number of letters in volumes 2 and 3 refer to the setting up of the
        British Library of Political and Economic Science at the London School
        of Economics. These include letters appealing for funds, proposals
        for a special collection on railways and characteristic letters to
        B. M. Headicar, the librarian, about library matters. In addition,
        letters in volume 2 refer to the Fabian book-box scheme, which sup-
        plied small circulating collections of books on economics and politics
        to local Fabian groups, Independent Labour Party branches and co-
        operative societies.

LONDON. NEW COLLEGE

(2577) G. F. Nuttall. New College, London, and its library: two lectures.

(2578) Sotheby and Co. Catalogue of printed books (including 'The Property of New College, London').

LONDON. SCHOOL OF SLAVONIC AND EAST EUROPEAN STUDIES

(2448) [Obituary of Heinz Schurer, 1910-1979]

2635 J.E.O. Screen and C. L. Drage. Church Slavonic and Russian books, 1552-1800, in the library of the School of Slavonic and East European Studies. Slavonic and East European Review 57 (3) 1979, 321-47.
> A checklist of the 113 titles dating from the 16th to 18th centuries, is prefaced by an account of the source of the books, the library of the Russian Orthodox Church in London, the Marsden Collection, formerly at King's College, London, and the library of the late Dr. Moses Gaster.

LONDON. ROYAL HOLLOWAY COLLEGE

(2374) [Obituaries of Florence Ellison, 1910-1978]

LONDON. UNIVERSITY COLLEGE

(2890) T. H. Hall. Search for Harry Price.

2636 J. Percival and W. A. Smeaton. Library and archive resources in the history of science at University College, London. British Journal for the History of Science Vol.11 1978, 191-5.
> Discusses the development of its scientific collections from its foundation in 1827.

2637 B. Tearle. The Law Library at University College London, 1829-1979. Law Librarian 10 (1) 1979, 3-7. bibliog.
> There is emphasis on the Library's early history, the re-organisation of 1908 and its subsequent development.

2638 J.A.B. Townsend. The Old Norse - Icelandic library at University College London. University of London Libraries Bulletin. 1 (16) 1979, 8-9, 14.
> The library of the Viking Society for Northern Research was transferred to University College, London, in 1931. Most books were destroyed in 1940, but the collection has been rebuilt.

(2891) A. Wesencraft. The Harry Price Library (in the University of London Library).

LONDON. WHITELANDS COLLEGE

2639 S. Ker. Whitelands.
In: University of London. Institute of Education Library. Education

Libraries Bulletin, Supplement 21, 1978. Books, libraries and teachers: towards a history of the London Institute of Education Area Library Service. Essays presented to Olive Stokes, edited by Margaret Couch, 58-70.

Whitelands College was established at Chelsea in 1841 as a Church of England institution for the training of schoolmistresses. In 1930 it moved to Putney. The writer was appointed College Librarian in 1948, and describes developments over the last 30 years in some depth, with observations on the college library scene in general.

LONDON. WYE COLLEGE

2640 Wye College. Library. A catalogue of agricultural and horticultural books, 1543-1918, in Wye College Library. Ashford, Kent, The Library, [1977]. [1], ii, 100p.

NOTTINGHAM

(2377) [Obituary of George Ellis Flack, 1893-1978]

OXFORD

2641 R.J.A. Finch. The development of libraries in the Universities of Oxford and Cambridge 1870-1939. Univ. College London, School of Library, Archive and Information Studies, 1974. [5], 55p. bibliog. [Thesis submitted as part requirement for M.A. degree. Typescript]

A broad survey of the copyright, college and specialist libraries between 1870 and 1918 and the inter-war period, concentrating on printed sources and accounts of university business, with only limited reference to manuscript materials and the internal working papers of the various libraries. During this period they evolved into modern research institutions, outgrowing their original semi-mediaeval context.

2642 N. R. Ker. Oxford college libraries before 1500.
In: The Universities in the Late Middle Ages, edited by Josef Ijsewijn and Jacques Paquet. Louvain, Louvain Univ. Press, 1978, 293-311.

Considers the collections of manuscripts at Oxford's ten secular colleges from the 13th century to 1375 and from 1375 to 1500, discussing their nature, date and how they reached the colleges.

2643 P. Morgan, compiler. Oxford libraries outside the Bodleian: a guide. 2nd ed. Oxford, Bodleian Library, 1980. xxi, 264p.
Rev. Lib.Hist. 5 (5) 1981, 168-9 (J. M. Fletcher)

Previous ed. Oxford, Oxford Bibliographical Society and the Bodleian Library, 1973 (see no. 1811).

(2652) A. Noel-Tod. The Bodleian Library in the eighteenth century, with
        reference to Oxford college libraries and the Radcliffe Library.

        OXFORD. BODLEIAN LIBRARY

 2644   N. Crum. Commonplace-books of Bishop William Lloyd, 1627-1717.
        Bod.Lib.Rec. 9 (5) 1977, 265-73. illus.
             An account of Bishop Lloyd's commonplace-books, many of which are in
             code, reflecting his reading and interests.

(2449) N. Davis. Dr. Robert Shackleton.

(2393) A. C. De La Mare and B. C. Barker-Benfield, editors.
        Manuscripts at Oxford: an exhibition in memory of Richard William Hunt
        (1908-1979).

 2645   R.J.W. Evans. Hungarica in the Bodleian: a historical sketch.
        Bod.Lib.Rec. 9 (6) 1978, 333-45.
             An account of the most important Hungarian printed books in the
             Bodleian.

(2856) J. F. Fuggles. Sir John Lambe's manuscripts in the Bodleian Library.

 2646   M. Heaney. The Bodleian classification of books.
        J. Librarianship 10 (4) 1978, 274-82.
             A description of E.W.B. Nicholson's decimal classification scheme for
             printed books. Dating from the 1880s, it is still used but is likely
             to be superseded soon.

(2389) J. M. Levine. Dr. Woodward's shield: history, science, and satire in
        Augustan England.

 2647   K. A. Manley. The Bodleian classification of manuscripts.
        J. Librarianship 10 (1) 1978, 56-9, 73.
             An account of E.W.B. Nicholson's scheme for arranging manuscripts
             according to broad subject, devised in the 1880s and still used.

 2648   K. A. Manley. A copyright problem for H. O. Coxe.
        Bod.Lib.Rec. 10 (1) 1978, 73-5.
             Two amusing poems are given, concerning a request by Bodley's Lib-
             rarian for the deposit of a book.

 2649   K. A. Manley. E.W.B. Nicholson and the Bodleian Facsimile Series.
        Bod.Lib.Rec. 9 (5) 1977, 279-91.
             In the 1880s E.W.B. Nicholson planned a grandiose scheme to issue
             cheap facsimiles of Bodleian manuscripts and printed books. Although
             the idea was never fully realised, it led to the introduction of
             photography into the Bodleian.

2650   K. A. Manley. Max Müller and the Bodleian sub-librarianship, 1865.
       Lib.Hist. 5 (2) 1979, 33-47.

       Max Müller arrived in London in 1846 to edit the Rig-Veda, settled in
       Oxford in 1848 and became Taylorian Professor of Modern European
       Languages in 1854. Against a background of factional intrigue and ·
       infighting within the University is recorded the appointment of
       Müller in 1865 as a sub-librarian of the Bodleian with special res-
       ponsibility for Oriental materials. He was Coxe's choice, and was
       approved by the Bodleian Curators, but opposed by many in Convocation,
       partly on the grounds of pluralism. However, Müller resigned in 1867
       because his health could not support two posts, literary labours and
       the Oxford climate.

2651   J. Morris, editor. The Oxford book of Oxford. Oxford U.P., 1978.
       xii, 402p. plates, map.

       Reproduces a number of contemporary references to the Bodleian Lib-
       rary, mainly of the 16th to 18th centuries.

2652   A. Noel-Tod. The Bodleian Library in the eighteenth century, with
       reference to Oxford college libraries and the Radcliffe Library.
       Aberystwyth, College of Librarianship Wales, 1980. [5], 42p. plates,
       plans, bibliog.
       Rev. **Lib.Hist.** 5 (5) 1981, 166-7 (P. Morgan)

       Begins by outlining the Bodleian's early promise and achievements of
       the 17th century, followed by reasons for inactivity during much of
       the 18th century. By contrast, several of the Oxford college lib-
       raries experienced renewal from the second quarter of the century,
       and the Bodleian itself showed a new level of activity and enterprise
       towards the end of the century.

(2390) [Obituary of Reginald Harrison Hill, 1894-1976]

(2394) [Obituary of Richard William Hunt, 1907-1979]

2653   I. G. Philip. The background to Bodleian purchases of incunabula at the
       Pinelli and Crevenna sales, 1789-90.
       Trans Cambridge Bibl.Soc. 7 (3) 1979, 369-75.

       Only in 1780 did the University of Oxford provide sufficient funds for
       the Bodleian to make large-scale purchases at important sales. This
       source, and an appeal to University members, produced the money needed
       to buy from the collections of Maffeo Pinelli (1736-85) and Pierre
       Antoine Crevenna.

2461) T. D. Rogers. Thomas Symonds to William Upcott.

(2785) A. G. Watson. Thomas Allen of Oxford and his manuscripts.

OXFORD. CHRIST CHURCH COLLEGE

(2799) A. Ashbee. Instrumental music from the library of John Browne (1608-1691), Clerk of the Parliaments.

2654 M. Chichester. The later development of Christ Church Library, Oxford.
Lib.Hist. 5 (4) 1980, 110-17.
Covers the development of the Library from the occupation of the new building in Peckwater Quadrangle in 1763, to date, tracing the extension of service to respond to the needs of the undergraduates as well as the senior members of the College. Administration, funding, special collections and catalogues are all considered.

OXFORD. KEBLE COLLEGE

2655 Keble College. The medieval manuscripts of Keble College, Oxford: a descriptive catalogue with summary descriptions of the Greek and Oriental manuscripts, compiled by M. B. Parkes. Scolar Press, 1979.
xxi, 365p. illus, plates, facsims.
Rev. T.L.S. Jan.23, 1981, 95 (A. I. Doyle)
All manuscripts bar one came to Keble College within the first 45 years of its foundation in 1870. The principal benefactors are recorded. Most were High Churchmen, sympathetic to the ideals of the founders, therefore liturgical works predominate.

OXFORD. LINCOLN COLLEGE

2656 V.H.H. Green. The Commonwealth of Lincoln College 1427-1977. Oxford U.P. 1979. xii, 746p. front., plates, map, ports.
The College was founded in order to train clergy in scholastic theology. The first donations of books were received in the 1430s.
A considerable amount of information about the library from this time until the conversion of All Saints church to house the collections in 1975, is given in appendix 7 and throughout the text.

OXFORD. MAGDALEN COLLEGE

(2849) N. R. Ker. The library of John Jewel.

OXFORD. MERTON COLLEGE

2657 J. M. Fletcher. Some further information about the medieval books of Merton College.
Bod.Lib.Rec. 10 (2) 1979, 84-6.
A note on several books found to be in the college library in the mid-15th century.

2658   H. W. Garrod and J.R.L. Highfield. An indenture between William Rede,
       Bishop of Chichester, and John Bloxham and Henry Stapilton, Fellows of
       Merton College, Oxford. London, 22 October 1374.
       Bod.Lib.Rec. 10 (1) 1978, 9-19.
           Bishop Rede gave to Merton College £100 and 100 books, here listed..

OXFORD. NEW COLLEGE

2659   R. W. Hunt. The medieval library.
       In: New College Oxford 1379-1979, edited by John Buxton and Penry
       Williams. New College, Oxford, 1979, 317-45.
           New College was the first Oxford or Cambridge college in which a
           library room was part of the original plan. A collection of books
           was provided by the founder, William of Wykeham. Early bequests are
           considered in some detail and the connection between the manuscripts
           and studies pursued by members of the College is discussed. Elsewhere
           in the book are found architectural details of the Founders Library,
           Upper Library and the new building of 1939.

OXFORD. ST. JOHN'S COLLEGE

2660   J. F. Fuggles. A history of the library of St. John's College, Oxford,
       from the foundation of the college to 1660. Oxford, Oxford Univ., 1976.
       185p. [Thesis submitted for B. Litt degree. Typescript]
           The College was founded in 1554. The building of the Library in 1596
           is described, together with the numerous benefactions received.

2661   J. F. Fuggles. The library of St. John's College, Oxford, 1555-1660.
       Lib.Assn Rare Books Group Newsletter 1 (13) 1979, 5-11.
           Both College and library were initially very poor, but by 1612
           probably possessed just under 2,000 volumes. William Laud provided
           money for a new building in the 1630s.

OXFORD. WORCESTER COLLEGE

(2922) R. Sayce. Another Oxford bibliophile: C. H. Wilkinson (1888-1960).

READING

2662   J. C. Holt. The University of Reading: the first fifty years. Reading,
       Reading U.P., 1977. xii, 372p. plates, plans, ports, bibliog.
           In 1892 the University Extension College was opened in conjunction
           with the Schools of Science and Art. The University Charter was
           granted in 1926. Appendix 4 reproduces Lady Stenton's personal and
           critical appraisal of the library's development since 1907. Elsewhere
           numerous passages supplement this account for the years since 1926, in

particular, relating to the early years of inadequate finance, the debate concerning the relative priority for a new Physics building and Library in the 1950s, the opening of the Library in 1963 and the growth of special collections in the 1960s and 1970s.

ST. ANDREWS

2663   E. K. Cameron. An early humanist edition of Aristotle at St. Andrews. _Bibliotheck_ 9 (2/3) 1978, 65-71.
The presence of this copy of Lefèvre's _Paraphrases_ of Aristotle at St. Andrews in the early 16th century gives an indication of the spread of humanism in Scotland. The book is described and its ownership traced.

2664   J. Durkan and R. V. Pringle. St. Andrews additions to Durkan and Ross: some unrecorded Scottish pre-Reformation ownsrship inscriptions in St. Andrews University Library.
Bibliotheck 9 (1) 1978, 13-20.
A list of ownership inscriptions from St. Andrews University Library which are not recorded in J. Durkan and A. Ross _Early Scottish libraries._ Glasgow, 1961.

SHEFFIELD

2665   C. K. Balmforth. University of Sheffield Library.
In: Encyclopedia of library and information science. Vol.27. New York, Dekker, 1979, 319-25. bibliog.
The University was created in 1905, an amalgamation of several earlier institutions. The history of their libraries is outlined, and fuller treatment is given to the development of the University Library from 1905 to the opening of the new library building in 1959.

SOUTHAMPTON

(2345) [Obituary of Herbert William Belmore, 1893-1978]

(2880) Parkes Library, University of Southampton.

LIBRARIES: Ecclesiastical

C A T H E D R A L

2666   E. A. Read. Cathedral libraries: a supplementary checklist.
        Lib.Hist. 4 (5) 1978, 141-63.
        This list supplements the previous checklist (see no.1078), con-
        taining some 250 additional items. Donors' books and borrowers'
        registers are now included, together with items pertaining to those
        cathedrals of modern foundation previously excluded.

        CANTERBURY

2667   M. Gibson. Lanfranc of Bec. Oxford, Clarendon Press, 1978. xii, 266p.
        front., map, bibliog.
        The weaknesses of the pre-Conquest library of Christ Church, Canter-
        bury, with its lack of Continental scholarship, its idiosyncratic
        survivals and absence of tradition of book production, is contrasted
        with the library as reformed by Lanfranc, who imported texts,
        especially canon law, from Bec, formed a scriptorium and developed
        the collections on systematic lines.

        CHICHESTER

(2811) M. Hobbs. More books from the library of John Donne.

        DURHAM

2668   B. Crosby. A 17th-century Durham inventory.
        Musical Times Vol.119 February 1978, 167, 169-70.
        Two rolls among the muniments of Durham Cathedral list the music
        books in use in the cathedral about 1665. Out of a possible 50 books,
        no fewer than 20 are still in their place of origin.

2669   R. C. Norris. Treasures of the cathedral.
        In: Durham Cathedral: resource material for schools collected by the
        Joint Curriculum Study Group of the Durham Education Assembly. New-
        castle, Graham, 1976, 4-18. plate, facsims.
        Durham became a Benedictine house in the 11th century, inheriting a
        tradition of learning and book collecting. Its manuscripts and early
        printed books are discussed and the various antiquarian collections,
        mostly dating from the 18th and early 19th century, which comprise the
        Dean and Chapter's historical and topographical collection, are
        described.

(2682) A. J. PIPER. The libraries of the Monks of Durham.

EXETER

2670 A. M. Erskine. Exeter Cathedral library and archives.
Devon Historian Vol.8 1974, 17-21.
> An outline history of the library from its 11th century foundation by
> Leofric, the first bishop of the diocese, together with details of
> subject coverage and its major treasures.

HEREFORD

(2416) F. C. Morgan's writings: a list published to mark his one hundredth
birthday.

(2417) P. Morgan. Frederick Charles Morgan.

(2418) [Obituaries of Frederick Charles Morgan, 1878-1978]

(2419) P. Whiteman. Eighty-one years a librarian.

LICHFIELD

2671 Lichfield Cathedral. Library. Lichfield Cathedral Library: a catalogue
of the Cathedral Library manuscripts, compiled by B. S. Benedikz.
Revised edition. Birmingham, University Library, 1978. [1] 43f.
Previous edition 1974.

ROCHESTER

(2683) R. Stockdale. Benedictine libraries and writers.

SALISBURY

2672 H. Bailey. Salisbury Cathedral Library: a brief account of its history
and contents. Salisbury, Friends of Salisbury Cathedral, 1978. 15p.

WINCHESTER

2673 F. Bussby. Winchester Cathedral 1079-1979. Southampton, Paul Cave,
1979. xvi, 352p. front., illus, plates, plans, facsims, ports.
> Several passages deal with the cathedral library at different periods,
> in particular, the revival of its fortunes in the 17th century under
> Bishop Morley. His large personal library came to the cathedral fol-
> lowing his death in 1684. The library was designed to be used by the
> prebendaries and the diocesan clergy, and its contribution to 18th
> century scholarship is demonstrated.

YORK

2674 C.B.L. Barr. The Minster Library.
In: A history of York Minster, edited by G. E. Aylmer and Reginald Cant.

Oxford, Clarendon Press, 1977, 487-539. illus, facsims, ports.

A general historical account from the 8th century library attached to
the cathedral school and the beginnings of a minster library proper
in the early 16th century, to the 1970s. It is particularly useful
for its account of 20th century developments, including the unfortunate episode of the sale of rare books in 1930 and the relationship of the library with the new University of York since 1964.

2675 York Minster. Library. A catalogue of the printed music published before
1850 in York Minster Library, compiled by David Griffiths. York, York
Minster Library, 1977. xxi, 118p. facsims, port.

The introduction and appendices mention previous catalogues, the Sharp
gift to make good the loss of music in the fire of 1829 and the gift
of music by William Priestley in 1835.

M O N A S T I C   A N D   R E L I G I O U S   O R D E R S

2676 W. R. Jones. Franciscan education and monastic libraries: some documents.

Traditio Vol.30 1974, 435-45

In the 13th century the English Franciscans compiled a form of union
catalogue of books, mainly patristic and theological, located in over
180 English and Scottish Monastic libraries. Various surviving
editions are described and discussed. The work is a precursor of
that compiled by John Boston of Bury in the 15th century, but the
writer concludes that "unlike the Franciscan catalogue, which was
part of a co-ordinated educational programme, Boston's catalogue is a
literary curiosity-piece - the unfinished work of a single monastic
bibliographer."

2677 F. S. Merryweather. Bibliomania in the Middle Ages ... A new and revised
edition prepared by H. B. Copinger ... Folcroft, Pa., Folcroft Library
Editions, 1974. 288p.

Facsimile reprint of the edition published in London by the Woodstock
Press, 1933. An account of mediaeval book production and the nature
and organisation of monastic libraries is followed by a discursive
tour of the latter, with particular mention of such monkish bibliophiles as Benedict Biscop and Boniface. The libraries of the
religious orders and of lay collectors are also noticed.

2678 L. S. Thompson. Scriptoria.
In: Encyclopedia of library and information science. Vol.27. New York,
Dekker, 1979, 139-59. facsims, bibliog.

In this general account of scriptoria, the carrel system, materials and techniques, there is some mention of English monastic and religious houses.

2679   R. M. Thomson. The reading of William of Malmesbury: addenda and corrigenda.
Revue Bénédictine 86 (3-4) 1976, 327-35.
For the main article see no.1852. This provides a supplementary list of authors and works known to William of Malmesbury.

2680   R. M. Thomson. The reading of William of Malmesbury: further additions and reflections.
Revue Bénédictine 89 (3-4) 1979, 313-24.
A further list of authors and works is followed by reflections on how the new material affects the general conclusions reached in 1975.

CAMBRIDGE

2681   N. R. Ker. Cardinal Cervini's manuscripts from the Cambridge friars.
In: Xenia medii aevi historiam illustrantia oblata Thomae Kaeppeli O.P., edited by Raymundus Creytens and Pius Künzle. Roma, Edizioni di Storia e Letteratura, 1978. Vol.1, pp 51-71.
Manuscripts forming part of the Ottoboni Collection in the Vatican Library are identified as originating from the libraries of the Dominican, Franciscan and Augustinian friaries in Cambridge. Apparently they were assembled, sent overseas and came into the possession of Cardinal Marcello Cervini some time before 1545. They form a large proportion of the manuscripts from English friaries which are still extant.

CANTERBURY

(2667) M. Gibson. Lanfranc of Bec.

DURHAM

2682   A. J. Piper. The libraries of the monks of Durham.
In: Medieval scribes, manuscripts and libraries: essays presented to N. R. Ker, edited by M. B. Parkes and Andrew G. Watson. Scolar Press, 1978, 213-49. facsims, map, plan.
Durham Cathedral Priory was founded in 1083. The first part of the article records the evolution, accommodation and arrangement of almost a dozen separate collections of books which existed within the monastic complex before the monastery's dissolution in 1539. The second part deals with book collections separate from service books, which are known to have existed at dependent cells at Oxford, Farne and

Lindesfarne.

ROCHESTER

2683   R. Stockdale. Benedictine libraries and writers.
In: The Benedictines in Britain. The British Library, 1980, 62-81.
illus, facsims.

    Particular reference is made to the library of the Benedictine cathe-
    dral priory of St Andrew at Rochester, a fairly typical library for
    its size. Over one hundred of its volumes have been identified in
    the British Library.

ST. ALBANS

2684   R. W. Hunt. The library of the Abbey of St. Albans.
In: Medieval scribes, manuscripts and libraries: essays presented to
N. R. Ker, edited by M. B. Parkes and Andrew G. Watson. Scolar Press,
1978, 251-77.

    Three documents are reproduced and discussed: excerpts from a 12th
    century catalogue, a leaf of a borrowers' list of the 15th century
    and a list of books sent to the Priory of Hertford, a cell of St.
    Albans. These, together with the surviving books and the chronicles,
    shed light upon the organisation and growth of the library up to the
    first half of the 15th century.

ST. ANDREWS

(2834) J. Durkan and J. Russell. John Grierson's book-list.

SAWLEY, Cambs

2685   D. N. Dumville. The sixteenth-century history of two Cambridge books
from Sawley.
Trans. Cambridge Bibl.Soc. 7 (4) 1980, 427-44.

    A description of two (both chronicles) of only three known surviving
    books from the Cistercian library at Sawley Abbey, established 1148.
    The books later had a variety of owners, including Archbishop Matthew
    Parker.

SYON

(2795) C. Garton. A Fifteenth century headmaster's library.

TORRE ABBEY, Devon

2686   D. Seymour. Torre Abbey: an account of its history, buildings, cartu-
laries and lands. Torquay, The Author, 1977. xvi, 303p. illus, plates,
facsims, maps, plans, bibliog.

A few facts about the library of Torre Abbey, together with remarks about Premontratensian libraries in general, are given in the addenda.

YORK

(2559) J. H. Moran. Education and learning in the city of York 1300-1560.

P A R I S H

2687 D.G.C. Allan and R. E. Schofield. Stephen Hales: scientist and philan-
thropist. Scolar Press, 1980. xi, 220p. bibliog.
    Stephen Hales (1677-1761) was one of the Associates of Dr. Bray from
    their genesis in 1723. The book touches on his involvement in the
    formation of parochial libraries.

2688 D. E. Gerard. Parish libraries.
In: Encyclopedia of library and information science. Vol.21. New York,
Dekker, 1977, 424-32. bibliog.
    The history of libraries associated with parish churches is divided
    into the periods pre-Reformation, 1550-1700 and 1700-1800. Due regard
    is paid to the work of Thomas Bray and his Scottish counterpart James
    Kirkwood.

2689 B. Heeney. A different kind of gentleman: parish clergy as professional
men in early and mid-Victorian England. Hamden, Conn.; Archon Books for
the Conference on British Studies and Wittenberg Univ., 1976. xii, 169p.
bibliog.
    Indicates ways in which the clergy sought to introduce working people
    to books for recreation and self-improvement, e.g. by reading rooms
    in church workingmen's institutes, village reading room and parish
    libraries. The Church of England Book Hawking Union founded in 1859
    took moral books to the rural poor.

2690 P. Morgan. Nineteenth-century church lending libraries in England.
In: Proceedings of the Lib.Assn Study School and National Conference,
Nottingham 1979. Lib.Assn, 1980, 29-31.
    Summarises what is known of 19th century collections of books kept in
    churches and parish rooms for lending to parishioners, drawn from the
    meagre sources which survive.

2691 D. M. Williams. English parochial libraries: a history of changing
attitudes.
Antiquarian Book Monthly Review 5 (4) 1978, 138-47. plates, facsims.
    A history of parochial libraries from mediaeval times to the mid-19th

century, citing many examples, is accompanied by post-War evidence of
an increasing acknowledgement of their importance and of the
restoration, cataloguing and re-housing of a number of them.

2692   D. M. Williams.   The use and abuse of a pious intention: changing
attitudes to parochial libraries.
In: Proceedings of the Lib.Assn Study School and National Conference,
Nottingham 1979. Lib.Assn, 1980, 21-8.

Deals with those parochial libraries which were founded between the
Reformation and the mid-19th century, recording fluctuating interest
shown in such collections, reference to them in reports and other
publications and losses and survivals.

BECCLES, Suffolk

(2535) M. Ellwood.   Library provision in a small market town, 1700-1929.

CAMBRIDGESHIRE

2693   A history of the county of Cambridge and the isle of Ely. Vol.6, ed. by
A.P.M. Wright. Oxford U.P. for the Institute of Historical Research,
1978. xvi, 314p. front., plates, maps, plans. (Victoria history of
the counties of England).

There is brief mention of ten parochial libraries and reading rooms
in villages in South East Cambridgeshire. Apart from one dating from
the early 18th century, they all date from c.1885-1910.

CASTLETON, Derbyshire

2694   Castleton Parish Library: the Farran Collection: a catalogue compiled by
Joan E. Friedman. Sheffield, Univ. of Sheffield, Postgraduate School of
Librarianship and Information Science, 1977. [4], v, 150p.

The core of the collection was the library of Frederick Farran, a
former vicar of Castleton, who died in 1817. He had been in the habit
of lending books to his parishioners. 700 volumes remain.

CASTLETOWN, Isle of Man

(2701) J. P. Ferguson. The parochial libraries of Bishop Wilson.

HATFIELD BROAD OAK, Essex

2695   A. Jones. Parochial learning.
Country Life Feb.16, 1978, 394. illus.

This letter provides brief details of the library at St. Mary's,
Hatfield Broad Oak, one of the four parochial libraries in Essex.
The library was built in 1708 to house the collection of books of the
incumbent, the Rev. George Stirling. The library consists of some 300

books, over the years further volumes having been added.

HITCHAM, Suffolk

2696   J. Russell-Gebbett. Henslow of Hitcham: botanist, educationalist and
clergyman. Lavenham, Dalton, 1977. 139p. illus, plates, facsims, ports.
In an attempt to improve the education of his parishioners, John
Stevens Henslow started a small lending library in 1840. He was also
involved in many other aspects of adult education, including museum
work, exhibitions, expeditions and adult literacy classes.

KING'S LYNN

2697   R. Wilson. St. Margaret's Church Library, King's Lynn: a short history.
King's Lynn, King's Lynn Public Library, 1977. [1] 12 leaves [type-
script]
The history of the libraries of St. Margaret's (f. 1631) and St.
Nicholas's (f. 1617). The latter was removed to St. Margaret's in
1797. Some light is thrown on the continuing debate between Church
and Corporation as to the matter of ownership. The writer also tells
how he removed the deteriorating collection from a damp attic to the
Public Library in 1965, and records its subsequent restoration.

LANGLEY, Bucks

2698   J. Harris. A rare and precious room: the Kederminster Library, Langley,
Buckinghamshire.
Country Life 162 (4195) 1977, 1576-9. illus.
A family pew with a library leading from it was built by Sir John
Kederminster possibly between 1613 and 1623. The library walls are
completely covered with over 250 painted panels which disclose eight
presses with doors painted on the back with tromp-l'oeil books. The
library consists of about 270 books, mainly Latin patristic works
published on the Continent in the early 17th century.

LLANBADARN FAWR, Dyfed

2699   E. G. Bowen. A history of Llanbadarn Fawr. Llanbadarn, Aberystwyth,
Ysgol Cwmpadarn Centenary Celebrations Joint Committee: llandysul, Gower
Press, 1979. xxii, 237p. illus, plates, facsims, maps, ports.
Includes a brief note on the parochial library established in the
Church at Llanbadarn Fawr in 1710.

MAIDSTONE

2700   J. M. Russell. The history of Maidstone. Rochester, Hallewell, 1978.
xi, 423p. front., illus, plates.

Facsimile reprint of 1st ed., Maidstone, Vivish, 1881. Pages 121-2
record the formation of a parochial library by Rev. Gilbert Innes,
who was curate of All Saints, 1692-1711. It was augmented by Rev.
Samuel Weller who arranged for the purchase of the library of Thomas
Bray following the latter's death. The collection was re-catalogued
and restored in 1810, and was removed to the Museum later in the
century.

MAN, Isle of

2701   J. P. Ferguson. The parochial libraries of Bishop Wilson. Douglas,
Shearwater Press, 1975. [8], 107p. port., bibliog.
Thomas Wilson (1663-1755) was consecrated Bishop of Sodor and Man in
1698, and was inspired by Dr. Thomas Bray to form parochial libraries
in 1699 for the instruction of his clergy. By 1740 each library consisted of approximately 40 works. These largely identical collections
are described. Their condition as reported in early visitation
returns is noted, and there is information on donors. Present day
traces of the collections are reported. A catalogue of the books in
the Library at Castletown in 1716 is reproduced in an appendix. Many
of the 830 volumes were acquired in the mid-17th century.

NANTWICH, Cheshire

2702   E. Garton. Nantwich in the 18th century: a study of 18th century life
and affairs. Chester, Cheshire Libraries and Museums, 1978. [6], 84p.
plates, maps, bibliog.
Pages 77-8 mention the library in Nantwich Parish Church, founded in
1704 to provide a reference library for use by the clergy of the
Deanery of Nantwich. Its history is outlined and there is a brief
analysis of its contents.

NEWCASTLE UPON TYNE

(3021) R. J. Charleton. Newcastle town.

REIGATE

2703   W. Hooper. Reigate: its story through the ages, including Redhill.
Dorking, Kohler and Coombes, 1979. [2], 217p. front., plates, facsims,
maps, plan, port.
Facsimile reprint of 1st ed., Guildford, Surrey Archaeological
Society, 1945. Reigate Parish Library, housed in the upper storey of
the old vestry, is recorded on pages 62-7. It was founded in 1701 by
Rev. Andrew Cranston, and in 1708 its administration was placed in the

hands of 44 trustees. There is mention of a number of distinguished donors and benefactors, indicating a wide level of support. Its readership was also wider than most parochial libraries, including parishioners, neighbouring clergy and gentry.

SUFFOLK

2704   A. E. Birkby, editor. Suffolk parochial libraries: a catalogue. Mansell, for the St. Edmundsbury and Ipswich Diocesan Parochial Libraries Committee, 1977 xxii, 129p. front., facsim.
Rev. Antiquarian Book Monthly Review 5 (4) 1978. (D. M. Williams).
The union catalogue is introduced by Canon Fitch, who provides an exemplary account of the fifteen parochial libraries which are known to have existed in Suffolk. Eight of these, dating from 1595 to 1773, survive almost intact, and their 1850 volumes are the subject of this catalogue. Some of them were personal libraries bequeathed by their owners. Canon Fitch also tells of recent steps taken to preserve the remaining parochial libraries. Five are now housed in the cathedral library and three still remain in their respective churches.

WIMBORNE

2705   D. M. Williams. A chained library.
Antiquarian Book Monthly Review 5 (9) 1978, 387-8.
Brief details of the history and present condition of the library of Wimborne Minster.

YORKSHIRE

2706   C.B.L. Barr. Parish libraries in a region: the case of Yorkshire.
In: Proceedings of the Lib.Assn Study School and National Conference, Nottingham 1979. Lib.Assn, 1980, 32-41.
A chronological survey of Yorkshire parochial libraries dating from mediaeval times to the 19th century, giving details of the collections, their donors and subsequent fortunes, including examples of wilful neglect. Their importance as collections rather than assemblages of odd volumes, is stressed, and steps taken in Yorkshire to secure their future are mentioned. There are many references to sources.

D I S S E N T I N G   C H A P E L S

LANCASTER

2707   M. Mullett. Historical records and early printed books at Lancaster Quaker Meeting House.
Gutenberg Jahrbuch 1978, 358-62.

Provides details of a lending library probably dating from the early
19th century, containing a number of volumes of the 17th and 18th
centuries.

LEEDS

2708   R. Mortimer. Leeds Friends' Old Library.
Lib.Assn Rare Bks Group Newsletter 1 (10) 1977, 13-14.
> Brief note of a collection of approx. 500 volumes, printed between
> 1651 and 1850, deposited in the Brotherton Library in 1976 by the
> Society of Friends.

LONDON. PADDINGTON

2709   H. E. Bonsall and E. H. Robertson. The dream of an ideal city: Westbourne Park 1877-1977. Westbourne Park Baptist Church, 1978. vii, 247p.
illus, ports.
> There is passing reference to Sunday school lending libraries and the
> library of the Westbourne Park Institute, associated with the church
> during Dr Clifford's pastorate. The latter issued some 2000 books
> annually to 200 readers. Students studied a wide variety of subjects
> in nearly 70 classes.

SOMERSET

2710   S. C. Morland, editor. The Somersetshire Quarterly Meeting of the
Society of Friends, 1668-1699. Somerset Record Society, vol.75 1978.
[9], 303p.
> There are references to the publication and distribution of Quaker
> literature, and the placing of copies of George Fox's Journal in
> meeting houses. It was also resolved to establish a library at
> Ilchester or elsewhere.

YORKSHIRE

2711   W. P. Thistlethwaite. Yorkshire Quarterly Meeting (of the Society of
Friends) 1665-1966. Harrogate, The Author, 1979. ix, 433, [19] p.
> There is much information about the distribution of books among
> Friends, particularly in the 17th and 18th centuries, and the forma-
> tion of a Quarterly Meeting Library and libraries at local meetings.
> At Hovingham village books were taken round and exchanged in 17
> neighbouring villages "by an energetic female connected with the
> Primitive Methodists, on the plan adopted by Tract-lending associa-
> tions."

DOWN

2712   J.R.R. Adams. Library provision for children in County Down prior to
        1850.
        Irish Booklore 4 (1) 1978, 20-23.

    Largely a study of Sunday school and school library provision in the
    early 19th century, with particular reference to the work of the
    Sunday School Society for Ireland (f. 1809) and the Society for Pro-
    moting the Education of the Poor in Ireland, better known as the Kil-
    dare Place Society (f. 1811).

LIVERPOOL

2713   J. E. Vaughan. The former St. Paul's Young Men's Friendly Society Lib-
        rary.
        Notes and Queries 24 (2) 1977, 129-30.

    The Society was founded in 1879, being housed at St. Paul's Church
    Institute, Miles Street, Liverpool, associated with St. Paul's,
    Princes Park. It formed part of a national organisation. The 136
    surviving titles date from 1812 to 1926, and are briefly analysed.

WINDSOR

2714   J. Callard. Catalogue of printed books, St. George's Chapel, Windsor.
        Library 32 (2) 1977, 161.

    A short letter of clarification on the author's "Catalogue of books
    (pre-1751) in the library of St George's Chapel, Windsor Castle" 1976,
    see no.1888.

YORKSHIRE

(2561) J. Smurthwaite. A collection of Yorkshire library catalogues.

LIBRARIES: Mechanics' institutes and other workers' institutes

(3091) J. Benson. British coalminers in the Nineteenth Century: a social history.

(3137) P. Corrigan and V. Gillespie. Class struggle, social literacy and idle time: the provision of public libraries in England.

2715 R. Lowery. Robert Lowery: Radical and Chartist, edited by Brian Harrison and Patricia Hollis. Europa Publications, 1979. vii, 283p. front., bibliog.

    Contains brief, but interesting references to various types of library provision for the working classes, of which he was a prominent advocate. He recalls that when he was a child his family had to choose between a weekly library subscription and a Sunday dinner.

2716 E. Nicholson. Working class readers and libraries: a social history 1800-1850. Univ.College, London. School of Library and Information Studies, 1976. [2], 125p. facsims, tables, bibliog. [Dissertation submitted as part requirement for MA degree in Library and Information Studies. Typescript]

    Attempts to discover English working class attitudes to libraries, particularly those of a paternalistic nature, to determine the extent to which libraries were established by working class groups, and to assess to what extent they met the needs of working class readers. Particular attention is paid to libraries of the Co-operative and Owenite movements and to those of Radicals and Chartists.

(2634) S. and B. Webb. The letters of Sidney and Beatrice Webb.

    IRELAND

(3099) P. Bolger. The Irish Co-operative Movement: its history and development.

    WALES

2717 H. Francis. News from the South Wales Miners' Library.
Llafur 2 (4) 1979, 100-1.

    Reports on several developments including the cataloguing of the International Brigade Collection and on the growing American collection.

2718 H. Francis. The origins of the South Wales Miners' Library.
Asst Libn 70 (12) 1977, 186-90, illus, port.

An edited version of the article which appeared in <u>History Workshop</u>
1 (2) 1976 (see no.1897).

BELFAST. PEOPLE'S CIRCULATING LIBRARY

(3101) H. G. Calwell. The People's Circulating Library.

CARLISLE

2719 B. Graham. Some aspects of working class adult education in nineteenth
century Carlisle. Nottingham, Univ.Faculty of Education, 1972. [Thesis
submitted for degree of M.Phil.]
> Includes a comparison of the facilities provided in the mid-19th
> century by the working men's reading rooms and the mechanics'
> institute. The former had more than twice the membership of the
> latter.

CLEVELAND

2720 M. C. Horton. The story of Cleveland: history, anecdote and legend.
Cleveland County Libraries, 1979. xxii, 568p. plates, facsims, map,
bibliog.
> There are several brief references to public libraries and to the
> libraries and reading rooms of mechanics' institutes.

DURHAM CO.

(2720) M. C. Horton. The story of Cleveland.

LEADHILLS, Lanarkshire. READING SOCIETY

(3109) P. Jackaman. The company, the common man, and the library: Leadhills and
Wanlockhead.

LEICESTER. MECHANICS' INSTITUTE

2721 C. E. Grewcock. The Leicester Mechanics' Institute, 1833-1870.
In: The adaptation of change: essays upon the history of nineteenth-
century Leicester and Leicestershire, edited by Daniel Williams.
Leicester, Leicestershire Museums, 1980, 13-34. charts.
> By 1839 the library consisted of 1600 volumes. Fiction, history,
> magazines, biography, and travel were most in demand. The Institute
> was beset by financial problems in the 1840s and from the 1850s was
> in continuous slow decline. Its library eventually formed the basis
> of the Leicester Free Library.

LONDON

2722 J. Noyce. Radicalism, literacy and a pint of coffee: working people's
coffee houses in London, 1830-c.1836.

<u>Studies in Labour History</u> No.4 1980, 25-39.

Discusses the part played by coffee houses in the everyday life of working people in the London of the 1830s. Particular attention is paid to those serving radically minded artisans and labourers. Their main object was the provision of liquid refreshment and food, the provision of newspapers, books and pamphlets, and acting as a forum for discussion and meetings.

LONDON. INFIDEL LIBRARY, Fleet Street

(3115) J. Noyce. Richard Carlile and the Infidel Library.

LONDON. LONDON SOCIETY OF COMPOSITORS

(3118) D. Mayall. The Library of the London Society of Compositors, 1855-1896.

LONDON. WORKING MEN'S ASSOCIATION

2723 G. Howell. A history of the Working Men's Association from 1836 to 1850: introduction by D. J. Rowe. Newcastle upon Tyne, Graham, [1972] 99p.

George Howell's manuscript, now in the possession of the Bishopsgate Institute, is printed for the first time. The history was never completed, the detailed account covering only the years 1836-7. The Association occupied premises near the Gray's Inn Road. The rules of the library and reading room are reproduced on pages 39-40. William Lovett allowed his library to be used by members. A circulating library was also formed, and a number of donations were received.

NEWCASTLE UPON TYNE

(3119) J. Knott. Newcastle-upon-Tyne newsrooms.

NOTTINGHAM

(3123) S. Dolman. History and social effects of Nottingham's libraries before 1850.

2724 J. J. Rowley. Drink and the public house in Nottingham, 1830-1860.
<u>Transactions of the Thoroton Society</u> Vol.79 1975, 72-83.

There is much useful information concerning operatives' libraries established at public houses. Several had seceded from other operatives' libraries which refused to purchase political or religious materials, and built up collections of several thousand volumes. The provision of newspapers and the employment of newspaper readers is also mentioned. The connection between these libraries and working class radicalism is stressed, and the full range of activities centred on public houses is surveyed. Libraries were also formed at temperance institutions.

STAFFORDSHIRE

2725   R. A. Lowe. The mechanics' institutions of the Potteries.
North Staffordshire Journal of Field Studies Vol.10 1970, 75-82.
A general survey of mechanics' institutes of the Potteries, with
particular reference to the Potteries Mechanics' Institution at
Hanley. Library and reading room facilities are mentioned. Such
institutions were usually small, and were linked in their activities
with the predominant local industry. Their general failure to gain
the confidence of the working classes is discussed.

WANLOCKHEAD, Dumfriesshire. MINERS' LIBRARY

(3137) J. C. Crawford. The restoration of the Wanlockhead Miners' Library.

(3138) J. C. Crawford. Wanlockhead Miners' Library: a guide book.

(3129) J. C. Crawford. Wanlockhead Museum Trust and the restoration of Wanlockhead Miners' Library.

(3130) J. C. Crawford and S. James. Library's history reflects changing
fortunes of a miners' village high in the Lowlands.

(3109) P. Jackaman. The company, the common man, and the library: Leadhills
and Wanlockhead.

(3131) P. Keating. A miners' library.

WOLVERHAMPTON. ATHENAEUM AND MECHANICS' LIBRARY

2726   M. Fogarty. An analysis of the reasons behind the decline and ultimate
collapse of the Wolverhampton Athenaeum and Mechanics' Library, (1847-
1869).
West Midland Studies Vol.12 1979, 32-9.
The origins of the Wolverhampton Athenaeum can be directly traced to
the foundation of the Wolverhampton Tradesmens' and Mechanics' Library
in 1827. Decline began about 1858. This was largely because it
reflected the interests and preoccupations of the dominant middle
class group. The majority had insufficient education to take full
advantage of the programme of lectures and classes and to be able to
appreciate the library facilities.

WORKSOP. READING SOCIETY AND MECHANICS' INSTITUTE

(3013) D. J. Thomas. Libraries of Worksop, 1830-1939.

YORKSHIRE

(2720) M. C. Horton. The story of Cleveland.

LIBRARIES: National

(2501) F. Strong. The Friends of the National Libraries.

2727 I. R. Willison. The history of the rare printed book and special collections in the copyright deposit libraries of the British Isles since the foundation of the British Museum Library in 1753.
In: The Library Association Centenary Conference: proceedings. Lib.Assn, 1977, 31-4.

> Rare book collections were not established in British copyright deposit libraries as separate administrative divisions until the 1960s. The theory and practice relating to the treatment of such materials is traced historically. The reason for such a late development is considered to be the essential archival function of such libraries as opposed to the service function, and its realisation was due to movements within the world of learning itself. The rôle of German positivist scholarship and the rise of historical bibliography is discussed.

ENGLAND

(2410) R. W. and G. P. Ackerman. Sir Frederic Madden: a biographical sketch and biobibliography.

2728 D. Anderson. Reflections on librarianship: observations arising from examination of the Garrick collection of old plays in the British Library.
Br.Lib.J. 6 (1) 1980, 1-6. illus.

> The Garrick collection was acquired in 1780. During the next 60 years several items were disposed of as 'duplicates' and others transferred, often, the author suggests, needlessly. Panizzi had the volumes rebound and 'improved'.

(2426) M. Borrie. Panizzi and Madden.

2729 British Library. Department of Manuscripts. Catalogue of additions to manuscripts 1946-1950. British Museum Publications, 1900. 3 vols.
Includes fourteen manuscripts containing catalogues of private libraries.

2730 British Library. Department of Manuscripts. Catalogue of additions to the manuscripts, 1756-1782, additional manuscripts 4101-5017. British Museum Publications, 1977. ix, 706p.

2731   British Library. Department of Manuscripts. Catalogue of dated and datable manuscripts c.700-1600 in the Department of Manuscripts, the British Library. [Compiled by] Andrew G. Watson. British Museum Publications, 1979. 2 vols. plates.

2732   British Library. Department of Oriental Printed Books and Manuscripts. Catalogue of Ethiopian manuscripts in the British Library acquired since the year 1877 [compiled] by S. Strelcyn. British Museum Publications, 1978. xvi, 184p. illus, plates, facsims.

(2427) British Library. Department of Printed Books. Sir Anthony Panizzi 1797-1879: an exhibition from 12 April to 15 July 1979.

(2828) British Library. Lending Division. The Edwin Gardiner chess collection.

(2428) A. C. Brodhurst. A side-light on Panizzi in the letters of Prosper Mérimée.

(2830) J. Brooke. King George III.

(2904) J. A. Clarke. Sir Hans Sloane and Abbé Jean Paul Bignon: notes on collection building in the eighteenth century.

2733   M. M. Foot. The Henry Davis gift: a collection of bookbindings. Volume 1, Studies in the history of bookbinding. British Museum Publications, 1979. 352p. illus.
Rev. Bk Coll. 29 (1) 1980, 119-21 (N. Barker)
    Library 2 (2) 1980, 240-3 (H. M. Nixon)
    Pap.Bibl.Soc.Am 75 (4) 1981, 498-9 (R. Nikirk)
    T.L.S. Jan.30, 1981, 123 (G. Barber)
The introduction states that Henry Davis spent over 25 years in building up one of the finest collections of bindings (from the 12th to the 20th centuries) in private hands. They came to the British Museum Library in 1968. There is an index of previous owners.

(2429) M.R.D. Foot. Gladstone and Panizzi.

2734   A. E. Gunther. The Royal Society and the foundation of the British Museum, 1753-1781.
Notes and Records of the Royal Society of London 33 (2) 1979, 207-16.
The influence of the Royal Society on the formative period of the British Museum is suggested by tables listing the executors of the will of Sir Hans Sloane, elected trustees of the British Museum and members of its Standing Committee, showing the high proportion of Fellows. In 1781 the Royal Society's Museum was given to the British

Museum.

2735 P. R. Harris. The Reading Room. British Library, 1979. 36p. front.,
illus, plates, plans, ports.
The history of the 1857 Reading Room to the present day, including its
construction, organisation, facilities, staff and readers, is preceded
by shorter accounts of its six predecessors.

2736 F. Hockey. Stolen manuscripts: the case of George Hillier and the
British Museum.
Archives 13 (57) 1977, 20-8.
Between 1853 and 1855 several sets of documents were sold to the
British Museum by George Hillier, antiquary and historian of the Isle
of Wight. The suspicion of the Keeper of MSS. was aroused, and it was
discovered that they had been stolen by Hillier from collections be-
longing to Lords Mostyn and Ellesmere.

2737 A. H. King. Printed music in the British Museum: an account of the collections, the catalogues, and their formation, up to 1920. Bingley,
1979. 210p. front., plate, facsims, tables, bibliog.
Rev. Bk Coll. 29 (2) 1980, 288-9 (N. Barker)
      Lib.Q. 50 (3) 1980, 389-91 (H. Lenneberg)
      T.L.S. Nov.21, 1980, 1343 (M. Cooper)
Covers the origin and growth of the printed music collections and the
acquisition policies followed at various times, also the cataloguing
of the collections and the evolution of technical procedures. The
year 1920 witnessed the retirement of William Barclay Squire, who had
been responsible for printed music since 1885. Several of the appendices deal with the music catalogues and the growth of the collections.

2738 P. F. Kornicki. Books from Japanese circulating libraries in the British
Library.
Br.Lib.J. 6 (2) 1980, 188-98. illus.
Kashikonya flourished from the 17th to the 19th century; 16 books are
identified as having formerly belonged to them.

(2475) A. Lunn. BNB/BSD 1949-1979: thirty years of bibliographic achievement.

(2430) E. J. Miller. Antonio Panizzi and the British Museum.

2739 E. J. Miller. The British Museum.
In: Education. General editor, G. Sutherland. Irish U.P., 1977, 112-24.
bibliog.
Brief notes and commentary on the Reports from the Royal Commission

and Select Committee on the British Museum, the texts of which are reprinted separately by the same publisher.

2740   J. Mirsky. Sir Aurel Stein: archaeological explorer. Univ. of Chicago Press, 1977. xiii, 585p. front., plates, maps, ports.

There is an intriguing account of his discovery of the library of Buddhist texts in the Caves of the Thousand Buddhas at Tun-huang, on the edge of the Gobi Desert. Many of the texts, which had remained hidden for 900 years, are now in the British Museum.

2741   K.M.E. Murray. Caught in the web of words: James A. H. Murray and the 'Oxford English dictionary'. Yale U.P., 1977. [14], 386p. front., illus, facsims, ports.

There is an interesting snippet of 'almost library history' in the passages recording Murray's attempt in 1864 and again in 1866-7, to obtain a post in the British Museum Library, without success. However, it is pertinent in illuminating the complicated nomination procedures involved.

(2905) M.A.E. Nickson. Sloane's codes: the solution to a mystery.

(2450) [Obituary of Noel Sharp, 1905-1978]

(2381) A. Olden. Among tyrants: Gosse at the British Museum.

(2375) J. G. Ollé. Arundell Esdaile: a centenary tribute.

(2431) A. Panizzi and S. Smirke. [Letters]

(2432) D. V. Reidy. Some hitherto unpublished Panizziana from Italy.

2742   D. E. Rhodes. Italian city and regional statutes, 1473-1600, in the British Library.

Br.Lib.J. 3 (1) 1977, 56-8.

Extant statutes are arranged by place and year.

2743   B. Rogers. Eric Partridge talks to Byron Rogers.

Daily Express Feb.5, 1977, 10. port.

Includes reminiscences of his daily attendance at the British Museum Reading Room over a period of forty years, particularly of other regular readers.

(2411) T. D. Rogers, editor. Sir Frederic Madden at Cambridge.

(2433) S. Schacht. Antonio Panizzi's librarianship and its representation in the pioneering library journals.

(2804) K. Sharpe. Sir Robert Cotton, 1586-1631: history and politics in early modern England.

(2359) G. Spinney. Frank Campbell 1863-1905.

(2805) C.G.C. Tite. The early catalogues of the Cottonian library.

(2434) P. J. Weimerskirch. Antonio Panizzi's acquisitions policies for the
library of the British Museum.

(2435) P. J. Weimerskirch. Sir Anthony Panizzi.

2744 I. R. Willison. The development of the British Museum Library to 1857
in its European context: a tour d'horizon. Bremen, Jacobi, 1977, 33-61.
Offprint from Wolfenbütteler Forschungen. Bd 2 1977. Traces the
development of the concept of the British national library from the
time of Leland to Panizzi, in its European context.

(2906) J. L. Wood. Sir Hans Sloane's books.

IRELAND

(2348) T. de Vere White. Richard Irvine Best and his Irish literary contemporaries.

(2850) P. Henchy. The Joly family - Jaspar Robert Joly and the National Library.

2745 Illustrations to the history of the National Library of Ireland 1877-
1977. Dublin, Stationery Office, 1979. 32p. illus, map, ports.
Early photographs and drawings of buildings and staff, with accompanying text.

2746 A. MacLochlainn. The National Library of Ireland, 1877-1977.
Irish University Review 7 (2) 1977, 156-67. illus, ports.
Concentrates largely on the creation of the National Library out of
the Royal Dublin Society, and the contribution made by its first two
librarians, William Archer 1877-1895 and Thomas William Lyster
1895-1920.

SCOTLAND

2747 P. Hardman. A mediaeval "Library in parvo."
Medium Aevum 47 (2) 1978, 262-73.
A description and analysis of MS. Advocates 19.3.1. which contains
three groups of booklets of the 15th century. They are thought to be
examples of three different kinds of works in uniform editions which
could be put together to form a small library.

2748 National Library of Scotland.
In: Encyclopedia of library and information science. Vol.27. New York,
Dekker, 1979, 98-109. illus, facsims, bibliog.

A brief history of the Advocates' Library is followed by subsequent developments and a description of the major collections.

WALES

2749   W.B.L. Evans. Early scientific books in the National Library of Wales.
        Lib.Assn Rare Books Group Newsletter 1 (12) 1978, 3-8.
        Brief description of a small collection, including a few books associated with John Dee.

2750   R. H. Lewis. Yr Eisteddfod a'r Llyfrgell Genedlaethol.
        In: Eisteddfota, 3: golygydd Ifor ap Gwilym. Abertawe, Gwasg Christopher Davies, 1980, 93-103.
        The author examines the extent to which resolutions passed at various National Eisteddfodau in the 19th century accelerated the eventual founding of the National Library of Wales in 1909.

2751   R. H. Lewis. Trem yn ôl: Llyfrgell Genedlaethol i Gymru.
        Barn 205 Chwefror 1980, 22-5.
        Sketches the general background to the founding of the Library.

2752   W. J. Lewis. Born on a perilous rock: Aberystwyth past and present.
        Aberystwyth, Cambrian News Ltd., 1980. xvi, 264p. illus, facsims, maps, ports.
        The National Library of Wales is covered on pp.105-90, and literary societies and the Public Library on pp.182-4.

LIBRARIES: Private

2753   E. Armstrong. English purchases of printed books from the Continent
1465-1526.
English Historical Review   94 (371) 1979, 268-90.
Evidence is given for the purchase of printed books from 1465 onwards,
mainly by English ecclesiastics on diplomatic missions to the Continent. From 1477 customs records indicate the import of Continental printed books on a commercial scale. The source and nature
of such books and their relation to books printed in this country is
discussed, and details of individual collectors are provided.

2754   T. H. Aston, and others. The Medieval alumni of the University of
Cambridge.
Past and Present   No.86 1980, 9-86.
Pages 63-6 discuss the authorship and ownership of books. Evidence
indicates that the incidence of ownership among secular clergy was
more or less identical at Oxford and Cambridge. However, the rate of
recorded ownership was much lower among regulars at Cambridge than
Oxford, largely due to the greater prominence at Cambridge of friars.

2755   R. Billcliffe. Charles Rennie Mackintosh: the complete furniture,
furniture drawings and interior designs. Lutterworth Press, 1979.   252p.
[4] p. illus, plates, facsims, bibliog.
Contains illustrations and descriptions of furniture and interiors of
domestic libraries and of the library of the Glasgow School of Art.

(2704)   A. E. Birkby, editor. Suffolk parochial libraries: a catalogue.
British Library. Department of Manuscripts. Catalogue of additions to
manuscripts 1946-1950.

2756   B. Capp. Astrology and the popular press: English almanacs 1500-1800.
Faber, 1979. 452p. facsims, bibliog.
Rev. Antiquarian Book Monthly Review   6 (10) 1979, 436-7   (A. Payne)
The general development and ownership of almanacs is dealt with in
chapter 2. The golden age was from 1640 to 1700. They were purchased
by almost every social group.

(3136)   P. Clark. English provincial society from the Reformation to the
Revolution: religion, politics and society in Kent 1500-1640.

2757   P. Clark. The ownership of books in England, 1560-1640: the example of some Kentish townsfolk.

In: Schooling and society: studies in the history of education, edited by Lawrence Stone. John Hopkins Univ. Press, 1976, 95-111. tables.

Analyses inventories of personal goods, taken after death by appraisers, for residents of Canterbury, Faversham and Maidstone. Tables indicate such factors as the expansion of book ownership, the wealth and occupation of owners, the subject matter of the collections and their location within the house.

2758   J. Cooper. Under the hammer: the auctions and auctioneers of London. Constable, 1977. 248p. front., plates, facsims, ports, bibliog.

Contains a number of anecdotes relating to the book sales of Samuel Baker (later Sotheby's) since 1745.

2759   J. Cornforth. English interiors 1790-1848: the quest for comfort. Barrie and Jenkins, 1978. 144p. illus.

Contemporary watercolours, many of them reproduced in colour, have been chosen to illustrate English interiors of the period. Many libraries, studies and library-drawing rooms are included. They throw light on the way rooms were used and changing fashions of furniture arrangement. The accompanying notes are particularly helpful.

2760   K. Dent. The private library of the landed classes; its role in informal education in the eighteenth century.

In: Informal agencies of education: proceedings of the 1977 Annual Conference of the History of Education Society of Great Britain. Leicester, The Society, 1979, 37-60. tables, facsim.

The primary agencies of the informal education of the gentry are seen as the private library, the family, private tutors, travel and circles of association. Case studies are presented which analyse the private library by subject field, consider the relationship between family interests and titles owned, evidence of library use, etc.

(2810)   T. F. Dibdin. Thomas Frognall Dibdin: selections.

2761   A.S.G. Edwards. The influence and audience of the Polychronicon: some observations.

Proceedings of the Leeds Philosophical and Literary Society: Literary and Historical Section 17 (6) 113-9.

Quotes examples of ownership of the Polychronicon by churchmen, scholars, antiquarians and bibliophiles from the 15th to the 17th century.

2762   C. Gilbert. The life and work of Thomas Chippendale. Studio Vista,
        1978. 2 vols. plates, facsims, plan, port., bibliog.
           The major part of volume 1 consists of detailed records of furniture
           supplied to particular patrons, based on extant accounts, receipts,
           letters, etc. Most of the commissions were for country houses.
           Volume 2 consists of plates. Library furniture of all kinds features
           in both.

2763   M. Girouard. Life in the English country house: a social and archi-
        tectural history. Yale U.P., 1978. vii, 344p. illus, plates, plan.
           The development of library accommodation from the 16th century closet
           off the bedchamber to the communal library cum living room, is seen
           as reflecting a change in attitude towards the book collection. From
           being the personal equipment of the owner of the house, it had become
           the common property of the family and his guests.

2764   J. Harthan. Books of hours and their owners. Thames and Hudson, 1977.
        192p. facsims, bibliog.
           Thirty-four manuscript books of hours, many of them French, are illus-
           trated and commented upon, including mention of their original and
           subsequent ownership by the laity of various social classes and the
           use to which they were put.

2765   F. Herrmann. Sotheby's: portrait of an auction house. Chatto and
        Windus, 1980. xxvi, 468p. plates, facsims, ports.
           This is the official history of Sotheby's, written after a long
           period of gathering together all extant source material. Sotheby's
           was founded by the bookseller Samuel Baker in 1733, largely as a book
           auction house, and so it remained for the first century. They were
           the premier auctioneers of antiquarian books throughout the 19th
           century. The book contains a great deal of relevant information about
           such sales as the Sunderland, Hamilton Palace, Crawford, Libri,
           Britwell Court etc. and about Sotheby's handling of private sales
           e.g. Pierpont Morgan's purchase of the library of Richard Bennett.
           There are sideways looks at book auctions conducted by other
           auctioneers, a full account of Quaritch's, and details of Thomas
           James Wise's dealings with Tom Hodge, one of Sotheby's partners.

2766   L. Jardine. Humanism and the Sixteenth century Cambridge Arts Course.
        History of Education 4 (1) 1975, 16-31.
           Some 200 itemised 16th century booklists contained in inventories of
           decease for members of the University who died in residence during
           the period 1535-90, are housed in Cambridge University Archives. Here

they are used to discover what were the standard textbooks at Cambridge at the time, in order to throw light upon the nature of humanistic education. Examples of two such inventories dated 1557/8 and 1565 are appended.

2767   G. R. Keiser. Lincoln Cathedral Library MS. 91: life and milieu of the scribe.
In: Studies in bibliography, edited by Fredson Bowers. Vol.32.
Bibliographical Society of the Univ. of Virginia, 1979, 158-79.
The manuscript is associated with Robert Thornton, the apparent compiler and scribe, who lived in the North Riding of Yorkshire in the early 15th century. The work is an anthology, and the article considers how the various texts for copying were obtained. The ownership of books by those with whom he came into contact is investigated, and the limitations of the use of wills for evidence of book ownership is pointed out. The article generally throws light upon the new importance of books for the middle classes at that time.

(3078) A. H. King. The history of music libraries in the United Kingdom.

2768   B. N. Lee. British bookplates: a pictorial history. David and Charles, 1979. 160p. facsims, bibliog.
Rev. <u>Antiquarian Book Monthly Review</u> 6 (9) 1979, 385 (P. Delaney)
Following a brief introductory survey, 261 bookplates and book labels of the 16th to 20th centuries are reproduced and annotated. The great majority relate to personal collectors.

2769   F. Mehlman. Library furniture.
<u>Antique Collector</u> 49 (10) 1978, 84-7. illus.
A brief historical survey of furniture designed specifically for the domestic library, accompanied by illustrations and details of bookcases, tables, desks, steps and globes, mainly of the late 18th and early 19th centuries.

2770   A. and P. Miall. The Victorian nursery book. Dent, 1980. 192p. illus, plates, facsims.
Long quotations describing the ideal schoolroom, its furnishing and library, are taken from "The English Schoolroom" by Rev. Anthony Thomson.

2771   E. J. Miller. The National Trust's libraries.
<u>National Trust</u> 1 (28) 1977, 15. illus.
Of the 200 odd houses now in the Trust's possession, some 30 contain libraries of varying size and importance. Some of the more

interesting are mentioned in this brief survey.

2772   J. S. Moore, editor. The goods and chattels of our forefathers: Frampton Cotterell and district probate inventories, 1539-1804. Chichester, Phillimore, 1976. xx, 364p. tables.

> A number of the 400 probate inventories have general references to books.

(2559) J. H. Moran. Education and learning in the city of York 1300-1560.

2773   A.N.L. Munby. Essays and papers: edited, with an introduction, by Nicolas Barker. Scolar Press, 1977. xiii, 241p. front., facsims.

> Rev. Bk Coll. 26 (4) 1977, 589-90 (D. J. McKitterick)
>> Lib.Assn Rec. 79 (8) 1977, 434 (I. Maxted)
>> Lib.Rev. 26 (4) 1977, 371-2 (P. Davison)
>> T.L.S. June 24, 1977, 760 (A. Bell)

> Most of the delightful essays and papers here reprinted reflect Dr. Munby's abiding interest in the condition of bibliomania particularly as it afflicted British noblemen, scholars and men of letters. The eighteen items were first published between 1948 and 1976 and include nos 399, 477, 1189. The collection opens with an appreciation of Dr. Munby's life and work, and closes with a list of his publications.

2774   A.N.L. Munby and L. Coral, editors. British book sale catalogues 1676-1800: a union list. Mansell, 1977. xxv, 146p. front., bibliog.

> Rev. Irish Booklore 4 (1) 1978, 64-8 (W. G. Wheeler)
>> Library 33 (4) 1978, 336-8 (R. J. Roberts)
>> Papers of the Bibliog.Soc.of America 73 (2) 1979, 279-82 (R. J. Gemmett)

> Retail sale catalogues are included with auction catalogues. The arrangement is chronological with indexes of consignors and auctioneers and booksellers.

2775   H. Muthesius. The English house. Edited with an introduction by Dennis Sharp and a preface by Julius Posener. Translated by Janet Seligman. Crosby Lockwood Staples, 1979. xxiii, 246p. illus, plates, plans.

> "Das Englische Haus" was originally published Berlin, Wasmuth, 1904-5. 3 vols. Hermann Muthesius' perceptive comments on "The library as smoking-room and male preserve" appear on pages 87-8. The furnishing of the late 19th century domestic library is discussed and illustrated on pages 219-22.

(2469) H. M. Nixon. Five centuries of English bookbinding.

2776   H. M. Nixon and W. A. Jackson. English 17th-century travelling lib-
        raries.
        Trans. Cambridge Bibl.Soc. 7 (3) 1979, 294-321. illus.
            Four Jacobean travelling libraries, all surviving with their cabinets
            and contents complete, are described and illustrated. Their com-
            mission is ascribed to William Hakewill, M.P. (1574-1655), who
            apparently presented them to Sir Thomas Egerton, Baron Ellesmere
            (c.1540-1617), Sir Julius Caesar (1558-1636), and to unidentified
            members of the Madden and Bacon families. The contents are examined
            (though the cabinets no longer survive) of similar libraries be-
            longing to Prince Charles (later Charles I) and his brother, Prince
            Henry. A smaller such library, owned by the Fountaine family and
            made c.1640, is also recorded.

2777   R. O'Day. The English clergy: the emergence and consolidation of a
        profession, 1558-1642. Leicester, Leicester U.P., 1979. xvi, 272p.
        tables.
            Pages 185-6 refer to the ownership of books by parochial clergy and
            the occurrence of studies in parsonages. The situation of the laity
            is contrasted.

(2516) Oxford University Society of Bibliophiles. The Warden's meeting: a
        tribute to John Sparrow.

(2883) Pepys - and after.

(3080) M. C. Ricklefs and P. Voorhoeve. Indonesian manuscripts in Great
        Britain: a catalogue of manuscripts in Indonesian languages in British
        public collections.

2778   E. Sangwine. The private libraries of Tudor doctors.
        Journal of the History of Medicine and Allied Sciences 33 (2) 1978,
        167-84.
            Inventories of the books of six eminent Tudor physicians are analysed
            and related to medical education and practice of the time. As the
            century progressed, the impact of classicism becomes more evident.

2779   L. S. Thompson. Private libraries.
        In: Encyclopedia of library and information science. Vol.24. New York,
        Dekker, 1978, 125-92. Illus, facsims, ports, bibliog.
            Pages 153-64 are devoted to English collectors from the Renaissance
            to the late 19th century.

(3085) J. L. Thornton and R.I.J. Tully. Scientific books, libraries and collectors: a study of bibliography and the book trade in relation to
science.

2780 P. Thornton. Seventeenth-century interior decoration in England, France
and Holland. Yale U.P., for the Paul Mellon Centre for Studies in
British Art, 1978. xii, 427p. illus, plates, plans.
Studies and libraries (mainly private) are discussed on pages 303-15,
with illustrations, demonstrating the evolution of book shelving and
other items of library furniture in the three countries.

(2518) J. Turner. The Roxburghe Club.

2781 G. Walkling. Bookcases.
Connoisseur 201 (810) 1979, 268-71. illus.
A brief survey of English domestic bookcase design from the late 17th
century to Ambrose Heal, including such items as revolving and move-
able bookcases. It was not until the late 18th century that such
furniture was considered appropriate for use outside the confines of
the library, and was adapted for the parlour and drawing room.

2782 M. I. Wilson. The English country house and its furnishings. Batsford,
1977. 216p. front., illus, facsims, plans, bibliog.
Contains brief references to the domestic library of various periods.
The provision of a library is seen as being an increasingly important
part of house planning since 1660, especially since the combined influences of the Grand Tour and Palladianism had prompted an interest
in classical learning.

John Rowland ABBEY, 1894-1969

2783 Sotheby and Co. Catalogue of the celebrated library, the property of the
late Major J. R. Abbey. 10th portion: 34 MSS of the 11th-19th century.
Sotheby, 20 June, 1978. 81p. front., plates.
The first of two sales which will complete the dispersal of the manuscript collection of the late Major Abbey. No fewer than 22 of these
34 MSS are 'in their first or medieval bindings'. The foreword emphasises that many of the MSS survived remarkable hazards: a Gospel
lectionary in Greek was almost certainly rescued from the sack of
Constantinople in 1453, while a Sacramentary for Cistercian use
'survived possession by John Ruskin'.

John ADAM, 1721-1792

(2784) I.R.M. Mowat. An eighteenth century private library: the books of
William and John Adam at Blair Adam.

William ADAM, 1689-1748

2784   I.R.M. Mowat. An eighteenth century private library: the books of
William and John Adam at Blair Adam.
Lib.Rev. Vol.28 Spring 1979, 8-13.

The library of the founder of the Adam family of architects and his
eldest son, as recorded in a catalogue published in 1883.

Thomas ALLEN, 1540-1632

2785   A. G. Watson. Thomas Allen of Oxford and his manuscripts.
In: Medieval scribes, manuscripts and libraries: essays presented to
N. R. Ker, edited by M. B. Parkes and Andrew Watson. Scolar Press,
1978, 279-314. facsims, port.

An account of the collection of manuscripts owned by the Oxford
antiquary and mathematician Thomas Allen. It was particularly rich
in manuscripts of a scientific nature, many of them formerly the
property of monastic houses and Oxford Colleges. Allen's catalogue
of 1622 is examined, and a complete list of the manuscripts is
appended. Most of them were bequeathed to Sir Kenelm Digby, who
gave them to the Bodleian; 21 were given by Allen to the Bodleian on
its foundation.

Admiral Sir Francis BEAUFORT, 1774-1857

2786   A. Friendly. Beaufort of the Admiralty: the life of Sir Francis
Beaufort 1774-1857. Hutchinson, 1977. 362p. illus, plates, maps, ports,
bibliog.

Chapter 7 discusses his intellectual and spiritual development during
the 1790s, in particular, his reading as revealed in his letters. His
growing library accompanied him aboard ship and included books on
navigation, astronomy, philosophy, literature and history. Theology
and devotional works were particularly well represented.

William BECKFORD, 1759-1844

2787   B. Fothergill. Beckford of Fonthill. Faber, 1979. 387p. plates, ports.
There are many scattered references to his book collecting activities.
His first major purchases took place at Paris in 1784 at the Duc de
Vallière sale, and numerous books were bought on his extensive

Continental travels. Topography, travel and the occult were
particularly sought after, and his library reflected his considerable
linguistic abilities. Many books were sold at times of financial
crisis.

2788   Sotheby and Co. Catalogue of ... autograph letters, literary manu-
        scripts etc. London. Sotheby, 5 and 6 July 1977. Lot No. 272.
            Includes the Beckford papers, pp.143-50. The Hamilton Palace sales
        of 1882-3 disposed of William Beckford's books and manuscripts. This
        collection is the most comprehensive archive of Beckford's papers
        remaining in private hands, the Hamilton family. (On Beckford's
        death his library and papers passed to his daughter, the Duchess of
        Hamilton.) The literary manuscripts, correspondence and personal
        papers here listed are of enormous interest to textual scholars,
        while historians of book collecting should note, in particular,
        Beckford's reading notes, manuscript catalogues and receipts re-
        lating to his collection.

2789   J. Turner. William Beckford of Fonthill.
        <u>Antiquarian Book Monthly Review</u> 7 (11) 1980, 524-5, 527. illus, bibliog.
            Briefly discusses Beckford's significance as a book collector,
        modern sales of Beckfordiana and the attractions of such material for
        the collector of today.

        Davis Evan BEDFORD, 1898-1978
2790   Royal College of Physicians of London. The Evan Bedford Library of
        Cardiology: catalogue of books, pamphlets and journals. Royal College
        of Physicians, 1977. xi, 245p. front., facsims.
            Dr. Bedford's cardiological library was built up over the period 1926
        to 1971, forming the greatest benefaction to be received by the Col-
        lege this century. Dr. Bedford contributes an account of its forma-
        tion.

        William BLAKE, 1757-1827
2791   G. E. Bentley, Jr. Blake books. Oxford, Clarendon Press, 1977. 1079p.
        front.
        Rev. <u>Pap. Bibl. Soc. Am.</u> 72 (3) 1978, 396-400 (M. D. Paley)
            Part V lists 44 books owned by Blake, and six more, the editions of
        which have not been identified. Other books formerly believed to
        have belonged to Blake are now believed to have belonged to another

person with the same name. The work thus amends the same author's "A Blake Bibliography" 1964 and Keynes "Blake Studies" 2nd ed., 1971 (see no. 1980).

Myles BLOMEFYLDE, 1525-1603

2792 J. C. Coldewey. Myles Blomefylde's library: another book. English Language Notes Vol.14 June 1977, 249-50.

The book in question is a translation of Boccaccio's Philocopo printed in 1566. The writer observes that "it is indeed becoming more and more apparent that Blomefylde's collection of books and manuscripts was one of the most important of the smaller libraries in Elizabethan England."

2793 D. J. McKitterick. The books of Myles Blomefylde. Library 32 (3) 1977, 270.

A letter amending the account of two items given in the article by D. C. Baker and J. L. Murphy in Library 31 (4) 1976 (see no. 1981).

Saint BONIFACE, 680-754

2794 J. C. Sladden. Boniface of Devon, Apostle of Germany. Exeter, Paternoster Press, 1980. 254p. bibliog.

Contains brief details of Boniface's collection of books which he carried with him on his missionary travels. They were mainly books of the Bible, commentaries, writings of the Fathers, volumes of conciliar canons and papal decrees.

BOWDLER family

(2624) L. J. Harris and B. Ll. James. The library of St. David's University College, Lampeter.

John BRACEBRIDGE

2795 C. Garton. A Fifteenth Century headmaster's library. Lincolnshire History and Archaeology Vol.15 1980, 29-38. facsims.

John Bracebridge was a priest, Vicar Choral at Lincoln Cathedral and Headmaster of Lincoln School. In 1420 he retired to the Brigettine monastery in Middlesex, which was soon to move to Syon. His large collection of 112 volumes helped to lay the foundation of Syon's library. They are listed in the Syon Catalogue, but only two survive. The books are described: theology, Biblical commentaries, Latin grammars and medical books are particularly well represented.

Robert BRIDGES, 1844-1930

2796　R. Bridges and W. B. Yeats. The correspondence of Robert Bridges and
W. B. Yeats, edited by R. J. Finneran. Macmillan, 1977. xviii, 68p.
ports.

> Appendix B lists nine Yeats volumes in Bridges's library and appendix
> C lists 12 Bridges's volumes in Yeats's library.

Thomas BRITTON, 1654-1714

2797　W. A. Campbell. The chemical library of Thomas Britton 1654-1714.
Ambix　24 (3) 1977, 143-8. facsims, port.

> A brief account of the life of Thomas Britton, musical small-coal man
> and enthusiastic amateur chemist, is followed by an analysis of the
> chemical items in the 1694 and 1715 sale catalogues of his library.
> They numbered 260 out of a total collection of nearly 3,000.

BRODIE family

2798　Sotheby and Co. Catalogue of printed books (including 'The Property of
Brodie of Brodie, removed from Brodie Castle', lots 1-173). Sotheby,
2 October, 1978, 5-22.

> An important collection of 18th and 19th century novels is the strong
> point of this further sale of Brodie books. At least three of the
> novels appear to be unique recordings. Brodie Castle, the family
> seat, is situated in Forres, Morayshire.

BROOKE family

(2965)　B. Baumfield. Raising the wind - or Lyttleton redivivus.

John BROWNE, 1608-1691

2799　A. Ashbee. Instrumental music from the library of John Browne (1608-
1691), Clerk of the Parliaments.
Music and Letters　Vol.58 January 1977, 43-59. tables.

> Examines manuscript music in the library of Christ Church, Oxford and
> the Rowe Library, King's College, Cambridge, which once belonged to
> John Browne, seeking to identify the various copyists present. It
> forms one of the largest and most comprehensive collections of its
> kind. Much of it reached Christ Church among the collections of
> Henry Aldrich and Richard Goodson, both bequeathed in the early 18th
> century.

Sir Thomas BROWNE, 1605-1682

2800   G. Richmond. Sir Thomas Browne's library.
Antiquarian Book Monthly Review Vol.4 1977, 2-9. facsims; 52-4.
bibliog.

The writer suggests various ways in which Browne brought his library
together e.g. by the gifts of friends and disciples. The 1711 sale
catalogue of his library also includes the books of his son Edward.
Many of the more notable books are discussed, particularly in the
field of classical studies, Biblical studies and theology, occultism,
philosophy, science and medicine.

Sir Richard BURTON, 1821-1890

2801   Royal Anthropological Institute. A catalogue of the library of Sir
Richard Burton, K.C.M.G., held by the Royal Anthropological Institute,
edited by B. J. Kirkpatrick. The Institute, 1978. xi, 170p. facsim.
The Library was accepted from the Royal Borough of Kensington in
1955.

Edward Norman CARROTHERS, 1898-1977

2802   K. Jamison. Edward Norman Carrothers (1898-1977): an appreciation.
Irish Booklore 4 (1) 1978, 5-6.

Best known as a field botanist, E. N. Carrothers was also a great
collector, particularly of Victorian books, glass, ceramics, and
printed ephemera of all kinds. He brought together an important collection of book illustrations of the 1860s and of Irish book plates.

Henry CAVENDISH, 1731-1810

2803   R. A. Harvey. The private library of Henry Cavendish (1731-1810).
Library 2 (3) 1980, 281-92. plates.

Cavendish assembled a collection of predominantly scientific works
in his London home. It was transferred to Chatsworth during the 19th
century, where it remains today. The catalogue, classification and
storage of the books are discussed. Cavendish himself took a close
interest in the library and used it extensively.

COKE family

(2412) M. F. Schmidt. Passion's child: the extraordinary life of Jane Digby.

Sir Robert Bruce COTTON, 1571-1631

2804   K. Sharpe. Sir Robert Cotton, 1586-1631: history and politics in early modern England. Oxford U.P., 1979. xiv, 293p. bibliog.

Rev. Library 3 (2) 1981, 164-5 (G. Williams)

Chapter 2 discusses his library of manuscripts collected over a period of 30 years, representing a monopoly of the most important material for the study of early English history. The make-up of the collection, its acquisition by purchase, gift and exchange, its binding, arrangement and cataloguing are all covered, and it is argued that it formed an important centre of research for scholars, courtiers and politicians.

2805 C.G.C. Tite. The early catalogues of the Cottonian library.
Br.Lib.J. 6 (2) 1980, 144-57.

Descriptions are given of 14 manuscript catalogues or lists compiled before the first printed catalogue of 1696; several pre-date the compilation of the famous 'Emperor' classification in the 1630s.

Nathaniel CURZON, 1st Baron Scarsdale, 1726-1804
2806 J. Hardy and H. Hayward. Kedleston Hall, Derbyshire - 3.
Country Life Feb. 9, 1978, 322-5. illus.

There is a photograph and a description of the library designed by Robert Adam in 1760. It was described by the visiting Duchess of Northumberland in 1766 as being furnished 'with bookcases filled with well-chosen, entertaining and instructive, rather than curious, books.'

Edward Davies DAVENPORT, 1778-1847
2807 J. Cornforth. Capesthorne Hall, Cheshire.
Country Life 162 (4183) 1977, 535-8. illus, port.
               162 (4184) 1977, 607-10. illus.

Edward Davies Davenport obtained Blore's services to transform Capesthorne Hall in the 1830s. Watercolours were painted to record the newly created main rooms, and those of the east and west libraries are reproduced in the first article. Davenport's library was rich in illuminated manuscripts and early printed books, especially Italian. A large part of it was sold in 1903.

Henry DAVIS,   -1977
(2733) M. M. Foot. The Henry Davis gift: a collection of bookbindings.

2808 M. Vowles. The Henry Davis Collection of the New University of Ulster.
An Leabharlann 6 (3/4) 1977. 91, 93-4.

Henry Davis was a London manufacturer who also had a factory in Belfast, and it was to the New University there that he bequeathed this collection. It consists of some 200 items illustrating the development of printing from the 15th to the 20th century, and includes 60 incunabula.

Thomas DEVEY, 1681-1705

2809 J. L. Salter. The books of an early eighteenth-century curate.
Library 33 (1) 1978, 33-46.
Transcription of the probate inventory of a young Warwickshire curate, Thomas Devey, of Coleshill. It comprises 130 items and the value of each is marked. An introduction is added.

Thomas Frognall DIBDIN, 1776-1847

2810 T. F. Dibdin. Thomas Frognall Dibdin: selections compiled by Victor E. Neuburg. Scarecrow Press, 1978. [2], viii, 245p. front., facsims, bibliog.
Rev. J.Lib.Hist. 14 (1) 1979, 90-2 (P. A. Metzger)
Aims to provide a balanced selection from Dibdin's enormous bibliographical output, including his Bibliomania, the 1st edition of which is reprinted in toto, Bibliophobia, never before reprinted, and passages from Reminiscences of a Literary Life. William Jerdan's contemporary account of Dibdin is reproduced in Appendix B. The introduction discusses his life and the significance of his work in the context of bibliophily in its heyday.

Philip DODDRIDGE, 1702-1751

(2577) G. F. Nuttall. New College, London, and its library: two lectures.

John DONNE, 1573-1631

2811 M. Hobbs. More books from the library of John Donne.
Bk Coll. 29 (4) 1980, 590-2.
A list of 15 titles in Chichester Cathedral Library which, although not signed by him, show characteristics to suggest that they may have belonged to Donne. The present note supplements one in Bk Coll. 27 (4) 1978 (see no.2813)

2812 G. Keynes. More books from the library of John Donne.
Bk Coll. 26 (1) 1977, 29-35. plates.
Details of ten volumes once in the possession of Donne, in addition

to those described in the author's "Bibliography of Donne" 4th ed., 1973.

2813   G. Keynes. More books from the library of John Donne.
       Bk Coll. 27 (4) 1978, 570-2.
       A list of a further twelve volumes in addition to those reported above.

       John DONNELLY,   -1748
2814   H. Fenning. The library of a preacher of Drogheda: John Donnelly, O.P.
       (d. 1748)
       Collectanea Hibernica Nos 18-19, 1978 for 1976-7, 72-104.
       Donnelly had taught at Louvain before coming to Ireland in 1719, and his books were largely French or Latin and mostly by Jesuits, and homiletical in nature.

       Gavin DOUGLAS, 1474?-1522
2815   P. Bawcutt. The 'library' of Gavin Douglas.
       In: Bards and makars: Scottish language and literature: medieval and renaissance, edited by Adam J. Aitken, Matthew P. McDiarmid, Derick S. Thomson. Glasgow, Univ. of Glasgow Press, 1977, 107-26.
       It is believed that no books once belonging to him survive. However, over 70 authors are referred to in his works, providing evidence for books he either owned or borrowed. Latin and Italian writers and British poets predominate.

       Sir Charles EASTLAKE, 1793-1865
2816   D. Robertson. Sir Charles Eastlake and the Victorian art world.
       Princeton, N.J., Princeton U.P., 1978. xvii, 468p. front., illus, plates, ports, bibliog.
       Contains brief references to his personal art library, which, valued at £2,008, was offered to the National Gallery and purchased in 1870.

       EDWARD IV, King of England, 1442-1483
(2843) G. Kipling. The triumph of honour: Burgundian origins of the Eliza-bethan renaissance.

       EGERTON family
2817   Tatton Park. Library. A catalogue of the library at Tatton Park, Knutsford, Cheshire, the property of the National Trust, compiled by

Shirley Pargeter. Cheshire Libraries and Museums, 1977. [11], 409p.
Tatton was the home of the Egerton family from 1598 to 1958. The
present building was erected between 1780 and 1825. The 12,000
volume collection is discussed in the short introduction. Dating
mainly from the 18th century, it contains much earlier material, including the remains of Sir Thomas Egerton's own 16th century collection. It is outstanding for its wealth of works on classical
antiquities and for the number of books in their original state.

Albert EHRMAN, 1890-1969

2818   Sotheby and Co. Catalogue of valuable printed books from the Broxbourne
Library illustrating the spread of printing: the property of Albert
Ehrman, Esq. 2 portions. London, Sotheby, 14 and 15 November, 1977.
220p. front., plates; 8 and 9 May, 1978, 260p. front., plates.
Happily arranged (alphabetically by town of imprint) this great
modern collection of 15th and 16th century European printing contains
many gems, notably a block-book of 48 leaves probably printed in
Germany before 1470. There are four separate indexes for authors and
short titles, printers, Hain-Copinger-Rechling numbers and provenance.

George ELIOT, 1819-1881

2819   W. Baker. The George Eliot - George Henry Lewes Library: an annotated
catalogue of their books at Dr. Williams's Library. Garland, 1977.
lxix, 300p. plates.
Rev. J.Lib.Hist. 14 (1) 1979, 92-4 (A. L. Ashby)
     Library 2 (4) 1980, 475-6 (B. Dennis)
     Lib.Hist. 4 (6) 1978, 185-6 (P. S. Morrish)
Over 2000 volumes from the library of George Eliot and George Henry
Lewes were donated to Dr. Williams's Library in 1882 by the latter's
son Charles Lee Lewes. A detailed analysis of the collection is
provided in the introduction.

2820   K. K. Collins. Sources of some unidentified offprints in the George
Eliot - George Henry Lewes Library.
Pap.Bibl.Soc.Am. 73 (4) 1979, 468-73.
Identifies 32 serial offprints listed in William Baker's catalogue
above.

Sir Richard ELLYS, 1688?-1742

(2846) National Trust. Blickling Hall, Norfolk.

John EVELYN, 1620-1706

2821   Christie, Manson and Woods Ltd. The Evelyn Library sold by order of the
        wills of J.H.C. Evelyn, deceased and Major Peter Evelyn, deceased.
        4 parts. London, Christie, 22/23 June 1977. 124p. front., plates;
        30 November/1 December, 1977. 155p. front., plates; 15/16 March
        1978. 178p. front., plates; 12/13 July, 1978. 114p. front., plates.
        Contains the nucleus of Evelyn's own collection at his death and also
        some inherited from his son at the latter's death in 1699. The books
        are fully representative of the many-sided intellectual currents of
        Evelyn's age. His close connections with the Royal Society are
        apparent from the impressive list of Robert Boyle's works, all the
        gifts of the latter, and by other contemporary works of science by
        Nehemiah Grew and others. The books inherited from his father-in-law
        Sir Richard Browne, enhance the importance of the library as one which
        is splendidly bound and embellished with specially designed tools by
        Abraham Bosse. Part 4 has an important section of books written by
        Evelyn.

(3038) Sion, Evelyn, and what next?

        EVELYN family

2822   Christie, Manson and Woods Ltd. The Evelyn family library. Sold by
        order of the Trustees. 314 lots. London, Christie, 12 October, 1977.
        56p. front.
        Contains those books acquired by the Evelyn family subsequent to the
        death of John Evelyn in 1706. Scientific books are prominent, but
        the largest category is topographical. The library contained copies
        of John Evelyn's own works.

2823   Christie, Manson and Woods Ltd. Valuable printed books ... (including
        'The Property of The Evelyn Family Trusts', lots 1-86). Christie,
        8 November, 1978, 5-27. front., plates.
        A further collection of books acquired by the family subsequent to the
        death of John Evelyn in 1706. For the most part they are English
        literary works, but, as in the earlier sale of 12th October 1977 from
        the family library, there are many of Evelyn's own works, the in-
        scription in one indicating that it was Evelyn's own copy. Other
        works, including Harris's Lexicon Technicum 2 vols. (1704-10), were
        also Evelyn's copies rather than general family property.

Richard FARMER, 1735-1797

2824   T. A. Lister. Richard Farmer's copy of Percy's edition of the Earl of
Northumberland's household book.
Bk Coll. 27 (3) 1978, 402-3.
An additional note to L. J. Lloyd's article below.

2825   L. J. Lloyd. Dr. Richard Farmer, 1735-1797.
Bk Coll. 26 (4) 1977, 524-36. port. (Portrait of a bibliophile, 21)
After Farmer's death his library was sold by auction in 8155 lots.
This article examines the prices paid for some of the items and the
identities of the purchasers. Farmer's library was extensive and
well-used, but its great strength lay in examples of early printing
and early English literature.

James Black FINDLAY

2826   Sotheby and Co. Catalogue of the J. B. Findlay collection: books,
periodicals, manuscripts etc. on conjuring and the allied arts. Part 1:
A-O (500 lots); Part 2: P-Z and miscellaneous (500 lots); London, 5 July
and 4 October, 1979. 2 vols. illus. plates. Part 3: Posters and play-
bills. London, 3 July 1980, 25-96. front., plates.
An extraordinarily specialised collection, the section on catalogues
of apparatus in Part 2 being of subject and typographical value.

Sir Herbert George FORDHAM, 1854-1929

2827   M. J. Freeman and J. Longbotham. The Fordham Collection at the RGS:
an introduction.
Geographical Journal July 1980, 218-31. maps, tables, port.
The collection consists of some 800 road-books and maps bequeathed to
the Society in 1929 by Sir Herbert George Fordham (1854-1929). An
outline of his life and carto-bibliographical studies and the nature
and chronology of his collecting activities, is followed by a discussion and analysis of his collection with particular attention to
the road-books.

Edwin GARDINER, 1896-

2828   British Library. Lending Division. The Edwin Gardiner chess collection:
catalogue by J. E. Vickery and C. A. Webb. Boston Spa, British Library
Lending Division, 1977. [2], 110p.
The collection was purchased by the National Central Library in 1970.
It consists of 891 monographs published between 1804 and 1960 on all

aspects of chess, and including many foreign titles.

GASKELL family

2829   M. D. Wheeler. Mrs. Gaskell's reading, and the Gaskell sale catalogue
in Manchester Central Library.
Notes and Queries 24 (1) 1977, 25-30.
> An examination of the sale catalogue of 1914 occasioned by the death
> in 1913 of Margaret Emily, second daughter of William and Elizabeth
> Gaskell. An attempt is made to distinguish those of the 4,000 total
> which belonged to Elizabeth.

GEORGE III, King of Great Britain and Ireland, 1738-1820

2830   J. Brooke. King George III. Constable, 1972. xix, 411p. front.,
plates, ports.
> Pages 304-6 record his book collecting activities. In 1762 he
> purchased the Thomason tracts and presented them to the British
> Museum. His own collections were designed to form the nucleus of a
> national library. In 1765 he purchased Joseph Smith's collection of
> incunabula. His representation of contemporary literature is dis-
> cussed. Sums of money from the Privy Purse devoted to the library
> are mentioned. At his death it contained about 65,000 books and 450
> manuscripts.

2831   J. H. Plumb and H. Wheldon. Royal heritage: the story of Britain's
Royal builders and collectors. B.B.C., 1977. 360p. illus, plates,
facsims, ports.
> George III's book collecting activities are described, and his
> generosity to visiting scholars is indicated. Some of the chief
> treasures are mentioned and illustrated.

Edward GIBBON, 1737-1794

2832   J.A.W. Bennett. Essays on Gibbon. Cambridge, The Author, 1980. vii,
85p. front.
> Chapter 1 features Gibbon as bookman and bibliophile and mentions
> collectors of Gibboniana and the wandering of copies from Gibbon's
> library. Other chapters devoted to English authors and the classics
> also refer to books owned by him.

2833   G. Keynes. The library of Edward Gibbon: a catalogue edited and introduced by Geoffrey Keynes. 2nd ed. Godalming, St. Paul's Bibliographies,

1980. [4], 293p. front., plates, facsims.

Rev. <u>Lib.Rev.</u> 30 (2) 1981, 119-20 (R. Norris)

    <u>Private Lib.</u> 3 (4) 1980, 170-2 (A. R. Hodges)

A facsimile of 1st ed., Cape, 1940 using Sir Geoffrey's own copy, in which a few corrections in ink have been made, and with the addition of some new entries in an appendix and a new preface which refers to a previously unknown manuscript catalogue in the Pierpont Morgan Library in New York. The long introduction records the formation of his libraries at Bentinck Street and Lausanne, largely to assist him in writing his <u>Decline and Fall</u>, and their dispersal following his death. The sources from which the books in Gibbon's possession at various times can be largely reconstructed, are discussed. One such source consists of a catalogue written on the back of 1676 playing cards.

John GRIERSON,   -1564?

2834 J. Durkan and J. Russell. John Grierson's book-list.

<u>Innes Review</u> 28 (1) 1977, 39-49. facsims.

John Grierson was Provincial of the Dominican Order in Scotland from 1523 until the Reformation. A list of his books is here reproduced which considerably augments the number of those books previously known to have been in his possession, and consequently in the Black-friars Library at St. Andrews. It seems that the books were assembled and their titles recorded in or about 1522.

Edmund GRINDAL, Archbishop of Canterbury, 1519-1583

2835 P. Collinson. Archbishop Grindal, 1519-1583: the struggle for a Reformed Church. Cape, 1979. 368p. plates, facsims, ports.

His books included editions of the Fathers, Reformed theology acquired during his exile on the Continent, and various chronicles. Some 80 volumes were bequeathed to Queen's College, Oxford, and others, mainly Greek works, to Pembroke Hall. Some went to a fellow of Pembroke, some to his chaplain, and others to a servant.

Field-Marshall Douglas HAIG, 1st Earl Haig of Bemersyde, 1861-1928

2836 Christie, Manson and Woods Ltd. Miscellaneous books (including 'The Property of Field-Marshal The Earl Haig of Bemersyde', lots 1-100). London, Christie, 21 December, 1977, 5-20.

A military library collected by Haig from subaltern days in India to more exalted rank in the Great War. Included are five Bibles, one printed in Edinburgh, 1758 with a richly ornamented contemporary

Scottish binding.

James Orchard HALLIWELL-PHILLIPS, 1820-1889

2837   W. F. Engel. J. O. Halliwell-Phillips and the Edinburgh University
Library.
Library 2 (2) 1980, 193-8.
Edinburgh University Library contains two collections formerly the
property of the 19th century Shakespearian scholar, Halliwell-Phillips.
One was acquired in 1872-89 as a benefaction of its owner, the other
by purchase in 1964.

Edward HARLEY, 2nd Earl of Oxford, 1689-1741

2838   W. J. Bate. Samuel Johnson. Chatto and Windus, 1978. xxii, 646p.
front., plates, ports.
Pages 224-6 record Johnson's contribution towards the cataloguing of
the printed books of the Harleian Library prior to their resale by
Thomas Osborne, his 'General Account' of the library published in
1742 and his selection and preparation for publication of the
'Harleian Miscellany'. It was during an altercation concerning the
latter that Johnson felled Osborne to the floor with the aid of a
folio Greek Bible.

2839   A general idea, at once magnificent and confused.
Lib.Assn Rec. 80 (2) 1978, 59, 62.
Reprint of proposals in 1742 to print the first two volumes of the
catalogue of Harley's library. Subscription arrangements and the
importance of the collection are indicated.

2840   National Trust. Wimpole Hall, Cambridgeshire. The National Trust, 1979.
62 [2] p. illus, map, plan, ports, bibliog.
James Gibbs's library designed in 1719 and his alterations to an
earlier orangery in order to form the book room, which acts as an
anteroom to the library, are described and illustrated. They were
created to house the greater part of Lord Harley's library, considered the finest of its time in England.

Gabriel HARVEY, 1550?-1630

2841   V. F. Stern. Gabriel Harvey: his life, marginalia and library. Oxford,
Clarendon Press, 1979. xii, 293p. facsims, bibliog.
Rev. Bk Coll. 29 (4) 1980, 598-600 (M. Hunter)
Library 3 (4) 1981, 348-53. facsims. (D. McKitterick)
Contains a catalogue of his books and manuscripts compiled from a

variety of sources, accompanied by a general description of his library and an estimate of its size. Appendix D lists additional books probably owned by him. His library was essentially the working library of a learned man of all-encompassing interests. His habits in annotating are also discussed, and typical kinds of marginalia are given.

William HARVEY, 1874-1936

2842   Sotheby and Co. Catalogue of rare ... Scottish books ... [including] the library of William Harvey J.P., F.S.A., Scot. (1874-1936). Edinburgh, 28 September, 1979. 270 lots. 20p. illus.

From his base at Dundee, Harvey collected a formidable library of chapbooks and all works that illustrated the local vitality of Scottish life. His fine book-plate adapted a chapbook 'character' in a frame of thistles.

HENRY VII, King of England, 1457-1509

2843   G. Kipling. The triumph of honour: Burgundian origins of the Elizabethan renaissance. The Hague, Leiden U.P., 1977. xiv, 188p. front., illus, facsims.

Chapter 2 is entitled "The first Royal Library". It describes how Edward IV developed the book collecting habit during his exile in Flanders, and how Henry VII transformed a small collection of books into a library worthy of a Flemish bibliophile. This he did with the assistance of Quentin Poulet, a Fleming, who occupied the new office of Royal Librarian.

HIGHMORE family

2844   J. E. Gordon. The medical Highmore family and their books.
The Practitioner Vol.213 December 1974, 858-63. facsim., ports.

In 1954 the Royal College of Surgeons of England was given a small collection of medical books written by members of the Highmore family who lived from the 17th to the 20th century. Biographical details of the physicians are provided, with mention of their books.

HILDYARD family

2845   J. Cornforth. Flintham Hall, Nottinghamshire - 3: the seat of Mr. Myles Thoroton Hildyard.
Country Life 167 (4304) 1980, 18-21. illus.

Deals with the two-storied library and the conservatory which are part

of the remodelling of the Regency house carried out in 1853-7 for
Thomas Blackborne Thoroton Hildyard by T. C. Hine. The design,
decoration and furnishing of the remarkable library are well described and illustrated. Unfortunately, neither Colonel Hildyard nor
his son was interested in books, but they inherited a good library
from elsewhere.

HOBART family

2846 National Trust. Blickling Hall, Norfolk. National Trust, 1978. 62p.
illus, plans, ports, bibliog.

Sir John Hobart, 1st Earl of Buckingham (1693-1756) inherited the
library of Sir Richard Ellys the Calvinist theologian and antiquarian. They were enriched by the Hobarts' own collection and by
accessions from another family house, Gunton. The collection of
over 12,000 volumes is briefly described, together with the fittings
designed by John Hungerford Pollen for the 8th Marquess of Lothian in
1860-1.

Alfred HOLLICK, 1887-1979

2847 Sotheby Parke Bernet and Co. Catalogue of printed books including a
collection of books and pamphlets by Jonathan Swift and his contemporaries. London, 19 and 20 May 1980, 112p.

The property of Thomas Alfred Hollick (1887-1979), who had collected
Swiftiana since 1943.

JARDINE family

2848 A. Rowan. Castlemilk, Dumfriesshire 2: a former home of the Buchanan
Jardine family.
Country Life 162 (4181) 1977, 422-5. illus.

Castlemilk was built in the late 1860s for Sir Robert Jardine by the
architect David Bryce. There is a photograph and a brief description
of its magnificent library decorated in the Jacobean manner.

John JEWEL, 1522-1571

2849 N. R. Ker. The library of John Jewel.
Bod.Lib.Rec. 9 (5) 1977, 256-65. illus.

84 books are identified as having formerly belonged to John Jewel,
Bishop of Salisbury. All except two are now in Magdalen College,
Oxford.

Jaspar Robert JOLY, 1819-1892

2850   P. Henchy. The Joly family - Jaspar Robert Joly and the National Lib-
        rary.
        Irish University Review 7 (2) 1977, 184-98. facsims, port.
            Joly was a council member of the Royal Dublin Society, and in 1863
            gave the Society the greater part of his library on the understanding
            that if a national library were created, the library would form part
            of its permanent collections. The collection consisted of 23,000
            printed volumes plus unbound papers and prints. It was particularly
            rich in Irish history, topography and biography, Irish and Scottish
            song music, Napoleonic literature and books on the French Revolution.
            Joly became one of the first Trustees of the National Library.

Ben JONSON, 1573?-1637

2851   C. McKelvie. An unrecorded book from Ben Jonson's library.
        Irish Booklore 3 (2) 1977, 124-6. facsims.
            A copy of Chalcidius' commentary on Plato's Timaeus (Leyden, 1617)
            bearing Jonson's motto and ownership inscription has come to light in
            Armagh Public Library. Its provenance is discussed, and reference is
            made to other volumes from Jonson's library in Irish collections.

James JOYCE, 1882-1941

2852   R. Ellmann. The consciousness of Joyce. Faber, 1977. [9], 150p.
            The appendix lists about 600 items which comprise all or nearly all
            the library that Joyce left behind him in Trieste when in June 1920
            he moved to Paris.

John KEATS, 1795-1821

2853   F. N. Owings. The Keats library: (a descriptive catalogue). Keats-
        Shelley Memorial Association, [1978]. 67p. front., facsims.
            His books numbered less than a hundred, as Keats was often hard
            pressed for money. Some books he gave to Fanny Brawne before em-
            barking for Italy in 1820. His chest of books was divided among his
            friends after his death. Each volume is traced from leaving Keats's
            hands to its present location.

Andrew KIPPIS, 1725-1795

2854   G. Walters. The auction sale catalogue (1796) of the library of Andrew
        Kippis, 'Literary ornament of the Dissenters'.
        The Price-Priestley Newsletter No.3, 1979, 71-7.

An assessment of the content of the sale at which several noted collectors were present, among them Gossett, Astle, Gough and Heber.

Sir Thomas KNYVETT, c1539-1618

2855   D. J. McKitterick, editor. The library of Sir Thomas Knyvett of Ashwell-thorpe, c.1539-1618. Cambridge, Cambridge Univ.Library, 1978. [4], v, 186p. facsims, ports.

Rev. J.Lib.Hist. 14 (3) 1979, 378-80 (N. H. Krivatsy)

Library 1 (3) 1979, 287-8 (G. Williams)

Lib.Hist. 5 (1) 1979, 15-18 (T. A. Birrell)

The 1618 catalogue of his printed books and the 1634 catalogue of his manuscripts are reproduced. The long introduction seeks to provide a detailed reconstruction of Knyvett's library and collecting career, pointing out its strengths and weaknesses and comparing it with contemporary private collections. The library consisted of 70 MSS and over 1400 printed books at his death. Its fortunes whilst in the hands of his descendants are outlined. It was acquired by John Moore, Bishop of Ely in the 1690s. Much of it later came into the possession of George I, who presented it to Cambridge University in 1715.

Sir John LAMBE, c1566-1647

2856   J. F. Fuggles. Sir John Lambe's manuscripts in the Bodleian Library.
Bod.Lib.Rec. 10 (2) 1979, 109-12.

21 manuscripts are tentatively identified as having entered the · Bodleian in 1632 from the collection of Sir John Lambe.

LEVESON-GOWER family

2857   Sotheby and Co. Catalogue of valuable printed books (including 'the property of His Grace the Duke of Sutherland, T.D., D.L., lots 195-305). Sotheby, 31 October, 1977, 37-48.

Travel, topography and natural history constitute the mainspring of this basically 19th century collection, which also includes editions of the major English literary figures.

George Henry LEWES, 1817-1878

(2819)   W. Baker. The George Eliot - George Henry Lewes Library: an annotated catalogue of their books at Dr. Williams's Library.

(2820)   K. K. Collins. Sources of some unidentified offprints in the George
          Eliot - George Henry Lewes Library.

          LEWIS family
2858   L. Lewis. The private life of a country house (1912-1939). David and
        Charles, 1980. 184p. illus, plates, ports.
            Lesley Lewis describes with near-total recall the household in which
            she lived as a child, Pilgrims' Hall, near Pilgrims' Hatch, Essex.
            She mentions the range of magazines displayed in the hall, with Brad-
            shaw and the ABC, the books in the schoolroom, and describes the
            smoking room in detail with its sets of Austen, Trollope, O Henry
            etc., books on history, biography and topography, books on the French
            Revolution, furniture, volumes in the Badminton Library and con-
            temporary bestsellers.

          Edward LHUYD, 1660-1709
2859   B. F. Roberts. Edward Lhuyd's collection of printed books.
        Bod.Lib.Rec. 10 (2) 1979, 112-27.
            Lhuyd, naturalist and Keeper of the Ashmolean Museum, Oxford, pos-
            sessed a large working collection of books. Though now dispersed,
            many are identifiable. Even during his travels to Celtic regions, he
            kept in touch with booksellers.

          Thomas LINACRE, c1460-1524
2860   G. Barber. Thomas Linacre: a bibliographical survey of his works.
        In: Linacre studies: essays on the life and work of Thomas Linacre
        c.1460-1524, edited by Francis Maddison, Margaret Pelling and Charles
        Webster. Oxford, Clarendon Press, 1977, 290-336. facsims.
            Includes details of twenty printed books and manuscripts bearing
            evidence of his ownership.

          Alexander William Crawford LINDSAY, 25th Earl of Crawford and
          8th Earl of Balcarres, 1812-1880
2861   N. Barker. Bibliotheca Lindesiana: the lives and collections of
        Alexander William, 25th Earl of Crawford and 8th Earl of Balcarres, and
        James Ludovic, 26th Earl of Crawford and 9th Earl of Balcarres. Quaritch
        for the Roxburghe Club, 1977. xviii, 415p. illus, plates, facsim, table,
        ports.

Rev. <u>Antiquarian Book Monthly Review</u> 6 (4) 1979, 160-1 (R. McLean)

<u>Bk Coll.</u> 27 (4) 1978, 575-8 (R. Birley)

<u>T.L.S.</u> June 23, 1978, 719 (A.R.A. Hobson)

Detailed studies of the book collecting activities of the 25th Earl (1812-1880) and the 26th Earl (1847-1913). The former began collecting before he was ten, and until he was eighteen he was a bibliomaniac. He then decided to build up a fine working library. It was particularly strong in Bibles and liturgical books. The 26th Earl built up a fine collection of books on mathematics and astronomy, manuscripts, incunabula, broadside ballads and documents of the French Revolution and the Napoleonic era. Much was dispersed in the sales of 1887 and 1889 and the manuscripts were sold for £150,000 in 1901. The sales of the 1920s and of 1947-8 almost completed the disposal. Much of the detail is drawn from the extensive family archives, particularly their correspondence with booksellers.

James Ludovic LINDSAY, 26th Earl of Crawford and 9th Earl of Balcarres, 1847-1913

(2861) N. Barker. Bibliotheca Lindesiana: the lives and collections of Alexander William, 25th Earl of Crawford and 8th Earl of Balcarres, and James Ludovic, 26th Earl of Crawford and 9th Earl of Balcarres.

(3030) Crawford Library. Catalogue of the Crawford Library of the Royal Observatory, Edinburgh. Supplement.

Clement LITILL, 1527/8?-1580

2862 C. P. Finlayson. Clement Litill and his library: the origins of Edinburgh University Library. Edinburgh, Edinburgh Bibliographical Society and the Friends of Edinburgh Univ.Lib., 1980. [5], 62p. illus, facsims.
Records all that is known of the Edinburgh lawyer Clement Litill and the ways in which he acquired his large collection of mainly theological and legal books. Following his death in 1580, the former were given to the Town Council. Following the foundation of the University, which received its first students in 1583, Litill's books became the nucleus of its library. An inventory of the original bequest of 276 volumes follows, some of which are no longer extant.

William LLOYD, Bishop of Worcester, 1627-1717

(2644) N. Crum. Commonplace-books of Bishop William Lloyd, 1627-1717.

LUCY family

2863   H. Summerson. The Lucys of Charlecote and their library.

In: National Trust Studies 1979. Sotheby Parke Bernet, 1978, 148-59.
illus, facsim, ports.

The seriousness of the 16th and 17th century Lucys is demonstrated by
the library catalogue of 1681. It records a remarkably wide range of
theological opinion, together with French books, legal works, etc.
In the early 18th century some of the books were sold and the library
reorganised. When Charlecote passed to John Hammond in 1786 he
brought with him the library of his bibliophilic father. In the
second quarter of the 19th century George Lucy refurbished the house
and augmented the library so as to be worthy of its setting rather
than for any studious purpose. In spite of subsequent sales, the
Charlecote library today is much the same as it was when George Lucy
died in 1845.

MacLACHLAN family of Kilbride

2864   J. Bannerman. The MacLachlans of Kilbride and their manuscripts.
Scottish Studies Vol.21 1977, 1-34. facsims, table, bibliog.

Major John MacLachlan of Kilbride who died c.1803 is known to have
possessed a collection of 22 mediaeval Gaelic manuscripts. A detailed history of the family is given, and an effort is made to as-
certain when the various manuscripts came into their possession. It
is thought possible that this occurred as early as the 15th or 16th
century.

John MAITLAND, 1st Duke of Lauderdale, 1616-1682

2865   P. Thornton and M. Tomlin. The furnishing and decoration of Ham House.
Furniture History Society, 1980. [9], 194p. plates, plans.

Pages 137-8 describe the antechamber to the Queen's bedchamber,
formerly the old library. Pages 152-4 describe the library and
library closet fitted out in 1673 with shelves from the old library,
plus an additional 522 feet of shelving. Furniture recorded in the
inventories of 1677, 1679 and 1683 is mentioned. The library is also
illustrated.

Tom MARTIN, 1697-1771

2866   P. Grinke. John Ives and the library of 'Honest' Tom Martin.
In: The Warden's meeting: a tribute to John Sparrow. Oxford, Oxford
University Society of Bibliophiles, 1977, 39-42.

The writer describes a volume in his possession which consists of annotated copies of the catalogues of various sales held in London, Diss and Norwich, of the library of the antiquary Tom Martin of Palgrave. They throw light upon the dispersal of his 8,000 books and manuscripts.

Sir William Stirling MAXWELL, 1818-1878

(2618) H. M. Black. The Stirling Maxwell Collection of emblem books in Glasgow University Library.

Andrew MELVILLE, 1545-1622

2867 J. Durkan and J. Kirk. The University of Glasgow, 1451-1577. Glasgow, Univ. of Glasgow Press, 1977. xiv, 498p. front., facsims, map.
Appendix 1 lists some of the books belonging to Andrew Melville. Elsewhere there are brief references to the University's library, in particular to donations.

METHUEN family

2868 F. J. Ladd. Architects at Corsham Court: a study in revival style architecture and landscaping, 1749-1849. Bradford-on-Avon, Moonraker Press, 1978. xv, 184p. front., plates, ports, bibliog.
Includes details of Lancelot Brown's provision within the existing West wing of a library in the gothic rococo style to house Sir Paul Methuen's collection of books. This dates from 1760-1763, and may be based on the plans of Henry Keene. The room was converted into a breakfast room by John Nash in 1797, who created the New Library at the same time.

Benjamin MILDMAY, Earl Fitzwalter, 1672-1756

2869 A. C. Edwards. The account books of Benjamin Mildmay, Earl Fitzwalter. Regency Press, 1977. [4], xii, 13-213, 11p. front., illus, facsims.
Pages 177-87 consist of a transcript of all entries dating from 1724 to 1754 relating to books. Interesting as a record of the purchases of a modest collector, who spent ten times as much on claret as on books.

Sir Thomas MORE, 1477/8-1535

2870 J. B. Trapp and H. S. Herbruggen. 'The King's good servant': Sir Thomas More 1477/8-1535. Ipswich, Boydell Press, 1977. 147p. front., illus, facsims, ports.

Published in connection with the exhibition held at the National
Portrait Gallery from 25th November 1977 to 12th March 1978. More's
enemies were successful in almost extinguishing his library. Of the
six extant books known, or believed to have been his, five are re-
united for the first time in this exhibition, and are described here.

John MORICE, 1768-1844

2871 A. Davis. John Morice, F.S.A., 1768-1844.
      Bk Coll. 29 (1) 1980, 36-49. port.
      Morice's library comprised about 4,000 books and was particularly
      strong in history and topography, many of them extra-illustrated.
      The growth of the collection is described against the background of
      his life. Some of the more important items are described from the
      catalogue of the sale after his death.

MOSTYN family

2872 Sotheby and Co. Catalogue of ... printed books comprising the property
      of Col. J. F. Williams-Wynne, C.B.E., D.S.O., J.P. London, 3 April, 1979.
      360 lots. 66p. front., illus, plates.
      English antiquarian books from the Penbedw and Peniarth-Hengwrt lib-
      raries, the majority of them carrying bookplates representative of
      the three hundred years history of this important library. Many of
      the classic works of Welsh lexicography and other aspects of Welsh
      literary history are present.

Sir Isaac NEWTON, 1642-1727

2873 J. Harrison. The library of Isaac Newton. Cambridge U.P., 1978. xiv,
      286p. facsims, tables, bibliog.
      Rev. Bk Coll. 29 (4) 1980, 604-7 (P. B. Wood)
          J.Lib.Hist. 15 (2) 1980, 222-4 (A. E. Skinner)
          Lib.Rev. 28 (3) 1979, 175 (P. B. Freshwater)
      The catalogue is preceded by three chapters, the first of which con-
      siders the use made by Newton of his working library and of other
      Cambridge libraries. Chapter 2 covers the fate of his books from the
      time of their purchase after his death by John Huggins, Warden of the
      Fleet Prison, until 1943, when the remaining half of the library was
      given to Trinity College, Cambridge. Chapter 3 looks at the com-
      position of the collection with subject and language analyses.

Frederick NORTH, 5th Earl of Guilford, 1766-1827

2874   M. Partridge. An English eccentric and some Slavs and Slavists.
Wiener Slavistisches Jahrbuch   Bd 21 1975, 202-13.
   An account of the career of the 5th Earl of Guilford, who was res-
   ponsible for bringing into being what was probably the finest early
   collection of Slavonic books and manuscripts assembled by a private
   English collector.

Edgar OSBORNE, 1890-1978

(2423) [Obituaries of Edgar Osborne, 1890-1978]

Wilfred OWEN, 1893-1918

2875   D. Hibberd. Wilfred Owen's library: some additional items.
Notes and Queries 24 (5) 1977, 447-8.
   After Owen's death in 1918 his small collection of books was care-
   fully preserved by his family, and was listed by Harold Owen in 1920.
   It was presented to the English Faculty Library at Oxford in 1975,
   after Stallworthy had listed it in his biography of Owen, below.
   Four more items are here recorded.

2876   J. Stallworthy. Wilfred Owen. Oxford U.P. and Chatto and Windus, 1974.
xiv, 333p. front., illus, facsims, ports, bibliog.
   Appendix C, pages 308-23, lists Wilfred Owen's working library.

John PARKER, 1548-1618/19

2877   S. Strongman. John Parker's manuscripts: an edition of the lists in
Lambeth Palace MS. 737.
Trans. Cambridge Bibl.Soc. 7 (1) 1977, 1-27. plates.
   The manuscripts described belonged to John Parker, son of Archbishop
   Matthew Parker, and include chronicles and lives of the saints.

Matthew PARKER, Archbishop of Canterbury, 1504-1575

2878   R. I. Page. Christopher Marlowe and the library of Matthew Parker.
Notes and Queries 24 (6) 1977, 510-14
   A detailed examination of conflicting evidence as to the year in
   which Parker's library came to Corpus Christi College, Cambridge.
   There is no clear conclusion. It may have been in 1578 or 1593 or
   in batches during his lifetime and then between 1578 and 1593.

PARKER family

2879 National Trust. Saltram, Devon. 10th ed. The National Trust, 1978. 37p. plates, plans.

There is mention of the exchange of positions of the Library and Eating Room in 1780 and further alterations to the Library in 1796 and 1819.

James William PARKES, 1896-1981

2880 Parkes Library, University of Southampton.
Bull. ABTAPL 1 (12) 1978, 3-4.

Provides a brief historical account of the collection of books on Jewish history, antisemitism and allied subjects formed from 1928 onwards by Rev. James Parkes. It was given to the University of Southampton in 1964.

John PARKHURST, Bishop of Norwich, 1512-1575

(2585) D. M. Sturley. The Royal Grammar School Guildford.

PASTON family

2881 Paston letters and papers of the fifteenth century, edited by Norman Davis. Oxford, Clarendon Press, 1971-6. 2 vols. front., facsims.
Rev. J.Lib.Hist. 13 (2) 1978, 234-6 (T. Lawler)

Contains a number of references to the private ownership and borrowing of books. John Paston II, 1442-1479 was the first of the family who revealed a lifelong interest in books, in owning them, borrowing them, lending them and evaluating his holdings. An inventory of his books made c.1475 appears in volume 1 page 516-8.

Samuel PEPYS, 1633-1703

2882 Magdalene College, Cambridge. Catalogue of the Pepys Library at Magdalene College, Cambridge. General editor Robert Latham. Vol.1: Printed books, compiled by N. A. Smith ... Ipswich, Brewer, 1978. xiii, 201p.
Rev. Analytical and Enumerative Bibliography 3 (2) 1979, 120-9 (M. A. Shaaber)
    T.L.S. Nov.24, 1978, 1375 (R. Ollard)

2883 Pepys - and after
Bk Coll. 28 (4) 1979, 487-500.

A discussion of the Pepys collection in the light of the publication of N. A. Smith's Catalogue of the Pepys Library at Magdalene College,

<u>Cambridge</u>, vol.1 1978, above. The article also considers the role of
library sale catalogues in reconstructing private collections, with
special reference to the 17th century. The rationale of such reconstruction is also discussed.

2884   E. M. Wilson. Samuel Pepys and Spain.
<u>Trans. Cambridge Bibl.Soc.</u> 7 (3) 1979, 322-37.
   Pepys's library in Magdalene College, Cambridge, contains 185 Spanish
   items, including 76 chapbooks. He himself visited Spain in 1684 to
   buy books.

   Sir Thomas PHILLIPPS, 1792-1872
(2593) J.M.G. Blakiston. Sir Thomas Phillipps and Winchester College.

2885   D. Chambers. Sir Thomas Phillipps and the Middle Hill Press.
<u>Private Lib.</u> 1 (1) 1978, 2-38. facsims.
   One of the most avid collectors ever, Sir Thomas's library numbered
   some 60,000 manuscripts and 50,000 printed books, many of which were
   recorded in catalogues printed at his Middle Hill Press in Worcestershire. The article traces the history of the press and includes 19
   facsimiles.

   Henry Graham POLLARD, 1903-1976
2886   Sotheby and Co. Catalogue of valuable printed books. Sotheby, 3/4 July,
   1978. 73p. front., port.
   This collection is a representative cross-section of the riches of
   English literature. Graham Pollard was the most influential and acute
   historian of the book trade, and his library, though not particularly
   accented towards any one author, is a vivid panorama of choice
   editions and seminal works.

   Solomon POTTESMAN, 1904-1978
2887   O. F. Snelling. Potty.
<u>Antiquarian Book Monthly Review</u> 7 (1) 1980, 26-30. facsim., port.
   Personal reminiscences of Solomon Pottesman, who lived an eccentric,
   vagrant-like existence at various lodgings in the Bloomsbury area,
   where he frequented the British Museum Reading Room, auction rooms
   and antiquarian booksellers. His life was devoted to the collection
   of incunabula, and his most valuable treasures were kept in various
   safe deposits and vaults dotted about London.

2888   Sotheby and Co. Catalogue of ... incunabula and sixteenth-century printed books, comprising the property of Mr. S. Pottesman, deceased. London, 15 and 16 October, 1979. 417 lots. 141p. front., illus, plates.

The collector sought to obtain as wide a geographical range of incunabula imprints as possible. A revered and eccentric antiquarian bookman, his collection was characterised by The Times as a 'poor man's Broxbourne library'.

2889   A. G. Thomas. Solomon Pottesman.
Bk Coll. 28 (4) 1979, 545-553. port.
Another largely anecdotal appreciation.

Harry PRICE, 1881-1948

2890   T. H. Hall. Search for Harry Price. Duckworth, 1978. x, 237p. front., plates, facsims, ports.

The author would appear to apply the methods of Sherlock Holmes to the book collecting, as well as to other aspects of Price's career. He believed himself to be the owner of the foremost collection of conjuring books in the world. Chapter 12 questions Price's reliability as a commentator on the books in his collection. Chapter 13 discusses the Burmese MS purporting to deal with conjuring. Chapter 14 considers his bookplates, including one alleged fake, and the presence in his collection of books with the bookplate of the Society of Psychical Research. Chapter 20 records the growth of the collection and its transformation from a library of rare conjuring books to over 10,000 items covering all aspects of the occult, and the circumstances in which it finally came into the possession of the University of London.

2891   A. Wesencraft. The Harry Price Library (in the University of London Library).
Libraries Bulletin, Univ. of London 1 (12) 1978, 10-13;
                                    1 (13) 1978, 5-9, 15

Records how in 1922 Price purchased a valuable collection of 160 conjuring books whilst on holiday in Berlin, and ingeniously and audaciously spirited them past the customs officers. The contents and scope of Price's library is delineated under the following headings: juvenile literature; conjuring books; witchcraft and the occult; psychical research and spiritualism; miscellaneous.

John RASTELL,   -1536

2892 R. J. Roberts. John Rastell's inventory of 1538.
<u>Library</u> 1 (3) 1979, 34-42.

> An inventory of Rastell's books now in the Public Record Office is
> reprinted and the items identified. Rastell was a printer, and some
> of the books appear to be his sale stock and some his personal lib-
> rary.

R.E.D. RAWLINS, 1917-1979

2893 Sotheby Parke Bernet and Co. Catalogue of well-known collection of
autograph letters, historical documents and signed photographs formed
between 1930 and 1979 by the late R.E.D. Rawlins, Esq. London, 2, 3 and
4 June 1980. 347p. illus.

> The collection of R.E.D. Rawlins (1917-1979), dubbed "the unofficial
> autographer Royal", numbered some 30,000 items. Lot 1053 is a 6-page
> manuscript library catalogue, dated 1789, of mainly theological books
> owned by Joshua Brookes, the eccentric divine.

William Henry RIDER, 1909-1980

2894 [Obituary]
<u>Antiquarian Book Monthly Review</u> 7 (4) 1980, 206.

> In addition to details of his work as a novelist and bibliographer,
> there is information concerning his collection of fine printing,
> especially private press books from William Morris to about 1945,
> which he formed from the 1930s.

Cecil ROTH, 1899-1977

(2627) P. S. Morrish. The Brotherton Library, its Judaica and Cecil Roth.

Ferdinand James de ROTHSCHILD, Baron, 1839-1898

2895 R. Myers. The library of Waddesdon Manor.
<u>Private Lib.</u> 2 (3) 1979, 115-20. plate, bibliog.

> The collection of some 785 books is largely a social history of
> aristocratic 17th and 18th century France, rich in memoirs and books
> about great houses and the theatre, and including many fine bindings.
> A descriptive catalogue of immense scholarship, initiated by the late
> Graham Pollard, is in course of preparation.

James A. de ROTHSCHILD, 1878-1957

2896 James A. de Rothschild Collection at Waddesdon Manor. Illuminated

manuscripts: the James A. de Rothschild Collection at Waddesdon Manor
[compiled by] L.M.J. Delaissé, James Marrow, John de Wit. Friboug,
Office du Livre for the National Trust, 1977, 608p. facsims.
Rev. T.L.S. July 28, 1978, 871 (J.J.G. Alexander)

> This collection was part of that formed by Baron Edmond de Rothschild
> of Paris, and was inherited by his son James A. de Rothschild. All
> of the 26 manuscripts are housed at Waddesdon Manor, which was be-
> queathed to the National Trust at his death in 1957. Each manuscript
> is described in detail and illustrated in colour.

John Frederick SACKVILLE, 3rd Duke of Dorset, 1745-1799

2897 W. K. Ford. Music at Knole.
In: National Trust Studies, 1979. Sotheby Parke Bernet, 1978, 160-79.
illus, facsims, ports.

> In the context of the musical tradition at Knole, there is a dis-
> cussion of an incomplete and undated catalogue of a collection of
> music formed by the third Duke. Its main interest lies in the wealth
> of instrumental music it records, both chamber and orchestral.

Michael SADLEIR, 1888-1957

2898 R. Stokes. Michael Sadleir, 1888-1957. Scarecrow Press, 1980. [1], v,
154p.

> Extracts from his works and the biographical introduction throw
> light upon his collecting activities in the field of 19th century
> fiction. Collecting was not an end in itself, but a preliminary to
> exposition and recording. There is a checklist of his writings.

Hans and Tanya SCHMOLLER

2899 Schmollers' Penguins.
Bk Coll. 28 (2) 1979, 252-5.

> Since about 1949 Hans and Tanya Schmoller have aimed at assembling a
> complete collection of Penguins. They are at present 300 volumes
> short of the total of 11,000 required. The collection is being trans-
> ferred in instalments to the British Library of Political and Economic
> Science.

Henry SCRIMGEOUR, 1505?-1572

2900 J. Durkan. Henry Scrimgeour, Renaissance bookman.
Edinburgh Bibl.Soc.Trans. 5 (1) 1978, 1-31, facsim.

> Scrimgeour was born in Dundee, but most of his life was spent abroad.

He was a diplomat and university teacher, and was in charge of the Fugger collection. The fate of his personal library and notes is discussed.

SEYMOUR family, Dukes of Somerset

2901 A. McCann, editor. The Petworth House archives; a catalogue. Vol.2. Chichester, West Sussex County Council, 1979, xi, 112p. front., plates, facsims.

Several catalogues of the library at Petworth are listed. They date from the late 17th to the early 19th century.

Yeshayahu SHACHAR, 1936-1977

2902 Sotheby Parke Bernet and Co. Catalogue of the well-known collection of Hebrew books, the property of the late Dr. Yeshayahu Shachar. London, 17 and 18 November 1980. 90p.

The library of Dr. Shachar, historian of Jewish art, was noted for its collections on the Hasidic movement and anti-semitism, and included the library of the Hasidic scholar, Prof. Joseph G. Weiss (1919-1969).

SHORE SMITH family

2903 H. Oliver. The Shore Smith family library; Arthur Hugh Clough and Florence Nightingale.
Bk Coll. 28 (4) 1979, 521-9.

The Shore, Smith, Clough and Nightingale families were all interrelated. Their relationships are explained in order to show how the existing library came to be formed. The chief interest of the books is that many of them contain signed and dated inscriptions, including some by the poet A. H. Clough. Many of the books came from the home of Florence Nightingale.

Sir Hans SLOANE, 1660-1753

2904 J. A. Clarke. Sir Hans Sloane and Abbé Jean Paul Bignon: notes on collection building in the eighteenth century.
Lib. Q. 50 (4) 1980, 475-82.

Concerns correspondence between Sir Hans Sloane and Abbé Jean Paul Bignon, master of the King's Library at Paris. The most fruitful aspect of this correspondence was the exchange of both retrospective and current research publications. Such books and periodicals were transmitted through diplomatic channels or through the good offices of travellers or merchants.

2905   M.A.E. Nickson. Sloane's codes: the solution to a mystery.
Factotum 1 (7) 1979, 13-18.
Using an autograph Sloane notebook discovered in the Department of
Manuscripts, code letters and signs following place and date of
purchase written on the fly-leaves of his books are proved to in-
dicate the price paid for them.

2906   J. L. Wood. Sir Hans Sloane's books.
Factotum 1 (2) 1978, 15-18.
Lists 28 books identifiable as some of Sloane's earliest acquisitions, and mentions a work which is, in effect, an author
catalogue of his medical books, and which does not appear to have
been noted previously.

Adam SMITH, 1723-1790

2907   M.C.T. Simpson. Books belonging to Adam Smith in Edinburgh University
Library: a survey of newly discovered items, with a general discussion.
Bibliotheck 9 (6) 1979, 187-99.
Adam Smith's library of about 3,200 volumes was dispersed on the
death of his heir. Some 1600 of his books are now in Edinburgh
University Library, of which over 70 have hitherto not been recorded
as having been his property. These items are discussed against the
background of his personal library practice.

Lawrence STERNE, 1713-1768

2908   E. A. Swaim. Sterne's books.
Library 32 (4) 1977, 381
A letter amplifying W. G. Day's article in _Library_ 31 (3) 1976 (see
no. 2076), suggesting a further source from which Sterne might have
acquired some of his books.

STEWART family

2909   K. C. Crawford. The Dugald Stewart collection (Edinburgh University
Library).
Bibliotheck 10 (2) 1980, 31-4.
A brief description of the collection formed by the Edinburgh
philosopher, Dugald Stewart, his father and his son. It came to the
University Library in 1910.

Sir William STIRLING-MAXWELL, 1818-1878

2910   Sotheby and Co. Catalogue of ... printed books ... [including] the property of William Stirling, Esq. (from the collection formed by Sir William Stirling Maxwell, 1818-1878). First portion: 81 lots; second portion 143 lots. London, 11 December 1978 and 30 January 1979, 2 vols.
    The catalogue notes that the books bear one or other of the specially designed stamps, bookplates or labels.

Sir Richard TEMPLE, 1634-1697

2911   G. R. Abernathy. Sir Richard Temple and the Stowe Library.
Huntington Library Quarterly 40 (1) 1976, 45-58.
    In spite of the fact that Sir Richard inherited considerable debts from his father, from that time until his death he never ceased collecting books. Details of his library are obtained from ledgers, bills, receipts and catalogues. At his death his library consisted of from 2200 to 2400 titles. It was particularly strong in the fields of law, history, divinity, politics and economics, and was of a practical nature rather than scholarly or antiquarian, being of use to his immediate family, relatives, friends, neighbours, and his household and estate staff.

Sir Charles TENNANT, 1823-1906

2912   Sotheby Parke Bernet and Co. Catalogue of valuable printed books comprising books from the library formed by Sir Charles Tennant (1823-1906) ... London, 24 and 25 November 1980. 100p.
    A collection of mainly literary and religious interest.

Alfred TENNYSON, 1st Baron TENNYSON, 1809-1892

2913   J. C. Hixson and P. Scott. Tennyson's books.
Tennyson Research Bulletin 2 (5) 1976, 190-9.
    Analyses the 2091 titles owned by Tennyson and relates them to the 368 extant titles from the library of his father's Somersby Rectory. The writer concludes that Tennyson made conscious efforts to be both more modern and more inclusive than the older literary culture in which he had been raised.

2914   S. Shatto. Tennyson's library.
Bk Coll. 27 (4) 1978, 494-513. illus, facsims.
    The bulk of Tennyson's personal collection has been preserved intact in the Tennyson Research Centre, Lincoln. His use of books and their

influence on his work are discussed.

Ellen TERRY, 1848-1928

2915   F. T. Bowyer, compiler. Catalogue of the working library of Ellen Terry
at Smallhythe Place, Tenterden, Kent. The National Trust, 1977. 63p.
The Smallhythe estate was bequeathed to the National Trust by Ellen
Terry's daughter Edith Craig, in 1939. The presence of annotation is
noticed. The foreword briefly discusses provenance, etc.

THYNNE family

2916   J. Collins. A short account of the Library at Longleat House, War-
minster, Wilts. Sotheby Parke Bernet, 1980. 36p. front., illus,
facsims.
Traces the book collecting activities of the Thynne family from
William Thynne during the reign of Henry VIII, to the present
Marquess of Bath. Several booksellers' and binders' invoices are
reproduced. The collections of Bishop Thomas Ken and Beriah Botfield
also came to Longleat.

2917   Sotheby and Co. Catalogue of ... printed books, duplicates from the
library at Longleat House. London, 11 June, 1979. 180 lots. 82p.
front., illus, plates.
The first sale of books from Longleat. They are designated
'duplicates' by the present Marquess of Bath, but clearly are often
unique by virtue of provenance, binding, etc. The present works are
mostly topographies and natural history.

Thomas TURNER, 1729-1793

2918   T. Turner. The diary of a Georgian shopkeeper. A selection by R. W.
Blencowe and M. A. Lower, with a preface by Florence Mavis Turner:
second edition with a new introduction by G. H. Jennings. Oxford U.P.,
1979. xxxii, 95p. front.
1st ed., Bodley Head, 1925. Turner was a draper of the parish of
East Hoathly in Sussex. His most entertaining diary covers the
period 1754-65 and provides evidence of the purchase and reading of
books by a small tradesman. He was particularly fond of works of
divinity, politics and literature.

Horace WALPOLE, 4th Earl of Orford, 1717-1797

2919   J. Cornforth. The Cowles-Lewis House, Farmington.

<u>Country Life</u>   April 27, 1978, 1150-3. illus, ports; May 4, 1978, 1230-3.
illus, ports.

>An account of the home of Mr. Wilmarth S. Lewis at Farmington,
>Connecticut.   Over the last 54 years Mr. Lewis has built up a vast
>collection of Walpole's books from Strawberry Hill, his letters,
>Strawberry Hill press books, portraits, prints and relics. The
>collections, which are made available to scholars, are described.

2920   W. S. Lewis. Rescuing Horace Walpole. Yale U.P., 1978. ix, 251p.
illus, facsims, ports.

>Wilmarth Lewis writes about 26 objects from his collection of Wal-
>poliana at Farmington, Connecticut, the largest of its kind in
>existence. Included are items from Walpole's library at Strawberry
>Hill, about which much background information is provided.

Izaak WALTON, 1593-1683

2921   J. Bevan. Some books from Izaak Walton's library.
<u>Library</u> 2 (3) 1980, 259-63. plates.

>A list of books formerly in Walton's possession which formed the
>basis for a talk to the Bibliographical Society.

Cyril Hackett WILKINSON, 1888-1960

2922   R. Sayce. Another Oxford bibliophile: C. H. Wilkinson (1888-1960).
In: The Warden's meeting: a tribute to John Sparrow. Oxford, Oxford
University Society of Bibliophiles, 1977, 86-9.

>Colonel Wilkinson's book collecting activities in the field of
>English literature, history and criticism from the 16th to the 20th
>centuries, are outlined. He was also librarian of Worcester College,
>Oxford, for nearly forty years. His own interests coincided very
>nearly with the strongest areas of the Worcester Library, and he left
>to Worcester a number of items to fill gaps in the College col-
>lections.

WILLIAM IV, King of Great Britain and Ireland 1765-1837

2923   C. Wainwright. The furnishing of the Royal Library Windsor.
<u>Connoisseur</u> 195 (784) 1977, 104-9. illus.

>Sir Jeffry Wyatville was commissioned by William IV to create the
>suite of rooms at Windsor Castle which comprise the Royal Library.
>However, most of the furniture was not specifically designed for
>Windsor but was originally made for the library at Carlton House.

The nature of the furniture and the identification of its designer is discussed.

WILLIAMS-WYNNE family
(2872) Sotheby and Co. Catalogue of ... printed books comprising the property of Col. J. F. Williams-Wynne, C.B.E., D.S.O., J.P.

Edward Meryon WILSON, 1906-
2924 Sotheby and Co. Catalogue of Spanish books. Sotheby, 19 June, 1978. 40p. illus.
Dr. Wilson was Cervantes Professor of Spanish at the University of London 1945-53 and subsequently Professor of Spanish at Cambridge. The importance of the collection is in its emphasis on Spanish books of the 16th-18th centuries and on English and other books dealing with Spain. Bibliographical works were a notable part of the sale.

Mary WILSON (née Macro), 1688-1761
2925 P. S. Morrish. Mary Macro's books.
Notes and Queries 26 (6) 1979, 535-6.
Lists 21 titles belonging to Mary Wilson née Macro, of Bury St. Edmunds, reproduced from her son's papers now in the possession of the Brotherton Library, Leeds. Her brother Cox Macro was an antiquary and bibliophile. However, the books in question are largely juvenilia.

Thomas WOODWARD, 1665?-1728
(2389) J. M. Levine. Dr. Woodward's shield: history, science, and satire in Augustan England.

William WORDSWORTH, 1770-1850
2926 C. L. Shaver and A. C. Shaver, editors. Wordsworth's library: a catalogue, including a list of books housed by Wordsworth for Coleridge from c.1810 to c.1830. Garland, 1979. xliii, 363p. front., plates.
Rev. Lib.Hist. 5 (3) 1980, 87-9 (P. Vavigueur)
The main part of the catalogue is a composite list of his books based on several sources which are fully described in the preliminaries. A subject analysis is attempted by the reviewer.

Edward WORTH, 1678-1733
2927 M. McCarthy. Dr. Edward Worth's library in Dr. Steevens' Hospital.

Journal of the Irish Colleges of Physicians and Surgeons 6 (4) 1977,
141-2, 144-5.

Dr. Worth, a Governor of Dr. Steevens' Hospital, Dublin, bequeathed
his library for the use of the physician and surgeon. The 4,500
volume collection, not exclusively medical, forms an almost unique
18th century Irish doctor's library exactly as he collected it. He
bought at many important auctions and had an eye for fine bindings.

WYNDHAM family, Earls of Egremont

(2901) A. McCann, editor. The Petworth House archives: a catalogue.

William Butler YEATS, 1865-1939

(2796) R. Bridges and W. B. Yeats. The correspondence of Robert Bridges and
W. B. Yeats.

LIBRARIES: Public

(2515) D. Aubrey. Enthusiasm has defeated apathy.

2928 J. Butler. Changes and chances.
Lib.Assn Rec. 79 (4) 1977, 193.
The writer compares the children's library service in 1947 and 1975.

(3138) B. Cottle. Popular reading and our public libraries: the abjured pre-scription.

(2532) H. Davies. Using 'public' libraries in Victorian England.

2929 M. Dewe. H. T. Hare: Edwardian library architect.
Lib.Rev. Vol.26 Summer 1978, 80-4
An outline of the career of Henry Thomas Hare (1860-1921), who designed nine public library buildings between 1897 and 1909. The buildings are listed and his ideas on public library planning are summarised.

(2465) R. J. Edwards. In-service training in British libraries: its develop-ment and present practice.

2930 A. Ellis. The finances and buildings of public libraries at the out-break of the First World War.
J. Librarianship 9 (2) 1977, 120-9.
The author argues that the financial position of public libraries between 1900 and 1914 was not as bad as previously thought, but that a decline began after the War. Many libraries spent substantial sums on newspapers at the expense of books. The article concludes that librarians had low expectations of the facilities they could provide, while open access cost more than could be afforded.

2931 A. Ellis. Public Libraries at the time of the Adams report. Stevenage, Clover Publications, 1979. [3], 88p. bibliog.
Rev. Lib.Assn Rec. 81 (7) 1979, 339 (J. Wilkie)
Lib.Hist. 5 (2) 1979, 66-9 (G. Jones)
Lib.Rev. 28 (3) 1979, 165 (J. S. English)
A situation report on public libraries in Great Britain in 1914, taking into account developments in the previous decade. The first chapter deals with the general and financial situation, emphasising

the decline in expenditure from 1908 to 1914 and discussing reasons
for this. Other chapters are devoted to buildings, library materials,
users and uses (including extension activities) and staffing
(largely conditions of service and the involvement of public librarians with the Library Association).

2932   A. Ellis. Rural library services in England and Wales before 1919.
       Lib.Hist. 4 (3) 1977, 69-80.

> Five corporate schemes are described, the first being the Yorkshire
> Village Library co-ordinated by the Yorkshire Union of Institutes in
> 1856. These were eventually assisted by the C.U.K.T., which also
> initiated its own experiments in county library provision before the
> passing of the 1919 Act. These latter are described and assessed.
> The legislation to create county libraries is seen as part of a wider
> policy to revitalise the countryside.

2933   A. Ellis. The users and uses of public libraries at the outbreak of the
       First World War.
       J.Librarianship 11 (1) 1979, 39-49.

> Discusses the use made, or often not made, of library resources,
> particularly the generally meagre extension activities. However, a
> few libraries were very active in the latter field.

2934   A. L. Farmer. The Board of Education Public Libraries Committee (1924-
       1927) and its report (the Kenyon Report). Loughborough, Loughborough
       Univ. of Technology, 1979. [5] 380, [34] p. tables, bibliog. [Thesis
       submitted in partial fulfilment of the requirements for an MLS degree.
       Typescript]

> Part One deals with the Committee itself, how it came to be appointed,
> its composition, including brief biographies of the committee members,
> and how it undertook its duties. Part Two deals with the Report, and
> contains a critical review of its findings and recommendations, the
> contemporary reaction to it, and the effects of its recommendations.
> The Committee's questionnaire is reproduced in an appendix.

2935   M. Garratt. Engineers and libraries.
       New Lib.World 28 (922) 1977, 69-70.

> Points out brief notes on public library activity which appeared in
> The Engineer between 1856 and 1858.

2936   P. D. Gratton. The public library from 1960 to 1980.
       In: Studies in library management. Vol.6. The coming of age of library
       management 1960-1980, edited by Anthony Vaughan. Bingley, 1980, 30-50.

> A general survey of trends, set against the social changes of the

period.

(2395) A guarded, pleasant life: an interview with F.G.B. Hutchings.

(2595) K. W. Humphreys. Special collections in university libraries (excluding copyright libraries) and in public libraries.

2937 E. J. Hunter. The rôle of the public library in the development of technical education in Great Britain and Ireland during the nineteenth century. Sheffield, Sheffield Univ., Postgraduate School of Librarianship and Information Science, 1973. xiv, 379p. illus, facsims, map, plans, bibliog. [Thesis submitted for the degree of Master of Librarianship. Typescript]

    The legal position surrounding the provision of technical education under the Public Libraries Acts is investigated. This is followed by an historical review of the provision of educational facilities by public libraries, including discussion of such questions as finance, buildings, administration, students, etc. Other relevant educational activities, e.g. lectures and the provision of technical books, are also discussed. Appendix 1 sets out a number of case studies.

2938 P. Jackaman. The catch 22 of Sunday service.
Lib.Rev. Vol.29 Summer 1980, 91-106.

    Traces the progress of the movement to open libraries, museums and galleries to the public on the Lord's Day, and the growth and subsequent decline of the practice of Sunday opening of public libraries from the mid-19th century to the present day. This is seen as one of the responses to the problem of making the service accessible to the working class. This is adequately set within the general social context, in particular, the changes in working hours and the scope of workers to indulge in recreational activities.

2939 P. N. Kaula. Library legislation in Great Britain.
Herald of Lib.Sci. 16 (4) 1977, 353-64.

    A chronological summary of public library legislation in England and Wales, including peripheral legislation such as the Malicious Damages Act of 1861. The salient features of such Acts are noted, and the recommendations of the Kenyon and subsequent reports are summarised.

2940 T. Kelly. Books for the people: an illustrated history of the British public library. Illustrations selected by Edith Kelly. Deutsch, 1977. 271p. front., illus, facsims, map, plan, ports, bibliog.
Rev. J.Lib.Hist. 15 (1) 1980, 109-10 (D. C. Dale)
    Lib.Assn Rec. 79 (8) 1977, 427-8 (J. G. Ollé)

Rev. T.L.S. Dec.30, 1977, 1532 (R. Hoggart)
  Largely a history of the public library service, with occasional
  reference to the national libraries, intended for a wider readership
  than his two previous volumes. The first chapter covers the precursors of the public library, including parish and town libraries,
  subscription libraries and working men's libraries. A considerable
  proportion of the book is devoted to post-war developments.

2941   T. Kelly. A history of public libraries in Great Britain, 1845-1975.
       2nd ed. revised. Library Association, 1977. xiii, 582p. illus, plates,
       map, ports, bibliog.
       Rev. J.Librarianship 10 (1) 1978, 67-9   E. Clough)
            J.Lib.Hist. 13 (3) 1978, 340-2 (P. J. Bassnett)
            Lib.Assn Rec. 79 (8) 1977, 427-8 (J. G. Ollé)
            Lib.Hist. 4 (4) 1977, 125 (P. S. Morrish)
            Lib.Rev. Vol.27 Winter 1978, 260-1 (H. McMullen)
            T.L.S. Dec.30, 1977, 1532 (R. Hoggart)
       Minor amendments throughout the original text of 1973 (see no.2102)
       and an additional chapter covering the years 1965 to 1975.

(2512) J. C. Kennedy. The Library Association, County Libraries Section: its
       inception, growth and influence 1920-1960.

2942   P. Larkin. Single-handed and untrained.
       Lib.Assn Rec. 79 (10) 1977, 531, 533, 539. illus.
       The author reminisces about his period as librarian of an un-named
       Urban District Council library near Birmingham in 1943-1946.

2943   S.L.M. Levy. The formative years of the English public library movement:
       a social history. Chicago, Univ. of Chicago Graduate Library School,
       1973. iv, 102p. tables, bibliog. [Dissertation submitted for M.A.
       degree. Typescript]
       Aims to relate the vision of the founders of the public library
       movement, especially Edwards and Ewart, to make books available to all
       segments of society, especially the lower classes and the newly
       literate, to the actuality of public library membership. This is done
       by analysing the membership statistics contained in the annual reports
       of Liverpool, Manchester and Birmingham public libraries for 1850-1870
       by age, sex, occupation and social class.

2944   J. D. MacFarlane. How the profession reacted: the McColvin Report of
       1942.
       Liv.Rev. 26 (4) 1977, 277-8.
       Mentions a review, Arundel Esdaile's editorial and E. V. Corbett's

letter in the <u>Library Association Record.</u> The Report was also widely reviewed in the general press.

2945   W. R. Maidment. Trade unionism in public libraries.
<u>J.Librarianship</u> 8 (3) 1976, 143-52.
> Covers the relationship between public library staffs and Nalgo since 1919. Librarianship was recognised in the national scheme of conditions of service agreed in 1946. Library participation in the 1974 London Weighting dispute is also discussed.

2946   E. J. Miller. Public libraries.
In: Education. General editor, G. Sutherland. Irish U.P., 1977, 125-36. bibliog.
> Brief notes and commentary on the Reports from Select Committees on Public Libraries 1849 and 1850-2, the texts of which are reprinted separately by the same publisher.

2947   R.J.B. Morris. Honest - but an outrageous opponent of reading for the masses.
<u>Lib.Assn Rec.</u> 79 (10) 1977, 574-5.
> A survey of the parliamentary career of Charles Sibthorp and his opposition to the Public Libraries Bill of 1850.

2948   R.J.B. Morris. Parliament and the public libraries: a survey of legislative activity promoting the municipal library service in England and Wales 1850-1976. Mansell, 1977. xiv, 477p. bibliog.
<u>Rev.</u> <u>Lib.Assn Rec.</u> 79 (10) 1977, 579, 581 (K. C. Harrison)
     <u>Lib.Hist.</u> 4 (5) 1978, 169-70 (W. A. Munford)
     <u>Lib.Q.</u> 49 (1) 1979, 73-8 (A. P. Young)
     <u>Lib.Rev.</u> Vol.27 Spring 1978, 53-4 (J. G. Ollé)
     <u>T.L.S.</u> Dec.30. 1977, 1533 (D.C.L. Holland)
> Based on the author's 1974 thesis (see no.2105). The main text covers the subject chronologically in five chapters. Appendix 4 provides a synopsis of the text, together with a tabulation of the procedural stages of all 66 Bills. Appendix 5 cites Parliamentary questions from 1865 to 1976 touching public libraries, with summaries of questions and answers, arranged chronologically.

2949   J. G. Ollé. Discourse on dirty books.
<u>New Lib.World</u> 81 (966) 1980, 237-9.
> Personal reminiscences of public lending libraries in the 1930s, especially concerning the woeful standards of the physical state of the bookstocks.

148

2950   G.I.J. Orton. An illustrated history of mobile library services in the
        United Kingdom: with notes on travelling libraries and early public lib-
        rary transport. Sudbury, Branch and Mobiles Group of the Lib.Assn, 1980.
        96p. illus, facsim., ports, bibliog.

> Chapter 2 is devoted to early municipal travelling libraries serving
> delivery stations e.g. that of Bradford (horse drawn) of 1902 and
> Glasgow (mechanical) of 1904 onwards, and mobile libraries from that
> of Manchester, 1931 onwards. Chapter 3 covers early county library
> book delivery vans and mobile libraries. Subsequent chapters record
> developments to date.

2951   W. B. Paton. Exciting times - another view of how the LA responded to
        the wind of change.
        Lib.Assn Rec. 79 (7) 1977, 364-5.

> A comment on the article by J. E. Pemberton (Lib.Assn Rec. 79 (4)
> 1977 below) in which the author, President of the Association in 1962,
> suggests that the Association had started to change its character
> before H. D. Barry's appointment as Secretary in 1959. He describes
> in detail the Association's relations with the Roberts Committee of
> 1957/58.

2952   J. E. Pemberton. A century of library politics.
        Lib.Assn Rec. 79 (4) 1977, 181, 184-5.

> An examination of the role of the Library Association as a political
> interest group. For the first eighty years of its existence it met
> political frustration in seeking reform of the public library
> service: examples are cited. With the appointment of H. D. Barry as
> Secretary in 1959 the position changed because of his conversion of
> the Association to a body representative solely of librarians.

2953   J. E. Pemberton. Politics and public libraries in England and Wales,
        1850-1970. Lib.Assn, 1977. x, 149p. bibliog.
        Rev. Aslib.Proc. 29 (7) 1977, 268-9
            J.Librarianship 9 (3) 1977, 215-9 (G. Jones)
            J.Lib.Hist. 13 (1) 1978, 105-10 (J. Wilkinson)
            Lib.Assn Rec. 79 (4) 1977, 211 (R. Brown)
            Lib.Hist. 4 (5) 1978, 170-1 (W. A. Munford)
            Lib.Q. 49 (1) 1979 73-8 (A. P. Young)
            Lib.Rev. 26 (4) 1977, 313-4 (W. S. Haugh)
            T.L.S. Dec.30 1977, 1533 (D.C.L. Holland)
        Its purpose is said to describe and analyse the political forces
        surrounding public library legislation for England and Wales. All

but the first chapter deal with the 20th century. Much attention is paid to the Roberts Report and the 1964 Act, analysing the various vested interests and relating the interaction between the parties involved to the political system in which they operated.

2954 R. Prichard. The Library Association, benefaction, and the public library movement.
In: One hundred years: a collection to celebrate the Library Association Centenary, by members of the library staff at CLW. Aberystwyth, College of Librarianship Wales, 1977, 1-11. bibliog.
Outlines the problems caused by the financial restrictions of the penny rate, indicates the nature of Victorian philanthropy and the ill-effects of certain kinds of benefactions on the progress of the public library movement. The Library Association is blamed for lack of leadership in this respect, failing to bring its members together as a body with a general understanding of direction and attitude, of policy and intent.

2955 F. B. Sessa. History of the public library.
In: Encyclopedia of library and information science. Vol.24. New York, Dekker, 1978, 267-91.
An outline history of British public libraries and their precursors is contained within pages 268-72.

(3159) R. P. Sturges. Do librarians care for their past?

2956 P. Sykes. The public library in perspective: an examination of its origins and modern role. Bingley, 1979. 184p. bibliog.
Rev. J.Lib.Hist. 15 (4) 1980, 496-9 (A. P. Robson)
   Lib.Assn Rec. 81 (6) 1979, 291-2 (E. V. Corbett)
   Lib.Q. 50 (3) 1980, 392-3 (P. Sullivan)
A controversial critique of the origins of the public library movement which contends that throughout its history it has failed to match the expectations of its protagonists. Reasons are given for the lack of support and for the apathy displayed by politicians and the public. A chapter is devoted to the memoirs of politicians, working class leaders and educationalists which demonstrate their unawareness of the potential of the service.

2957 J. Taylor. The architectural medal: England in the nineteenth century. An annotated catalogue, with accompanying illustrations and biographical notes on architects and medallists. Based on the collection of architectural medals in the British Museum. British Museum Publications, 1978. xiii, 244p.

150

Medals struck to commemorate the opening of several public libraries
are reproduced and described.

2958   C. M. Turner. The changing social and administrative position of the
public library in England and Wales as revealed by legislative activity,
with special reference to the contrasts between the Acts of 1850 and
1964. Univ.College, London, School of Library, Archive and Information
Studies, 1976. vii, 140p. tables, bibliog. [Thesis submitted for M.A.
degree. Typescript]

"Aims to identify the main legislators and campaigners and examine
their aims, motives and tactics, as well as those of their opponents;
to show how far they were embodied in the legislation and how they
have evolved over the period." An appendix lists, with notes, the
various bills concerning public libraries, both successful and un-
successful, which have come before Parliament since 1835.

2959   K. Weibel and others, editors. The role of women in librarianship 1876-
1976: the entry, advancement, and struggle for equalisation in one
profession. Mansell, 1979. xli, 510p. bibliog.

A useful sourcebook, consisting mainly of an anthology of periodical
articles. About one third relate to the United Kingdom, mainly to
public libraries, and deal with such subjects as librarianship as a
profession for women, the employment of female assistants, etc. The
arrangement is chronological, as is the very full annotated bibliography, pages 301-441, with its separate author, title and subject
indexes.

2960   R. Williams. Plus ça change: aspects of library equipment.
In: One hundred years: a collection to celebrate the Library Association
Centenary, by members of the library staff at CLW. Aberystwyth, College
of Librarianship Wales, 1977, 13-23. facsims, bibliog.

Various kinds of equipment of a century ago are discussed, including
indicators, book disinfecting apparatus, book rests, etc., also the
matter of lavatory accommodation and reading rooms.

IRELAND

2961   J. S. Powell. Social and political influences on library provision in
Ireland 1850-1925.
Lib.Rev. Vol.29 Spring 1980, 20-6. bibliog.

This deals largely with public libraries, beginning with the abortive
Act of 1853, the almost static period between the Act of 1855 and
1880, the progress between 1880 and 1914 and the Carnegie experiments

with county libraries from 1920, all explained within the Irish context.

SCOTLAND

2962   W. Scobbie. Scottish public libraries: the last fifty years.
In: Of one accord: essays in honour of W. B. Paton, edited by Frank
McAdams. Glasgow, Scottish Lib.Assn, 1977, 22-34.
    A general retrospective glance at developments in services, working
conditions, education for librarianship, library co-operation, etc.

ABERDEENSHIRE

(2406) [Obituaries of Neil Russell McCorkindale, 1921-1977]

ACTON

(2425) [Obituaries of Bernard Ira Palmer, 1910-1979]

2963   B. I. Palmer. They kept it going.
New Lib.World 78 (930) 1977, 233-4.
    Reminiscences of Acton Public Libraries, in particular, of Charles
Hocking, who was Deputy when Bernard Palmer started working there in
1927, and who became Chief Librarian in 1937.

AIRDRIE

(2437) W. E. Tyler. William Bryce Paton.

ANGUS

2964   N. Craven. The development of public libraries in Angus, 1870-1975.
Univ. of Strathclyde, Department of Librarianship, 1976. 2 vols.
[Thesis submitted for M.A. degree. Typescript]
    Traces the development of the six public library systems which were
operating in the County of Angus at the time of local government re-
organisation in 1975. Each is treated separately, but in a similar
manner. Each is prefaced by an outline sketch of libraries existing
before the adoption of the Acts.

BANBURY

(2422) [Obituaries of Thomas William Muskett, 1901-1977]

BEDFORD

(2384) [Obituary of Cyril Hargreaves, 1911-1977]

BEDFORDSHIRE

(2380) [Obituary of George Glazier, 1902-1978]

BIRMINGHAM

2965   B. Baumfield. Raising the wind - or Lyttleton redivivus.
        Lib.Assn Rec. 81 (2) 1979, 61.
        In 1926 a quantity of manuscripts and books from Warwick Castle were
        deposited on loan in Birmingham Public Library. In 1978 a number of
        the manuscripts were reclaimed by the present Lord Brooke and
        auctioned, while others were sold outright to the Library.

2966   H. A. Whatley. Non-librarianship: yesterday's closed libraries.
        Lib.Rev. Vol.28 Summer 1979, 78-87.
        The writer recalls his experience of lending library and newsroom
        routines in the inner ward libraries of Birmingham in the 1930s.

2967   H. A. Whatley. Stack routine: the shelves assistant.
        Lib.Rev. 26 (1) 1977, 10-15.
        Personal reminiscences of Birmingham Reference Library in the early
        1930s, in particular, such routines as the updating of the location
        books, coping with the problem of overcrowded shelves, the handling
        of recent additions, dusting and checking routines and the technique
        of retrieving books using tall ladders. The supervision of all of
        these duties was the responsibility of the Shelves Assistant.

BLACKBURN

2968   J. T. Heyes. Libraries in Blackburn: a history of the major library
        institutions from 1787 to 1974. Lib.Assn, 1979. [3], viii, 535p.
        illus, tables, maps, plans, facsims., bibliog. [Thesis submitted for
        Fellowship of the Library Association. Typescript]
        The major section (pages 139-427) is devoted to Blackburn Public
        Library. Other chapters cover circulating, subscription and
        mechanics' institute libraries. Various miscellaneous institutions
        e.g. churches, Sunday schools, factories, newsrooms, clubs, etc are
        grouped under mutual improvement societies.

BLACKPOOL

2969   J. Burkitt. Blackpool Libraries 1880-1980. Blackpool District Libraries, 1980. [1], 19p. illus.

A general history, with emphasis on early developments, the growth of
branch library provision, and the radical reorganisation which took
place in the late 1940s under F. E. Cronshaw.

BOLTON

2970   T. Dunne. Bolton Public Libraries, 1853-1978: one hundred and twenty-
five years in retrospect. Bolton, Arts Department of Bolton Metro-
politan Borough, 1978. 44p. illus, facsims, ports.
Rev. Lib.Hist. 5 (2) 1979, 65-6 (N. E. Willis)

Bolton Public Library was opened in 1853, following a poll in the
previous year. There was very little opposition to the proposals.
Of special interest are the quotations from the minutes of the fund-
raising committee of working men. Bolton was singular in running a
subscription library from 1853 to 1908 parallel with the free library
service, and its unfortunate consequences are discussed. The development of the library service is dealt with chronologically in five
chapters, most attention being given to the librarianship of James
Kirkbride Waite, 1870-1904 and the dynamic Archibald Sparke, 1904-
1931. Also included is a survey of libraries in Bolton prior to the
1850s, and mention of the abortive attempt to establish an Athenaeum
in 1846.

BOURNEMOUTH

(2438) [Obituary of Harold Neville Percival Pepin, 1899-1978]

BRISTOL

(2362) [Obituaries of Eric Allen Clough, 1914-1979]

CAITHNESS

2971   D. Hay. The distant decade: Caithness County, 1925-1935.
Lib.Rev. 28 (3) 1979, 151-4.

Personal reminiscences of a now vanished library service.

CAMBRIDGE

2972   Long-lived Cambridge.

Lib.Assn Rec. 82 (8) 1980, 351.

A brief note on the foundation in 1855 and the early years of the public library service in Cambridge.

CARDIGANSHIRE

(2373) A. R. Edwards. Yr hedyn mwstard: atgofion Alun R. Edwards.

(2752) W. J. Lewis. Born on a perilous rock: Aberystwyth past and present.

CARMARTHENSHIRE

(2537) D. F. Griffiths. History of 'public libraries' in Carmarthenshire.

CHELTENHAM

(2378) [Obituary of Harold Gould Fletcher, 1906-1978]

CHESHIRE

2973   A history of the county of Chester, edited by B. E. Harris. Vol.2. Oxford U.P., for the Institute of Historical Research, 1979. xvi, 266p. front., illus., plates, maps. (Victoria history of the counties of England).

Contains brief references to Cheshire County Libraries.

(2347) [Obituaries of Sidney George Berriman, 1911-1980]

CHIPPENHAM

2974   J. A. Chamberlain. Chippenham: some notes on its history. Chippenham, Charter Trustees, 1976. vii, 199p. plates, map, bibliog.

Pages 168-72 record the foundation of the Wiltshire County Library Service in 1919, and the development of the Chippenham Branch Library from 1926 to 1974.

CLEVELAND

(2720) M. C. Horton. The story of Cleveland.

CLYDEBANK

(2355) [Obituaries of John Brogan, 1940-1979]

COATBRIDGE, Lanarks

(2370) [Obituaries of Alexander Dow, 1902-1977]

CORNWALL

(2346) [Obituary of Winifred Mary Bennetts, 1902-1979]

COVENTRY

(2440) J. D. Hendry. S. A. Pitt: his contribution to libraries and librarianship.

(2445) J. G. Ollé. Ernest A. Savage: librarian extraordinary.

(2446) J. G. Ollé. Ernest Albert Savage.

CROSBY, Lancs

(2343) [Obituary of Jean Ballantyne, 1903-1976]

CROYDON

(2358) [Obituaries of Thomas Edward Callander, 1909-1978]

(2447) J. G. Ollé. William Charles Berwick Sayers.

DERBYSHIRE

2423) [Obituaries of Edgar Osborne, 1890-1978]

DONCASTER

(2540) A. Thrall. The history of adult education in 19th century Doncaster.

DUBLIN

2975 T. P. Dowd. The Gilbert Library and the Dublin city local collection.
An Leabharlann 7 (2) 1978, 42-54.
A description of the Gilbert library and the Dix and Yeates col-
lections.

DUMBARTON

(2414) [Obituaries of William McBarron Martin, 1917-1980]

DUMFRIESSHIRE

(2408) [Obituary of Mary McLean (née Duncan), 1903-1976]

DUNFERMLINE

2976 W. J. Murison. Novice in the 'Thirties.

<u>Service Point</u> 1 (14) 1977, 5-9.

Mr. Murison tells of his early experiences with Dunfermline Public Libraries in the 1930s. He commenced as an Assistant-in-Training and was promoted Depute Librarian in 1938.

DURHAM COUNTY

(2720) M. C. Horton. The story of Cleveland.

DYFED

(2373) A. R. Edwards. Yr hedyn mwstard: atgofion Alun R. Edwards.

EAST HAM

(2382) [Obituaries of James Green, 1918-1979]

EASTBOURNE

2977 J. C. Aspden. A municipal history of Eastbourne 1938-1974. Eastbourne, Eastbourne Borough Council, [1979] [2], 285p. front., plates, ports. Detailed consideration is given to post-war strategy, following the destruction of the Central Library in 1943, and the inadequacy of branch library provision, set against ever rising issues. The achievement of branch library extension and the opening of the new Central Library in 1964, is fully recorded.

EDINBURGH

(2366) [Obituaries of James Watson Cockburn, 1908-1980]

(2445) J. G. Ollé. Ernest A. Savage: librarian extraordinary.

(2446) J. G. Ollé. Ernest Albert Savage.

ESSEX

2978 A history of the county of Essex, edited by W. R. Powell. Vol.7. Oxford U.P., for the Institute of Historical Research, 1978. xx, 212p. front., illus, plates, maps. (Victoria history of the counties of England).

Covers the liberty of Havering-atte-Bower and Chafford hundred, with brief references to public libraries and reading rooms (19th-20th centuries) in Hornchurch, Rainham, Romford, South Ockendon and Upminster.

(2385) [Obituary of Edward Rhys Harries, 1897-1979]

GALASHIELS

(2406) [Obituaries of Neil Russell McCorkindale, 1921-1977]

GATESHEAD

(2997) J. Knott. The adoption of the Public Libraries Acts in Newcastle upon Tyne and Gateshead.

GLAMORGAN

(2463) [Obituaries of David Glyndwr Williams, 1912-1978]

2979 S. Scott. Public library development in Glamorgan 1920 to 1974: an area study with particular reference to Glamorgan County Library. Lib.Assn, 1979. xxv, 334p. plates, maps, tables, bibliog. [Thesis submitted for Fellowship of the Library Association. Typescript]
   Chapter one provides an outline history of library provision in Glamorgan up to the founding of the county's first rate-supported public library in 1862. Three chapters cover the independent public library authorities within the periods 1862-1923; 1923-1945 and 1945-1965. Two chapters cover the County Library during the early years and 1945-1965. The last chapter covers the period from the 1964 Act to the reorganisation of local government. Appendix 2 consists of a calendar of C.U.K.T. correspondence relating to the development of the County Library and other library authorities in the County, 1919-1947. This is a comparative study, assessing and trying to account for varying standards of service.

GLASGOW

2980 R. A. Gillespie. The Mitchell Library 1877-1977.
   S.L.A. News 1 (141) 1977, 339-41.
   A general outline history.

2981 Glasgow District Libraries. The Mitchell Library, Glasgow, 1877-1977. Glasgow, Glasgow District Libraries, 1977. viii, 114p. front., facsims.
   Rev. Lib.Rev. Vol.26 Summer 1978, 112-3. (J. C. Sharp)
   The first chapter is devoted to a general history of the Library, which had its origin in the bequest of the wealthy tobacco manu-facturer Stephen Mitchell who died in 1874. It was taken over by the

Glasgow Corporation under a special Act passed in 1899. More historical details, particularly concerning the collections, are found in subsequent chapters devoted to particular subject departments.

(2440) J. D. Hendry. S. A. Pitt: his contribution to libraries and librarianship.

(2351) [Obituaries of Charles Wilfred Black, 1909-1978]

GRAVESEND

(2439) W. A. Munford. Alex J. Philip.

GREENOCK

(2355) [Obituaries of John Brogan, 1940-1979]

(2437) W. E. Tyler. William Bryce Paton.

GUERNSEY

2982 H. Hughes. Towards a public library service in Guernsey.
J.Librarianship 12 (3) 1980, 171-8.
Though concentrating on future prospects, the author refers to the unsatisfactory state of library provision on the island since the Guille-Allès and Priaulx libraries were established in 1882 and 1889 respectively.

HALIFAX

(2456) [Obituary of Douglas Taylor, 1916-1978]

HAMILTON, Lanarkshire

(2454) [Obituaries of William Stewart, 1909-1977]

HAMPSHIRE

(2341) [Obituaries of Frank William Stuart Baguley, 1929-1980]

(2451) [Obituary of Herbert Msurice Sherry, 1893-1979]

HAWICK

2983 E. Robinson. Hawick Public Library until 1904.
Hawick Archaeological Society Transactions 1979, 3-10. illus, plates.

The Public Libraries Acts were adopted in 1878. The Library possessed
several unusual features; for instance, readers were illegally charged
for their tickets. The first librarian was a woman. A Carnegie
building was opened in 1904. The author mentions the Hawick Subscription Library, established 1762.

HEREFORD

(2418) [Obituaries of Frederick Charles Morgan, 1878-1978]

(2419) P. Whiteman. Eighty-one years a librarian.

HERTFORDSHIRE

(2422) [Obituaries of Thomas William Muskett, 1901-1977]

(2376) [Obituary of George Lancelotte Evans, 1919-1979]

HOVE

2984   J. Middleton. A history of Hove. Phillimore, 1979. [10], 272p. illus,
maps, bibliog.
   Pages 163-70 mention the opening of Hove Public Library in 1891, and
   describe the Carnegie financed building opened in 1908 and the
   Wolseley Room in 1925.

HULL

(2371) [Obituaries of Robert Forrester Drewery, 1907-1978]

JERSEY

(2369) [Obituary of Arscott Sabine Harvey Dickinson, 1893-1979]

KETTERING

(2388) [Obituary of Mary Haworth, 1915-1978]

KIDDERMINSTER

(2391) [Obituary of Leslie Williams Horsfall, 1905-1980]

KING'S LYNN

2985   R. Wilson. King's Lynn Library 1905-1974: a brief history. [Norfolk
County Library] 1980. 27p. illus.
Rev. Lib.Hist. 5 (5) 1981, 167-8. (R. P. Sturges)

A continuation of the author's Fellowship thesis <u>The Libraries of King's Lynn 1797-1905</u> (see no.990). Although the Public Libraries Acts were adopted in 1898, the cramped Stanley Library, re-opened as a Free Rate Supported Library, had to suffice until the Carnegie Library was opened in 1905. It was necessary to advertise for public subscriptions to furnish the Library, and lack of funds and poor standards persisted until the 1960s. The St. Margaret's Parochial Library was rescued in 1966, and gradually repaired and bound, and the Stanley Library was also restored about this time.

LANARKSHIRE

(2437) W. E. Tyler. William Bryce Paton.

LANCASHIRE

2986 J. D. Marshall, editor. The history of Lancashire County Council, 1889 to 1974. Martin Robertson, 1977. xiv, 456p.
Traces the progress of the County Library Service since its foundation in 1924-5.

(2367) [Obituary of Florence Elsie Cook, 1905-1980]

(2397) [Obituary of Raymond Irwin, 1902-1977]

LEEDS

(2396) [Obituaries of Frederick George Baxendale Hutchings, 1902-1978]

LEICESTER

2987 M. Elliott. Victorian Leicester. Phillimore, 1979. xvi, 192p. illus, plates, maps, plan.
Pages 152-3 briefly record opposition to the establishment of the public library which opened in the old Mechanics' Institute in 1871. Branch libraries were provided through the generosity of two wealthy individuals 20 years later. One grant was made on condition that the branch should open on the Sabbath, the other that it should remain closed.

LEICESTERSHIRE

(2492) L. M. Cantor and G. F. Matthews. Loughborough from College to University: a history of higher education at Loughborough 1909-1966.

LEIGH, Lancs

(2548) N. Ackers. The history of Leigh Library and its antecedents.

LICHFIELD

2988   H. Clayton. Cathedral city: a look at Victorian Lichfield. Lichfield,
The Author, 1977. [5], 171p. plates, facsims.
    Pages 102-4 contain de ails of the stone laying ceremony for the
public library in 1857, and a description of the completed building.

(2340) [Obituary of Hubert Appleyard, 1909-1979]

LONDON

2989   A. W. Ball. The public libraries of Greater London: a pictorial history,
1856-1914. Lib.Assn. London and Home Counties Branch, 1977. 108p. illus,
facsims, map, plans, ports, bibliog.
<u>Rev</u>. <u>Lib.Assn Rec.</u> 79 (8) 1977, 427-8 (J. G. Ollé)
    <u>Lib.Hist.</u> 4 (4) 1977, 121-2 (P. Lavigueur)
    <u>Lib.Rev.</u> Vol.27 Spring 1978, 54-6 (P. M. Whiteman)
    A delightful music hall romp, with such turns as stone laying cere-
monies, opening ceremonies, library buildings 'from the sublime to
the gorblimey', furniture and fittings, living on the job, library
staff, caretakers and cleaners, etc., carried along at a breathtaking
pace by our inimitably breezy M.C. Alan Ball.

2990   A. Service. London 1900. Granada Publishing, 1979. xiii, 274p. illus,
plates, maps, plans, bibliog.
    Major trends in public library architecture between 1890 and 1910 are
outlined and illustrated on pages 189-97.

LONDON. BETHNAL GREEN

2991   M. M. Chrimes. Libraries in Bethnal Green 1850-1922. Loughborough,
Loughborough Univ. of Technology, 1978. 150p. bibliog. [Thesis submitted in partial fulfilment of the requirements of MLS degree. Type-
script]
    The history of the public library movement in Bethnal Green is
traced up to the time of the opening of the first permanent public
library in 1922. The local movement is also related to public library development in general. Other local libraries are also discussed.

(2452) K. C. Harrison. Stanley Snaith: a memoir.

(2453) [Obituary of Stanley Snaith, 1903-1976]

LONDON. FULHAM

(2992) M. Dewe. Public library buildings in Hammersmith: benefactors and architects.

LONDON. HAMMERSMITH

2992 M. Dewe. Public library buildings in Hammersmith: benefactors and architects.

Fulham and Hammersmith Historical Record Autumn 1979, 1-4.

A brief account of three library buildings in the London Borough of Hammersmith and Fulham, two financed by Andrew Carnegie and designed by Henry Thomas Hare, and one financed by J. Passmore Edwards and designed by Maurice Bingham Adams.

LONDON. LAMBETH

(2413) [Obituary of Stanley Walter Martin, 1904-1978]

LONDON. PADDINGTON

(2407) [Obituaries of Francis Noel McDonald, 1910-1980]

2993 R. D. Williams. A history of Paddington Libraries 1850-1965. Loughborough, Loughborough Univ., Department of Library and Information Studies, 1978. [3], 87p.

Rev. Lib.Hist. 5 (4) 1980, 124-6 (D. F. Keeling)

Lib.Rev. Vol.29 Summer 1980, 123 (G. E. Maxim)

Paddington is one of the best examples of a local authority with a negative attitude towards public libraries. It achieved borough status in 1901, and as part of boundary changes, became responsible for the Queen's Park Branch Library. However, it did not adopt the Public Libraries Acts until 1920, and subsequent provision was modest. Sources are largely confined to vestry and council minutes and local newspapers.

LONDON. STEPNEY

(2443) C.A.R. Bostle. George Edward Roebuck: a critical study of his life and work.

LONDON. WALTHAMSTOW

(2443) C.A.R. Bostle. George Edward Roebuck: a critical study of his life and work.

LONDON. WESTMINSTER

2994 J. Cowell. A city's contribution to the LA's first hundred years. Lib.Assn Rec. 79 (6) 1977, 298-9, illus.
Librarians of the public library service and other librarians in Westminster who have played a significant part in the affairs of the Library Association from 1877 onwards.

(2407) [Obituaries of Francis Noel McDonald, 1910-1980]

LUTON

(2379) [Obituaries of Frank Gardner, 1908-1980]

MACCLESFIELD

2995 B. Brill. Macclesfield Library: the first 100 years. [Chester, Cheshire Libraries and Museums, 1978.] [48]p.
Rev. Lib.Hist. 4 (6) 1978, 186-7 (R. P. Sturges)
The library building opened in 1876, together with its initial bookstock of 10,000 volumes, was the gift of David Chadwick MP. Its development to date under successive librarians is recorded.

MALVERN

(2418) [Obituaries of Frederick Charles Morgan, 1878-1978]

(2419) P. Whiteman. Eighty-one years a librarian.

MIDDLESEX

(2347) [Obituaries of Sidney George Berriman, 1911-1980]

MONAGHAN

2996 Monaghan County Library. Monaghan County Library 1952-1973: a review. Clones, Monaghan County Library, [1977] 9 leaves. plates.
The main progress has been the inauguration in 1956 of the Republic's first Mobile Library Service and the completion of the Development Scheme prepared in 1962.

2997   J. Knott. The adoption of the Public Libraries Acts in Newcastle upon
Tyne and Gateshead.

In: LA 77: essays in librarianship edited by J. Knott. Newcastle upon
Tyne, Newcastle upon Tyne Polytechnic, Department of Librarianship, 1977,
19-35.

   Records the struggle to establish public libraries in Newcastle and
   Gateshead, drawing attention to the factors which stimulated or re-
   tarded the setting up of such services. "Initiative on and support
   for the public library came in both cases from liberals inside and
   outside the Council; they saw a clear link between educational
   developments and the library's role as a continuing means of self-
   culture, whilst conservative opposition was based on hostility to
   increased taxation and the notion of self-help."

2998   J. Knott. Newcastle upon Tyne City Libraries: the first 100 years.
Newcastle upon Tyne, Newcastle upon Tyne Polytechnic, School of Librarianship, 1980. [5], 92p. bibliog.

Rev. Lib.Assn Rec. 83 (2) 1981, 94 (J. Allred)
   Lib.Hist. 5 (5) 1981, 167 (R. P. Sturges)

   The first chapter was previously published as part of "The adoption
   of the Public Libraries Acts in Newcastle upon Tyne and Gateshead,"
   above. Both this and the following chapter, dealing with the
   establishment of the Library Service, are based on Knott's thesis
   (see no.2550). These are followed by four chronological chapters
   covering the period 1900 to 1980. The service stagnated somewhat
   during the latter part of the librarianship of Basil Anderton, which
   spanned the years 1894 to 1936. Newcastle Central Library was the
   last major library in England to be converted to open access, which
   took place in 1950.

(2460) [Obituaries of William Tynemouth, 1914-1977]

   NEWHAM

(2382) [Obituaries of James Green 1918-1979]

   NEWPORT, Isle of Wight

(3011) M. Howley and I. Orton. Seventy-five years: the first county library.
A history of the Isle of Wight County Library, 1904-1979.

2999 L. J. Mitchell. Oldest library.
      County Councils Gazette December 1979, 284. illus.
      Local landowner and philanthropist Sir Charles Seely (1833-1915)
      offered £5,000 to the County Technical Education Committee for the
      establishment of a free library at Newport. It opened in 1904.

      NORTHAMPTONSHIRE

(2397) [Obituary of Raymond Irwin, 1902-1977]

      NOTTINGHAM

3000 S. J. Best. Nottingham Public Libraries.
      In: Encyclopedia of library and information science. Vol.20.
      New York, Dekker, 1977, 274-84.
      A history of Nottingham Public Libraries since 1867 when the Public
      Libraries Acts were adopted and the town took possession of the
      Artisans' Library and of the collection of the Nottingham Naturalists'
      Society, which had been the earliest advocate of a Nottingham Free
      Library.

      OXFORD

3001 M. Graham. Public library facilities in Oxford before 1914.
      Oxoniensia Vol.43 1978, 222-40.
      There are details of early 19th century reading rooms, subscription
      and circulating libraries. The Public Library (Reference Library and
      Reading Room) was opened in 1854, and a Lending Department followed
      in 1857. Throughout this period the service was severely handicapped
      by inadequate finance, cramped premises and a bookstock consisting
      largely of donations, in spite of an interested Committee and a suc-
      cession of able and energetic librarians. Expansion was made possible
      by the opening of a new Central Library in 1895, but the building was
      badly designed, inflexible and soon proved to be inadequate.

      PAISLEY

3002 A. Scott. Small certainly, beautiful maybe: Paisley Reference Library.
      Lib.Rev. 26 (4) 1977, 273-6.
      Includes brief details of accommodation, book provision and staffing
      in Paisley Central Library at the time of its opening in 1871.

ROTHERHAM

3003 Rotherham's centenary.

Lib.Assn Rec. 82 (8) 1980, 350. illus.

A brief outline of the library service from its foundation in 1880.

RUGBY

(2396) [Obituaries of Frederick George Baxendale Hutchings, 1902-1978]

SEVENOAKS

(2401) [Obituary of George Henry Lawrence, 1920-1977]

3004 P. Swan. A short history of library services in Sevenoaks 1905-1980.
Kent County Library, 1980. 16p. illus, facsim., port., bibliog.

Brief mention is made of subscription and circulating libraries
existing in Sevenoaks in the latter half of the 19th century and
early 20th century. Sevenoaks adopted the Public Libraries Acts in
1903. The present building opened in 1905 was financed by Andrew
Carnegie. Particular attention is given to developments under the
librarianship of George Bennett (1920-1965).

SHEFFIELD

(2396) [Obituaries of Frederick George Baxendale Hutchings, 1902-1978]

3005 J. E. Vickers. A popular history of Sheffield - with a guide to places,
buildings and things of interest. East Ardsley, Wakefield, E.P. Publishing, 1978. xii, 264p. illus, bibliog.

An outline history of the Public Library Service from 1856 to 1976 is
given on pages 216-9.

SHETLANDS

(2404) [Obituary of George Watson Longmuir, 1910-1979]

SHROPSHIRE

3006 A history of Shropshire, edited by G. C. Baugh. Vol.3. Oxford U.P.,
for the Institute of Historical Research, 1979. xvi, 399p. front.,
illus, plates, maps. (Victoria history of the counties of England).

Includes a brief mention of the county library service.

SMETHWICK

3007   Times past, times present: a century of Smethwick.
Lib.Assn Rec. 79 (10) 1977, 514. illus.

A short outline of the history of Smethwick Public Library.

SOUTHAMPTON

(2362) [Obituaries of Eric Allen Clough, 1914-1979]

STOKE-ON-TRENT

(2415) [Obituary of Kennard Desmond Miller, 1915-1980]

STRATFORD-UPON-AVON

(2418) [Obituaries of Frederick Charles Morgan, 1878-1978]

(2419) P. Whiteman. Eighty-one years a librarian.

SWANSEA

(2441) [Obituary of Leslie Mervyn Rees, 1911-1978]

3008   G. Williams. Adoption at Swansea, 1868-1970.
Lib.Hist. 4 (3) 1977, 81-4.

The main interest in the struggle for adoption at Swansea is found in
the influence of topographical factors, allegations about the mani-
pulation of local opinion and the disputed voting at the adoption
meeting of 1870. A change of council led to the opening of the
public library being delayed until 1876. Other forms of library
provision are also mentioned.

3009   G. Williams. "The longest and most stormy meeting that Swansea ever had".
Gower Vol.30 1979, 18-21.

The first serious attempt at adoption of the Public Libraries Acts in
Swansea in 1868 was rejected. At a second attempt in 1870 a long and
heated meeting was held which eventually agreed to their adoption.

3010   G. Williams. Swansea: three chiefs in five decades.
Lib.Rev. 26 (2) 1977, 93-9.

Swansea adopted the Public Libraries Acts in 1870, but no service was
provided or librarian appointed until 1875. Frederick Cole, a headmaster, held the office of librarian for only three months, leaving
to become a schools inspector. Thomas John Lean, formerly librarian
of Cardiff, was librarian from 1876 to 1880, when he resigned because

of minor administrative discrepancies. Samuel Edward Thompson was
librarian from 1880 to 1919, during which time a new Central Library
was opened in 1887.

TAUNTON

(3126) R. Bush. The book of Taunton: the story of a county town.

WALLASEY

(2445) J. G. Ollé. Ernest A. Savage: librarian extraordinary.

(2446) J. G. Ollé. Ernest Albert Savage.

WIGHT, Isle of

3011   M. Howley and I. Orton. Seventy-five years: the first county library.
        A history of the Isle of Wight County Library 1904-1979. Newport, Isle
        of Wight County Library, 1980. [2], ii, 43p. illus, facsims, ports.
          There are details of several subscription, circulating, institute and
        other libraries dating from the early 19th century. In 1904 the Lib-
        rary and Technical Institute was opened at Newport, the first of a
        network of free public libraries financed by Sir Charles Seely and
        administered by the County Council. The Public Libraries Acts were
        adopted in 1924, and the subsequent development of the County Library
        Service is described in some detail.

WILTSHIRE

(2974) J. A. Chamberlain. Chippenham: some notes on its history.

WORCESTERSHIRE

3012   M. F. Nauta. A history of Worcestershire County Library 1923-1974.
        Lib.Assn, 1977. [7], iv, 280p. illus. map, bibliog. [Thesis approved for
        Fellowship of the Library Association. Typescript].
          Its history is recorded in a chronological sequence of eight chapters.
        An introductory chapter covers libraries in Worcestershire prior to
        the setting up of the County Library Service.

WORKSOP

3013   D. J. Thomas. Libraries of Worksop, 1830-1939. Loughborough, Lough-
        borough Univ. of Technology. Department of Library and Information
        Studies, 1978. [7], 106p. illus, map, plans, facsims, bibliog. [Thesis

submitted in partial fulfilment of the requirements for MLS degree.
Typescript]

Illustrates the problems of small libraries and their librarians.
Chapter 1 deals with the Worksop Reading Society and Mechanics'
Institute, founded in 1832 and revived in 1852. In 1896 it was taken
over to form the nucleus of a public library. The history of the
Public Library is recorded chronologically in four chapters, one of
which deals with the Worksop Rural Libraries Scheme sponsored by the
C.U.K.T., 1915-1918, and puts forward reasons for its failure. Pro-
vides a rare example of a librarian's dismissal for unseemly conduct.

YORKSHIRE

3014　B. J. Barber and M. W. Beresford.　The West Riding County Council, 1889-
1974.　Wakefield, West Yorkshire County Council, 1979.　[4], iv, 262,
[9] p. illus, maps, plans, tables, port.

Pages 76-81 chart the progress of the County Library Service from
1921 to 1973.

(2720)　M. C. Horton.　The story of Cleveland.

(2422)　[Obituaries of Thomas William Muskett, 1901-1977]

E N D O W E D　　P U B L I C　　L I B R A R I E S

(2932)　A. Ellis.　Rural library services in England and Wales before 1919.

ARMAGH

3015　C. McKelvie.　Early English books in Armagh Public Library: a short-
title catalogue of books printed before 1641.
Irish Booklore　3 (2) 1977, 91-103. facsims.

Lists 302 works printed within the British Isles or at English
presses operating abroad, with a brief introduction.

DUBLIN

3016　Archbishop Marsh's Library.　An exhibition of early European printings,
1472-1700.　Dublin, Archbisyop Marsh's Library, 1977.　56p. illus,
facsims, port., bibliog.

The development and spread of printing in Europe is demonstrated by
64 books selected from the various collections comprising Archbishop
Marsh's Library.　Historical information on the latter is provided in
the preface and notes.

(2542) D. Guinness. Georgian Dublin.

3017   M. McCarthy. All graduates and gentlemen: Marsh's Library. Dublin,
        O'Brien Press, 1980. 239p. illus, facsims, ports, bibliog.
        Rev. Lib.Assn Rec. 83 (1) 1981, 37 (D. Gerard)
            A summary of Archbishop Marsh's life and career is followed by an
            account of the library he began to build about 1701, and for which
            he purchased the 10,000 volume library of Dr. Edward Stillingfleet
            in 1705. It was incorporated as a public library by an Act of 1707.
            The history of the Library to the present day is followed by a great
            deal of information on incunabula and other famous books in the col-
            lection.

EAST LOTHIAN

3018   L. G. Durbidge. Brougham and Brown: a note.
        Lib.Hist. 4 (4) 1977, 115.
            The writer touches on the subject of how much Samuel Brown and his
            scheme of itinerating libraries in East Lothian influenced Lord
            Brougham's ideas as manifest in the Society for the Diffusion of
            Useful Knowledge, and whether Brown was himself influenced by the
            Society's publishing activities.

GLASGOW

(2980) R. A. Gillespie. The Mitchell Library, 1877-1977.

(2981) Glasgow District Libraries. The Mitchell Library, Glasgow, 1877-1977.

GUILDFORD

(2585) D. M. Sturley. The Royal Grammar School Guildford.

INNERPEFFRAY, Perthshire

3019   G. Thompson. The legacy of a Scottish Lord: Innerpeffray.
        Wilson Library Bulletin 51 (10) 1977, 844-7. illus.
            In 1680 Lord David Drummond transferred his private library to the
            priest's loft above the family chapel and made it available to
            students. In 1750 a library was built to house it. Its history is
            outlined and some of its chief treasures noted.

KINGS LYNN

(2697) R. Wilson. St. Margaret's Church Library, King's Lynn: a short history.

MANCHESTER

3020   Christie, Manson and Woods Ltd. Important books from Chetham's Library, Manchester. London, 26 and 27 November 1980. 147p. illus.

Comprises 415 lots, mainly of 18th century scientific and travel books.

NEWCASTLE UPON TYNE

3021   R. J. Charleton. Newcastle town. Newcastle upon Tyne, Graham, 1978. [2], iv, 443p. plates.

Facsimile reprint of 1st ed., London, Walter Scott, 1885. On page 104 is an account of the chained library in the vestry of St. Nicholas which was augmented in 1736 by the 1600 volume library of Dr. Thomlinson, lecturer of the church. They were bequeathed to the Corporation of Newcastle for public use. Its state of neglect in 1885 is well described. On page 136 there are brief details of the library of the Literary and Philosophical Society founded in 1792.

NORWICH

3022   D. Stoker. Doctor Collinges and the revival of Norwich City Library, 1657-1664.

Lib.Hist. 5 (3) 1980, 73-84.

Norwich City Library was founded in 1608 for the use of local Puritan preachers, but by 1655 it was neglected and unaccessible. This article describes the role of Dr. John Collinges, local Presbyterian minister and controversialist, in persuading the Municipal Assembly to reopen it and in reorganising it on a subscription basis. An appendix lists books purchased, sold and exchanged during this period.

LIBRARIES: Special

ACCOUNTANCY. INSTITUTE OF CHARTERED ACCOUNTANTS OF SCOTLAND, Aberdeen

3023   Institute of Chartered Accountants of Scotland. An accountant's book
collection 1494-1930. Catalogue of the Antiquarian Collection of the
Institute of Chartered Accountants of Scotland. With an introduction by
Anne B. G. Dunlop, Keeper of the Antiquarian Collection. 3rd ed.
Edinburgh, The Institute, 1976. xviii, 120p. front., facsims.
Rev. <u>Bibliotheck</u> 9 (1) 1978, 29-30 (T. A. Cherry)

> The nucleus of the collection was formed by Richard Brown (1856-1918),
> an Edinburgh chartered accountant, in his capacity as Secretary of the
> Society of Accountants in Edinburgh.

AFRICA

3024   J. H. Wynter. The development of Africana collections in British
learned libraries.
<u>African Research and Documentation</u> 1 (16-17) 1978, 1-11.

> Begins by mentioning the occurrence of Africana in country houses and
> subscription libraries in the 18th century, then considers the growth
> of such collections in learned society libraries and academic lib-
> raries up to the present.

AGRICULTURE. WYE COLLEGE, Ashford, Kent

(2640) Wye College. Library. A catalogue of agricultural and horticultural
books, 1543-1918, in Wye College Library.

ANTIQUARIAN STUDIES. SOCIETY OF ANTIQUARIES, London

3025   J. Hopkins. The Society of Antiquaries and its library.
<u>Libraries Bulletin, Univ. of London</u> 1 (9) 1977, 5-8.

> The Society was founded in 1707 and its library in 1717. Between its
> occupation of Somerset House in 1780 and the move to Burlington House
> in 1875, it had acquired 20,000 books and manuscripts and an equal
> number of prints and drawings.

ARCHITECTURE. ARCHITECTURAL ASSOCIATION, London

3026   E. Dixon. The Architectural Association Library 1862 to 1978. _Architectural Association Annual Review_ 1979, 13-79. illus, plans, facsims, ports.

      The Association was founded in 1847. The Library was formed in 1862 to promote the education and advancement of the younger members of the profession, and more than most libraries, it has always been predominantly user orientated. From the beginning the collection was a lending library, and a reference library was not formed until much later. A lantern slide collection was started in 1899. This detailed history is firmly set in the context of the Association's overall development, and is based on primary sources. Appendices list the Honorary Curators and Librarians and Honorary Assistant Librarians.

ARMY. Aldershot

3027   H. N. Cole. The story of Aldershot: a history of the civil and military towns. New ed. Aldershot, Southern Books (Aldershot) Ltd, 1980. xxx, 480p. illus, plates, maps, facsim, bibliog.

      First ed., Aldershot, The Wellington Press, 1951. There are brief accounts of two libraries formed for army personnel. Prince Consort's Library was opened in 1860, the building furnishing, books and librarian being paid for by the Prince. Details are also given of its librarians up to 1930. The Victoria Soldiers' Library was opened in 1851, stocked with books which came from libraries of the hospitals and recreation huts established in the Crimea.

ART. GLASGOW SCHOOL OF ART

(2755)   R. Billcliffe. Charles Rennie Mackintosh.

ART. NATIONAL GALLERY, London

(2816)   D. Robertson. Sir Charles Eastlake and the Victorian art world.

ART. VICTORIA AND ALBERT MUSEUM, London

3028   A. S. Cocks. The Victoria and Albert Museum: the making of the collection. Leicester, Windward, 1980. [6], 186p. illus, bibliog.

      Chapter 10 of this popular illustrated book is devoted to the National Art Library. It was founded in 1837, forming part of the

Schools of Design in Somerset House, the progenitor of the Museum, with a specifically educational and practical purpose. The evolution of its role to the present day, its librarians, early catalogues and bequests are covered. There are numerous colour illustrations of major treasures.

3029   E.M.B. King. The South Kensington Museum Art Library: a study of its origins and development until 1900. Univ. College London, School of Library, Archive and Information Studies, 1975. vi, 103p. tables, plans, bibliog. [Thesis submitted in part requirement for M.A. degree. Typescript]

The first two chapters cover the origins to 1858 and 1858 to 1898 respectively. Chapter 3 deals with the conception and compilation of the Universal Catalogue of Books on Art. Chapter 4 deals with the complementary subject catalogues, the photographic collections and the major bequests of Alexander Dyce and John Forster, which were particularly strong in the fields of the classics and English literature.

ASTRONOMY. ROYAL OBSERVATORY, Edinburgh

3030   Drawford Library. Catalogue of the Crawford Library of the Royal Observatory, Edinburgh. Supplement [compiled by] Mary F. I. Smyth and Michael J. Smyth. Edinburgh, Royal Observatory, 1977. [12], 112p.

A computer-produced index of books in the Crawford Collection published before 1800 and of manuscripts, broadsheets and works on comets published up to the early 1900s. It also includes, in addition to the works entered in the original catalogue of 1890, similar works acquired from other sources. The Crawford Collection was presented by the 26th Earl of Crawford in 1888.

BANKING. INSTITUTE OF BANKERS, London

3031   E. Green. Debtors to their profession: a history of The Institute of Bankers, 1879-1979. Methuen for The Institute of Bankers, 1979. xxi, 245p. front., illus, facsims, ports.

The progress of the Institute's library, in successive locations, is traced from its formation in 1879 to date. Its growth was particularly rapid under the librarianship of Miss Irene Shrigley, who was appointed in 1930 and retired in 1957.

CARTOGRAPHY. ROYAL GEOGRAPHICAL SOCIETY, London

(3043) I. Cameron. To the farthest ends of the earth: the history of the Royal
Geographical Society, 1830-1980.

CHEMISTRY. THOMAS BRITTON

(2797) W. A. Campbell. The chemical library of Thomas Britton 1654-1714.

CHESS. EDWIN GARDINER

(2828) British Library. Lending Division. The Edwin Gardiner chess collection.

CHRISTIANITY

(2711) W. P. Thistlethwaite. Yorkshire Quarterly Meeting (of the Society of
Friends) 1665-1966.

CHRISTIANITY. BRISTOL BAPTIST COLLEGE

(2573) N. S. Moon. Education for ministry: Bristol Baptist College, 1679-1979.

(2574) Sotheby and Co. Catalogue of Western Manuscripts (including 'The
Property of the Bristol Baptist College').

CHRISTIANITY. BRITISH AND FOREIGN BIBLE SOCIETY, London

3032 A. F. Jesson. The libraries of the British and Foreign Bible Society
and the American Bible Society, New York: a comparison. Loughborough,
Loughborough Univ. of Technology, 1977. [2], 88p. illus. [Dissertation
submitted in partial fulfilment of the requirements for an MLS degree.
Typescript]

The first chapter outlines the development of the Society from its
foundation in 1804, and its library from the appeal for donations
issued in December 1804, until 1976, when the number of volumes had
risen to 26,500. Other chapters discuss its role, particularly in
the context of the reappraisal of the early 1970s, and its catalogues.

CHRISTIANITY. DISSENTING ACADEMY, Northampton

(2579) M. Deacon. Philip Doddridge of Northampton, 1702-51.

CHRISTIANITY. DR. WILLIAMS' LIBRARY, London

3033 J. Creasey. Dr. Williams's Library.
Libraries Bulletin, Univ. of London 1 (10) 1977, 5-7.

An outline history from its foundation in 1729, indicating the nature
and provenance of its holdings.

3034   E. A. Payne. A venerable Dissenting institution: Dr. Williams's Library
1729-1979. Dr. Williams's Trust, 1979. 25p.
A biographical sketch of Dr. Daniel Williams is followed by an
historical account of the Library in its various homes, celebrated
trustees, major bequests, and its relationship to other libraries at
different periods.

CHRISTIANITY. EVANGELICAL LIBRARY, London

3035   A. Tyler. Evangelical Library 'serving a worldwide readership.'
British Weekly August 31, 1979, 6. illus, port.
A general account of the lending library with brief historical
details. It was started in 1928 by Geoffrey Williams of Biddington
Chapel, London, who stored the books in his own home, and subsequently made them available to the public. It moved to its present
premises in St. Marylebone in 1946 with 20,000 volumes: it now possesses 80,000. It is particularly rich in Puritan writings, de-
nominational history, commentaries and hymnology.

CHRISTIANITY. FREE CHURCH COLLEGE, Edinburgh
(2575) Sotheby and Co. Catalogue of rare ... Scottish books ... [including]
the property of The Free Church College, Edinburgh.

CHRISTIANITY. HENRY PHILLPOTTS

3036   E. B. and G. E. Bentley. Bishop Phillpotts Library, the Frank Parker
bequest and its extra-illustrated Macklin Bible, 1800.
Bk Coll. 29 (3) 1980, 363-94. plates.
Henry Phillpotts, Bishop of Exeter, left his theological library to
the clergy of Cornwall. It was opened in 1871, and was greatly augmented in 1883 by the bequest of Frank Parker, an incumbent in Devon.
The most unusual work is the Macklin Bible, grangerised from 6 to 63
volumes.

CHRISTINAITY. HEYTHROP COLLEGE, London
(2576) M. J. Walsh. Heythrop College Library.

CHRISTIANITY. NEW COLLEGE, London
(2577) G. F. Nuttall. New College, London, and its library: two lectures.

(2578) Sotheby and Co. Catalogue of printed books (including 'The Property of New College, London').

CHRISTIANITY. ST. DEINIOL'S LIBRARY, Hawarden

3037   A. R. Vidler. Scenes from a clerical life: an autobiography. Illustrations by George Murray. Collins, 1977. 208p. illus.

In chapter 7 Alec Vidler recalls the nine years beginning in 1939 during which he was Warden of St. Deiniol's Library. He also describes its foundation by Gladstone, and its development under his predecessors.

CHRISTIANITY. SION COLLEGE, London

3038   Sion, Evelyn, and what next?
Bk Coll. 26 (3) 1977, 319-28.

An editorial, with some historical notes, on sales of material from the libraries of John Evelyn and Sion College, both held in 1977. The reasons for such sales and possible remedies are suggested.

3039   Sotheby and Co. Catalogue of important and valuable printed books and manuscripts comprising the property of Sion College which will be sold by auction. London, Sotheby, 13 June 1977. 76 lots. 82p. front., plates, facsims.

This contentious sale was limited to some of the 'secular' books and manuscripts, illustrating by good provenance notes many of the library's distinguished donors, among them Sir Robert Coke and Richard Rawlinson. Important manuscript sources for the book trade included the memorandum book of Thomas Bennet and Henry Clements for the period 1686 to 1732, and the unique archives for early American libraries assembled by Thomas Bray (1635-1730) and bequeathed to the College by him.

CLUBS

3040   A. Lejeune and M. Lewis. The gentlemen's clubs of London. Macdonald and Janes, 1979. 298p. illus, facsim, ports.

Many random remarks about the libraries of individual clubs, sadly often referring to the retreat of books before the growing accommodation for ladies. Of greater importance is the photographic record, which is the chief feature of the book.

CLUBS. ORIENTAL CLUB, London

(3050) D. Forrest. The Oriental: life story of a West End Club.

(3051) F. M. Innes. Oriental Club: Library.

CLUBS. REFORM CLUB, London

3041 G. Woodbridge. The Reform Club, 1836-1978: a history from the Club's records. The Reform Club in association with Clearwater Publishing Company, 1978. [10], 185p. front., illus, facsims, plan, ports, bibliog. Chapter 8 is devoted to the Library, the period up to the First World War being covered in much greater detail than the period since. The building up of a library according to a settled plan was given high priority from the beginning, and by 1900, c.60,000 volumes were in stock. Parliamentary papers, history, politics and law were particularly well represented.

COMMERCE. CO-OPERATIVE REFERENCE LIBRARY, Dublin

(3099) P. Bolger. The Irish Co-operative Movement: its history and development.

CONJURING. JAMES BLACK FINDLAY

(2826) Sotheby and Co. Catalogue of the J. B. Findlay collection: books, periodicals, manuscripts etc on conjuring and the allied arts.

ECONOMICS. BRITISH LIBRARY OF POLITICAL AND ECONOMIC SCIENCE, London

(2634) S. and B. Webb. The letters of Sidney and Beatrice Webb.

FEMINISM. FAWCETT LIBRARY, CITY OF LONDON POLYTECHNIC

3042 A. Pritchard and D. Doughan. Access to the literature on women: the Fawcett Library and BiblioFem.
Asst Libn 72 (2) 1979, 22-8. facsims.
Since 1977 housed at the City of London Polytechnic, the Fawcett Library was formally inaugurated in 1926 as the Women's Service Library, the Library of the London and National Society for Women's Service, the direct descendant of the first Women's Suffrage Committee founded in 1866. The scope of the Library, the special collections which have gravitated to it, and its historical development into a form of national archive for the women's movement, is covered.

GEOGRAPHY. ROYAL GEOGRAPHICAL SOCIETY, London

3043 I. Cameron. To the farthest ends of the earth: the history of the Royal
      Geographical Society, 1830–1980. Macdonald, 1980. front., illus, plates,
      maps, ports, bibliog.

      The Society's library was assembled after its move to Waterloo Place
      in 1839, but it was not until the move to Savile Row in 1871 that it
      began to assume something of the reputation it enjoys today. Pro-
      gress under successive librarians is recorded and special collections
      are mentioned. The parallel history of the Society's famous map
      collection is also outlined.

(2827) M. J. Freeman and J. Longbotham. The Fordham Collection at the RGS: an
        introduction.

GEOLOGY. GEOLOGICAL SOCIETY OF LONDON

3044 Sotheby and Co. Catalogue of printed books (including 'The Property of
      the Geological Society of London', lots 245–319). Sotheby, 22 November,
      1977, 41–50.

      Mostly botanical and zoological works, including several by Thomas
      Pennant and one incunable, Regiomontanus <u>Epytoma in Almagestū</u>
      <u>Ptolomei</u> (Venice, 1496).

GEOLOGY. ROYAL GEOLOGICAL SOCIETY OF CORNWALL, Penzance

3045 Sotheby and Co. Catalogue of printed books (including 'the Property of
      the Royal Geological Society of Cornwall', lots 55–63). Sotheby, 4 July,
      1977, 12–13.

      A short list but interesting in showing the Society's holdings of
      important 19th century French treatises and journals such as <u>Annales</u>
      <u>des mines</u> (Paris, 1817–96).

GOVERNMENT. TREASURY SOLICITORS DEPARTMENT, London

(3061) Great Britain. Treasury Solicitors Department. Library. Catalogue of the
        Legal Library of the Treasury Solicitor.

GOVERNMENT. WAR OFFICE, London

(2400) [Obituary of Derrick William King, 1908–1980]

HOROLOGY. WORSHIPFUL SOCIETY OF CLOCKMAKERS, London

3046 Worshipful Company of Clockmakers. Library. The clockmakers' library:

the catalogue of the books and manuscripts in the library of the Worshipful Company of Clockmakers, compiled by John Bromley. Sotheby
Parke Bernet, 1977. xii, 136p. front., facsims, ports.

> The preface records the genesis of the library in 1813. It is now
> deposited with Guildhall Library.

HORTICULTURE. WYE COLLEGE, London

(2640) Wye College. Library. A catalogue of agricultural and horticultural
books, 1543-1918, in Wye College Library.

HUNGARICA. BODLEIAN LIBRARY, Oxford

(2645) R.J.W. Evans. Hungarica in the Bodleian: a historical sketch.

ICELANDIC STUDIES. UNIVERSITY COLLEGE, London

(2638) J.A.B. Townsend. The Old Norse - Icelandic library at University College London.

ICELANDIC STUDIES. UNIVERSITY OF LEEDS

(2626) Brotherton Library. A catalogue of the Icelandic Collection, University
Library, Leeds.

INDOLOGY. INDIA OFFICE LIBRARY, London

3047 India Office Library. Catalogue of Persian manuscripts in the Library
of the India Office. The Library, 1980. [1530]p.

> Facsimile reprint of 1st ed., Oxford, printed for the India Office by
> H. Hart, 1903-37. 2 vols.

3048 India Office Library. Catalogue of the Panjabi and Sindhi manuscripts
in the India Office Library, compiled by C. Shackle. India Office Library and Records, 1977. [3], ix, 79p.

3049 J. C. Lancaster. The scope and uses of the India Office Library and
Records with particular reference to the period 1600-1947.
Asian Affairs 1 (65) 1978, 31-43.

> The article is largely concerned with archival materials. The library
> dates from 1801, and the archives are invaluable for tracing its
> history and the provenance and acquisition of its materials. From
> 1867 to 1947 the India Office Library was a copyright library for
> books published in India. Post-war acquisition policy is discussed
> and many of the library's individual collections are mentioned.

(2462) M. Lloyd. Sir Charles Wilkins, 1749-1836

(2455) [Obituary of Stanley Cecil Sutton, 1907-1977]

INDOLOGY. ORIENTAL CLUB, London

3050 D. Forrest. The Oriental: life story of a West End Club. 2nd ed.
Batsford, 1979. 256p. front., illus, plates, ports, plans.
For 1st ed., 1968 see no.701. A supplement mentions the attempts
since 1969 to fill some of the gaps left by the drastic and in-
discriminate sale of books in 1961.

3051 F. M. Innes. Oriental Club: Library. Oriental Club, 1978. 10p.
[Privately printed for circulation among Club Members.]
Contains a fuller account of post-1961 developments than that contained in Forrest's Supplement, (above), together with a description
of the collection and some of its major treasures.

JUDAICA. UNIVERSITY OF LEEDS

(2627) P. S. Morrish. The Brotherton Library, its Judaica and Cecil Roth.

JUDAICA. UNIVERSITY OF SOUTHAMPTON

(2880) Parkes Library, University of Southampton.

JUDAICA. YESHAYAHU SHACHAR

(2902) Sotheby Parke Bernet and Co. Catalogue of the well-known collection of
Hebrew books, the property of the late Dr. Yeshayahu Shachar.

LAW. ADVOCATES LIBRARY, Edinburgh

(2748) National Library of Scotland.

LAW. COLLEGE OF ADVOCATES AND DOCTORS OF LAW, London

3052 G. D. Squibb. Doctors' Commons: a history of the College of Advocates
and Doctors of Law. Oxford, Clarendon Press, 1977. xv, 244p. front.,
plates, facsim., map, bibliog.
Sir Leoline Jenkins, in his will proved in 1685, left forty books to
form the basis of a library, and the collection was augmented by
several bequests in the first half of the 18th century. Chapter 6
records its history and method of financing, which was partly by
tarrifs paid by bishops on their consecration. The library consisted mainly of canon and civil law, and was sold in 1861 when the

College was dissolved.

LAW. GRAY'S INN, London

3053   P. Beddingham. The Library in Gray's Inn.
Antiquarian Book Monthly Review 7 (8) 1980, 390-7. illus, facsims.
Sketches the history of the Library from the first known reference
to it in 1555 in the will of Robert Chaloner, to the present day.
Rapid growth took place in the 19th century and a new building was
opened in 1929 to replace that built in 1842. The 1929 building was
destroyed in 1941, together with most of the bookstock apart from the
valuable printed books and manuscripts which had been evacuated. The
post-war period witnessed the opening of the new building in 1958 and
attempts at rebuilding the depleted bookstocks.

LAW. INNER TEMPLE, London

3054   Christie, Manson and Woods Ltd. Important travel and topographical
books (including 'The Property of the Honourable Society of the Inner
Temple', lots 15-51). London, Christie, 11 October, 1978, 8-14.
The voyages and travels, all classic works of the 18th to early 20th
centuries, indicate a more wide-ranging past accession policy than
would pertain today.

LAW. LINCOLN'S INN, London

3055   Sotheby and Co. Catalogue of printed books (including 'The Property of
Lincoln's Inn Library', lots 271-91). Sotheby, 10 November, 1978, 35-6.
An occasional sale, but the predominance of sets of the great
Victorian county archaeological and historical societies point to an
era when accession policy reflected a more wealthy and polymathic
profession.

3056   R. Walker. Lincoln's Inn Library.
Law Librarian 8 (1) 1977, 3-4.
An outline history of the library, its bookstock and staffing, from
1475 to date.

LAW. SIGNET LIBRARY, Edinburgh

3057   G. H. Ballantyne. The Signet Library Edinburgh and its librarians,
1722-1972. Glasgow, Scottish Lib. Assn, 1979. xv, 194p. illus, plates,
ports, bibliog.

Rev. Lib.Assn Rec. 81 (10) 1979, 493 (T. Shearman)

T.L.S. Apr.24, 1981, 471 (A. Bell)

The Signet Library originated as a law library for the Society of writers to the Signet, but had started to develop into a general library by the end of the 18th century. The five sections of the present work contain a background account of libraries in Edinburgh; an outline history of the Signet Library; its buildings; its librarians and its books and catalogues.

3058   Sotheby and Co. Catalogue of printed books ... the property of The Society of Writers to her Majesty's Signet. Sotheby, 12/14 April, 1978. 88p. illus.

This sale represents a further economic winnowing of a splendid private reference library. Earlier sales were in 1959-60 and 1962-4. The present catalogue reflects many of the varied and impressive purchases of earlier distinguished librarians, notably Macvey Napier, David Laing and T. G. Law. The Library remains a major legal and Scottish antiquarian collection.

3059   Sotheby and Co. Catalogue of printed books [from the Signet Library, Edinburgh.] Edinburgh, Sotheby, 8 and 9 March, 1979. 597 lots. 55p. illus, plates.

A sale of a further 25,000 volumes of wide subject interest. Noting that the Signet Library will henceforth concentrate on legal and Scottish literature, the introductory note looks on the present disposal as 'a phoenix pyre rather than an immolation'. There are interesting notes, too, on the Signet provenance at different stages in the library's history.

LAW. SOCIETY OF ADVOCATES OF ABERDEEN

3060   Sotheby and Co. Catalogue of printed books (including 'The Property of The Society of Advocates of Aberdeen,' pp.43-51; 5-17, lots 175-247; 1-83). London, Sotheby, 15 November 1976; 6 October, 1977. 247; 484 lots.

The volumes sold in these two sales illustrate that the Society collected not only in the field of Scottish law and history but in every phase of the Scottish Enlightenment, and more widely in the literary and topographical works of the 18th and 19th centuries.

LAW. TREASURY SOLICITOR'S DEPARTMENT, London

3061   Great Britain. Treasury Solicitors Department. Library.

184

Catalogue of the Legal Library of the Treasury Solicitor, compiled by
R. Toole Scott. 6th ed. The Department, 1977. 171p.
Previous ed., 1975.

LAW. UNIVERSITY COLLEGE, London

(2637) B. Tearle. The Law Library at University College London, 1829-1979.

MARINE

3062 H. M. Otness. Passenger ship libraries.
J.Lib.Hist. 14 (4) 1979, 486-95. illus.
There are references to libraries aboard British ships, including the
Queen Mary and the P and O liners serving Australia and New Zealand
around the turn of the century.

3063 J. Rose. Elizabeth Fry. Macmillan, 1980. [14], 218p. plates, table,
ports, bibliog.
There is an intriguing reference to the part played by Elizabeth Fry
and her husband Joseph in providing libraries for all the coast guard
stations in Great Britain between 1834 and 1836, and also to 48
cruisers.

3064 K. Turner. Hello sailors! - library services for British seamen
yesterday and today. Aberystwyth, College of Librarianship Wales, 1977.
[5], 21p. bibliog.
Covers libraries, both professional and recreational, aboard ships of
the Merchant and Royal Navies from the 16th century to the present,
together with library provision in boarding houses and seamen's missions. Particular attention is paid to the work of the Seafarers
Education Service since 1920.

MEDICINE

3065 L. J. Parr. Early libraries for nurses in England, 1860-1914.
J.Librarianship 12 (2) 1980, 102-14.
The increase in nursing literature led to the need for libraries for
nurses. Few existed during this period, but the foundations were laid
for future development.

2778) E. Sangwine. The private libraries of Tudor doctors.

MEDICINE. CHARING CROSS HOSPITAL MEDICAL SCHOOL

3066 L. S. Godbolt. At the end of all our work is a patient.

Lib.Assn Rec. 79 (2) 1977, 86-89. illus.

Charing Cross Hospital was founded in 1818, although there is no firm evidence as to the date of the creation of the Medical School library. The article reviews its history, paying particular attention to the period since 1945. The library moved several times before occupying its present site in Hammersmith in 1973.

MEDICINE. DR. STEEVENS' HOSPITAL, Dublin

(2927) M. McCarthy. Dr. Edward Worth's library in Dr. Steevens' Hospital.

MEDICINE. NOTTINGHAM MEDICO-CHIRURGICAL SOCIETY

3067 J. B. Cochrane, editor. Nottingham Medico-Chirurgical Society: 150th anniversary year. Nottingham, The Society, 1978. 92p. illus.

Chapter 3 covers the history of the Society's library to 1903. Elsewhere there are details of earlier medical book clubs.

MEDICINE. ROYAL COLLEGE OF PHYSICIANS OF LONDON

3068 L. M. Payne and C. E. Newman. The history of the College Library 1688-1727.
Journal of the Royal College of Physicians of London 5 (4) 1971, 385-96. facsim., port.

See also nos 1471-2, 2231. The major event of this period was the arrival of the Dorchester Library in 1688. In 1708 a Committee was appointed to make recommendations concerning the future management of the Library. A number of presidents and curators during this period were eminent bibliophiles and antiquaries.

3069 L. M. Payne and C. E. Newman. The history of the College Library 1760-1792: in the time of George III.
Journal of the Royal College of Physicians of London 8 (3) 1974, 283-93. facsims.

Largely a period of consolidation. The Statutes were revised in 1765. The activities of various beadle-librarians are recorded. In 1792 Dr. John Lathan was appointed to put the Library in order, and a number of bindings were repaired. Gifts of books are also mentioned.

3070 L. M. Payne and C. E. Newman. The history of the College Library: the last thirty years in Warwick Lane.
Journal of the Royal College of Physicians of London 9 (1) 1974, 87-98. facsim., port.

This was a period of increased activity, with greater expenditure on books and many donations. Two major bequests were the library of Dr. Thomas Gisborne who died in 1806 and, at the end of the period under review, that of Dr. Matthew Baillie, who died in 1823.

(2790) Royal College of Physicians of London. The Evan Bedford Library of Cardiology: catalogue of books, pamphlets and journals.

MEDICINE. ROYAL COLLEGE OF SURGEONS OF ENGLAND, London

(2844) J. E. Gordon. The medical Highmore family and their books.

MEDICINE. ROYAL SOCIETY OF MEDICINE, London

(2405) L. S. Godbolt. Sir John Young Walker MacAlister: (1856-1925): a biography.

MEDICINE. UNIVERSITY OF LONDON

(2630) R. M. Nicholas. The development of medical libraries within the University of London and associated institutes.

MEDICINE. WELLCOME HISTORICAL MEDICAL LIBRARY, London

3071 H. Turner. Henry Wellcome: the man, his collection and his legacy. The Wellcome Trust and Heinemann, 1980. [7], 96p. illus, ports.
Sir Henry Wellcome, 1853-1936, American-born pharmaceutical entre-preneur, came to England in 1880, and commenced the formation of a vast Museum of Mankind, served by a library on a similar scale. The Wellcome Historical Medical Library, opened to the public in 1949, is described, and the story of its formation, organisation and housing is outlined. It is particularly rich in Western and Oriental manu-scripts, incunabula and illustrative material.

3072 Wellcome Historical Medical Library. A catalogue of printed books in the Wellcome Historical Medical Library. Vol.3: Books printed from 1641 to 1850: F-L. The Library, 1976. 565p.
Rev. Bk Coll. 26 (4) 1977, 590-2 (E. M. Payne)
For previous volumes see no.729.

MILITARY SCIENCE. KING'S COLLEGE, London

(2632) A. M. Shadrake. The War Studies Library at King's College, London University.

3073   Sotheby and Co. Catalogue of printed books (including 'The Property of
        The Royal Artillery Institution', Lots 228-46; 112-27). Sotheby, 21
        November, 1977, 39-41; 19 December, 1977, 19-21.

    These two sales are indicative of the interests of the Institution
    Library, ranging from natural history to linguistic manuals and
    glosses. Early books of note are Aelianus De Militaribus (Venice,
    1552) and Vegetius De Re Military (Antwerp, 1585).

MILITARY SCIENCE. ROYAL MILITARY ACADEMY, Sandhurst

3074   G. A. Shepperd. Sandhurst: the Royal Military Academy Sandhurst and its
        predecessors. Country Life Books, 1980. 224p. illus, plates, ports,
        bibliog.

    The Royal Military Academy at Woolwich and the Royal Military College
    at Sandhurst were founded in the 18th century and were amalgamated in
    1947. There is a reference to the College Library in the 1870s with
    the Chaplain acting as Librarian. The Library was financed by
    officers and cadets, with different subscriptions and regulations.
    Other passages refer to changes in accommodation in the 20th century
    and the growth of the collections, until in the 1970s they formed the
    country's most important collection of military works outside London,
    with a stock approaching 100,000.

MILITARY SCIENCE. ROYAL UNITED SERVICES INSTITUTE, London

3075   Christie, Manson and Woods Ltd. Printed books (including 'The Property
        of the Royal United Services Institute', lots 1-264). Christie, 25
        October, 1978, 5-44.

    An impressive collection, notably strong in volumes of pamphlets and
    in regimental records. Topographical works, voyages and naval works,
    army lists, gazetteers, atlases, plans and drawings are the several
    points of interest, while chronologically the collection ranges from
    Du Bellay's Disciplina militare (1550) to the Militärgeographische
    Angaben 25 vols (1940-1) of the German General Staff.

3076   Christie's South Kensington Ltd. Printed books ... [including] ...
        from the library of the Royal United Services Institute. London, 10
        August, 1979. 99 lots. 15p; 28 November 1979. 31 lots 5p.

    Continuation of earlier sales.

MUSIC

3077 B.A.R. Cooper. Catalogue of printed music in Aberdeen libraries.
      Research Chronicle, Royal Musical Association Vol.14 1978, 2-138.
            Includes an historical account of collections in the University Lib-
            rary, the University Music Department and the City Library.

(3120) T. Fawcett. Music circulating libraries in Norwich.

3078 A. H. King. The history of music libraries in the United Kingdom.
      Fontes Artis Musicae 25 (3) 1978, 201-4.
            A survey of various kinds of collections of music which have been
            formed over the last 350 years and which have found their way into
            major British libraries. There is also brief mention of music
            circulating libraries of the late 18th and 19th centuries.

(3095) A. H. King. Music circulating libraries in Britain.

      MUSIC. BRITISH LIBRARY, London

(2737) A. H. King. Printed music in the British Museum: an account of the
      collections, the catalogues, and their formation, up to 1920.

      MUSIC. DURHAM CATHEDRAL

(2668) B. Crosby. A 17th-century Durham inventory.

      MUSIC. JOHN BROWNE

(2799) A. Ashbee. Instrumental music from the library of John Browne (1608-
      1691), Clerk of the Parliaments.

      MUSIC. JOHN FREDERICK SACKVILLE, 3rd DUKE OF DORSET

(2897) W. K. Ford. Music at Knole.

      MUSIC. ROYAL COLLEGE OF MUSIC, London

(2570) Miss Banner's Library.

      MUSIC. ST. MICHAEL'S COLLEGE, Tenbury Wells

(2591) Sotheby and Co. Catalogue of the Toulouse-Philidor Collection of manu-
      script and printed music.

      MUSIC. YORK MINSTER

(2675) York Minster. Library. A catalogue of the printed music published before 1850 in York Minster Library.

ORIENTAL STUDIES

3079 N. Matthews and M. D. Wainwright. A guide to manuscripts and documents
in the British Isles relating to the Far East, edited by J. D. Pearson.
Oxford U.P., 1977. xiv, 182p.

For previous volumes in this series see nos 1426, 1476. The arrangement is by town and then by institution, listing the major collections of manuscripts. Includes some historical notes on the collections.

3080 M. C. Ricklefs and P. Voorhoeve. Indonesian manuscripts in Great
Britain: a catalogue of manuscripts in Indonesian languages in British
public collections. Oxford U.P., 1977. xxix, 237p. bibliog.

The arrangement is by language and then by library. The manuscripts
are annotated, including details of provenance. The catalogue is
prefaced by notes on 25 prominent collectors.

ORIENTAL STUDIES. ROYAL ASIATIC SOCIETY, London

3081 C. F. Beckingham. A history of the Royal Asiatic Society, 1823-1973.
In: The Royal Asiatic Society: its history and treasures ... edited by
Stuart Simmonds and Simon Digby. Brill for the Society, 1979, 1-77.

Pages 39-44 mention many gifts of books and manuscripts to the
Society's library since 1824. Librarians and honorary librarians are
listed at the end of the chapter.

3082 C.E.J. Whitting. The Burton Collection at the Royal Asiatic Society.
In: The Royal Asiatic Society: its history and treasures ... edited by
Stuart Simmonds and Simon Digby. Brill for the Society, 1979, 145-54.
plate, port.

The collection of books by and about Sir Richard Burton formed by
Oscar Eckenstein, was purchased after his death in 1921 by Lewis C.
Lord, who presented it to the Society in 1939. It includes a number
of letters and books with annotations in Burton's hand.

PATENTS. PATENT OFFICE LIBRARY, London

3083 R.M.S. Hall. Woodcroft's heritage: the collections at the Science
Reference Library.
Br.Lib.J. 6 (1) 1980, 65-76.

A description of the kinds of material collected and services provided
by the Science Reference Library since its inception as the Patent

Office Library in 1855 under Bennet Woodcroft.

3084   J. Hewish. The indefatigable Mr. Woodcroft: the legacy of invention.
The British Library, Science Reference Library, [1980]. 40p. illus,
facsims, bibliog.

An outline of the life and career of Bennet Woodcroft (1803-1879) who
was appointed Assistant to the Commissioners of Patents in 1852, and
who was the decisive influence in the formation of the Patent Office
Library, ancestor of the Science Reference Library. At the beginning
it consisted of his own personal books supplemented by loans and
donations.

POLITICS. BRITISH LIBRARY OF POLITICAL AND ECONOMIC SCIENCE, London

(2634) S. and B. Webb. The letters of Sidney and Beatrice Webb.

PRINTING. LONDON SOCIETY OF COMPOSITORS

(3118) D. Mayall. The Library of the London Society of Compositors, 1855-1896.

SCIENCE

3085   J. L. Thornton and R.I.J. Tully. Scientific books, libraries and collectors: a study of bibliography and the book trade in relation to
science. Supplement 1969-75. Lib.Assn, 1978. vii, 172p. bibliog.

Supplements the 3rd ed., 1971 (see no.1480). Private libraries are
covered in chapter 10, institutional collections in chapter 12.

SCIENCE. CHESTER SOCIETY OF NATURAL SCIENCE

3086   E. G. Williams. The Chester Society of Natural Science founded by
Charles Kingsley in 1871, later becoming The Chester Society of Natural
Science, Literature and Art: its origin and development over one hundred
years. Chester, The Author, 1977. iii, 88, iiip.

There are scattered references to the Society's library, particularly
to its transfer, together with the library of the Archaeological
Society, to the City Library in 1939, and its subsequent fate. There
is also brief mention of the Mechanics' Institute Library and a subscription library.

SCIENCE. NATIONAL LIBRARY OF WALES, Aberystwyth

(2749) W.B.L. Evans. Early scientific books in the National Library of Wales.

SCIENCE. OLDHAM MICROSCOPICAL SOCIETY

3087   Christie, Manson and Woods Ltd. ... Travel and natural history books ...
[including] ... the property of the Oldham Microscopical Society.
London, 16 May, 1979. 13 lots. 3p.

SCIENCE. ROYAL DUBLIN SOCIETY

(2361)   [Obituary of Desmond John Clarke, 1907-1979]

SCIENCE. SCIENCE MUSEUM, London

3088   D. Follett. The rise of the Science Museum under Henry Lyons. Science
Museum, 1978. x, 167p. front., plates, plans.
Chapter 12 surveys the growth of the Science Library and controversy
concerning its role from 1920 to 1933, especially under the librarianship of Dr. S. C. Bradford.

(2352)   M. Gosset. S. C. Bradford, Keeper of the Science Museum Library 1925-
1937: recollections of a colleague whose memory may be at fault.

3089   Science Museum Library. A catalogue of books printed before 1641 in the
Science Museum Library compiled by Judit Brody: subject index compiled
by Judith Field and Judit Brody. Science Museum, 1979. [2], ii, 43p.

(2353)   D. J. Urquhart. S. C. Bradford.

SCIENCE. UNIVERSITY COLLEGE, London

(2636)   J. Percival and W. A. Smeaton. Library and archive resources in the
history of science at University College, London.

SHIPPING. NATIONAL MARITIME MUSEUM, Greenwich

3090   National Maritime Museum. Guide to the manuscripts in the National
Maritime Museum. Vol.1.: The personal collections, edited by R.J.B.
Knight. Mansell, 1977. xxiv, 234p. front.
The personal papers of 300 people connected with the Royal Navy and
the Merchant Shipping industry are described. Biographical notes and
details of provenance are provided.

SLAVONIC STUDIES

(2874)   M. Partridge. An English eccentric and some Slavs and Slavists.

SLAVONIC STUDIES. SCHOOL OF SLAVONIC AND EAST EUROPEAN STUDIES, UNIVERSITY OF LONDON

(2635) J.E.O. Screen and C. L. Drage. Church Slavonic and Russian books, 1552-1800, in the library of the School of Slavonic and East European Studies.

SOCIAL SCIENCES. BRITISH LIBRARY OF POLITICAL AND ECONOMIC SCIENCE, London

(2633) J. Harris. William Beveridge: a biography.

(2634) S. and B. Webb. The letters of Sidney and Beatrice Webb.

SPANISH LITERATURE. CAMBRIDGE UNIVERSITY LIBRARY

(2614) A.J.C. Bainton, compiler. 'Comedias sueltas' in Cambridge University Library: a descriptive catalogue.

TECHNOLOGY

(2563) R. V. Fox. The development of technological university libraries from the libraries of the colleges of advanced technology.

TECHNOLOGY. BRITISH SCIENTIFIC INSTRUMENT RESEARCH ASSOCIATION, London

(2383) [Obituary of Christopher Wharton Hanson, 1902-1979]

TECHNOLOGY. ROYAL DUBLIN SOCIETY

(2361) [Obituary of Desmond John Clarke, 1907-1979]

TECHNOLOGY. SCIENCE MUSEUM, London

(3088) D. Follett. The rise of the Science Museum under Henry Lyons.

LIBRARIES: Subscription

3091 J. Benson. British coalminers in the Nineteenth Century: a social
history. Dublin, Gill and Macmillan, 1980. [12], 276p. maps, bibliog.
Pages 152-4 discuss reading rooms, institutes and libraries, the most
important adult educational self-help institutions to be found in the
coalfields. They were "started by the employers as part of their
attack on what they saw as the miners' obdurate intemperance and
irresponsibility, as part indeed of a much larger entrepreneurial
offensive designed to turn the workers into a reliable factor of
production". A number of examples are cited, with details of accommodation, stock and subscription rates.

3092 M. J. Crump and R. J. Goulden. Four library catalogues of note.
Factotum 1 (3) 1978, 9-13. facsim.
Reports the discovery of Samuel Fancourt's Salisbury circulating
library catalogue of 1739, with the rules of the library printed on
the verso of the title page. Also, catalogues of the subscription
library and Harrod's circulating library at Stamford (1787 and 1790
respectively). The catalogue of Ann Yearsley's circulating library
in Bristol, dated 1793, has also been discovered.

3093 D. E. Gerard. Subscription libraries (Great Britain).
In: Encyclopedia of library and information science. Vol.29. New York,
Dekker, 1980, 205-21. bibliog.
The terms "subscription library" and "circulating library" are de-
fined, and the rise, development, decline and significance of each
type is demonstrated in the context of the changes in society, publishing and other forms of library provision. The time-scale covered
is from the early 18th century to the 20th (brief mention of the survival of certain notable proprietary libraries and the demise of the
circulating libraries by the 1960s).

(2689) B. Heeney. A different kind of gentleman: parish clergy as professional
men in early and mid-Victorian England.

(2421) T. Hubbard. "I hate you, Mr. Mudie."

3094 M. J. Jannetta. Footnotes on circulating libraries.
Factotum 1 (5) 1979, 16-17.

194

Details of John Rosen's circulating library at 54 St. Martin le Grand, advertised in a novel published in 1772, of Meyler's circulating library at Bath, that of William Bott at Buxton, and several such libraries at Weymouth.

(3078) A. H. King. The history of music libraries in the United Kingdom.

3095 A. H. King. Music circulating libraries in Britain.
Musical Times Vol.119 February 1978, 134-5, 137-8
A preliminary study of music circulating libraries in the late 18th and 19th centuries. Many of them were maintained by music publishers, and some of the collections were of very considerable size. There is a list of those in London and the provinces, with dates where known, and the regulations of some of them are reproduced. A supplementary note by P. S. MORRISH appears on pp 293 and 312.

(2715) R. Lowery. Robert Lowery: Radical and Chartist.

(3145) V. E. Neuburg. Popular literature: a history and guide from the beginning of printing to the year 1897.

3096 J. Sutherland. The economics of the Victorian three-volume novel.
Business Archives Vol.41 January 1976, 25-30.
The business archives of Richard Bentley's publishing house throw light upon the economics of fiction publishing. Detailed breakdowns are cited, and reference is made to the role of the circulating libraries.

3097 E. A. Swaim. "Circulating library": antedatings of O.E.D.
Notes and Queries 25 (1) 1978, 14-15.
The O.E.D.'s earliest citation of the term "circulating library" is a 1742 advertisement of Samuel Fancourt when he proposed to erect a public circulating library in London. The writer points out that Fancourt used the term in an advertisement in the "Salisbury Journal" in October 1740 and that an even earlier usage is found in the "York Courant" that same year.

(2634) S. and B. Webb. The letters of Sidney and Beatrice Webb.

(3150) R. M. Wiles. The relish for reading in provincial England two centuries ago.

MUDIE

(2421) T. Hubbard. "I hate you, Mr. Mudie."

3098   R. C. Terry. Anthony Trollope: the artist in hiding. Macmillan, 1977.
        xiii, 286p. plates, port.

> In questioning Sadleir's opinion that Trollope's popularity slumped
> seriously after the publication of his autobiography, in chapter
> three the author relates Trollope's rise and fall to the represen-
> tation of his novels in Mudie's catalogues from 1857 to 1935.

IRELAND

3099   P. Bolger. The Irish Co-operative Movement: its history and develop-
        ment. Dublin, Institute of Public Administration, 1977. xiv, 434p.
        illus, ports.

> Chapter 24 covers village circulating libraries promoted by the Irish
> Agricultural Organisation Society in 1900 and organised by local co-
> operative societies. Also mentioned is the Co-operative Reference
> Library, Dublin, set up in 1914 to provide information on co-
> operative organisation throughout the world.

ACTON. BEDFORD PARK CLUB

3100   M. J. Bolsterli. The early community at Bedford Park. Routledge and
        Kegan Paul, 1977. xii, 136p. plates, plan, facsims.

> There is brief mention of the Bedford Park Club 1879-1939. Reading
> room facilities were provided and books were supplied by the Grosvenor
> Gallery Library and later by Mudies.

BECCLES, Suffolk

(2535) M. Ellwood. Library provision in a small market town, 1700-1929.

BELFAST. PEOPLE'S CIRCULATING LIBRARY

3101   H. G. Calwell. The People's Circulating Library.
        Irish Booklore 3 (1) 1976, 61-2.

> Refers to Ronald Adams's note in _Irish Booklore_ 2 (2) 1975 (see no.
> 2269). The Library was one of the activities of the Belfast Working
> Classes' Association, the founder of which was Dr. Andrew George
> Malcolm (1818-56), a physician in the Belfast General Hospital. The
> Library was opened in 4 Castle Chambers in July 1847. The People's
> News-Room in the same premises had been open since June 1846. Brief
> details are given.

BIRMINGHAM. BIRMINGHAM AND MIDLAND INSTITUTE

3102   Sotheby and Co. Catalogues (dated 2 December 1975; 3 May, 7 June 1976;

24/25 January, 11/12 May, 2 June, 16/17 June 1977; 30 July 1979; each
including 'the property of the Birmingham and Midland Institute').
London, 1975-1979.

> The sales indicate the Library's notable holdings of works in the
> fields of natural history, science, travel, topography, archaeology
> and bibliographical reference, mainly of the 18th and 19th centuries.

CHESHIRE

3103   S. Harrop.   Community involvement in education in North-East Cheshire in
the late eighteenth and early nineteenth centuries.
Transactions of the Lancashire and Cheshire Antiquarian Society   Vol.80
1980 for 1979, 1-21. map.

> The late 18th century witnessed rapid growth in population and in the
> cotton industry.   The community was strongly influenced by dissent,
> and this independent spirit encouraged the formation of numerous
> examples of self help and informal agencies of education.   Brief
> mention is included of various society libraries, book clubs and
> village libraries.

DERBY. PHILOSOPHICAL SOCIETY

3104   D. King-Hele.   Doctor of revolution: the life and genius of Erasmus
Darwin.   Faber, 1977. 361p. illus, plates, facsims, ports, bibliog.

> Pages 160-1 refer to the Derby Philosophical Society of which Darwin
> was the president and leading spirit.   He encouraged the establish-
> ment of a library for which regulations were adopted in 1784.   A manu-
> script catalogue and charging ledger for 1786-9 survives.   By 1835
> the catalogue recorded 1200 volumes.

3105   R. P. Sturges.   The membership of the Derby Philosophical Society 1783-
1802.
Midland History   4 (3-4) 1978, 212-29.

> An analysis of the membership of the Society to the time of the death
> of its founder Dr. Erasmus Darwin, taking into account such factors
> as status, profession, education and religious affiliation, and con-
> sidering the reasons for members' interest in the Society and in
> natural philosophy in general.   There is brief reference to the lib-
> rary and its catalogues and loan register, and to the use made of it
> by William Brookes Johnson.   The article concludes with a bio-
> graphical appendix.

DOWN

(2541) J.R.R. Adams. A history of libraries in County Down from the earliest period to the year 1900.

ELY. PAMPHLET CLUB

3106 J. Feather. The Ely Pamphlet Club 1766-1776.
Trans. Cambridge Bibl. Soc. 7 (4) 1980, 457-63.
This club of 12 members was a typical small provincial book club.
There was little serious reading, fiction and travel being the most
popular categories. Never was more than £5 per annum spent, and the
club declined rapidly.

ESSEX

(2978) A history of the county of Essex, edited by W. R. Powell. Vol.7.

GRAVESEND

3107 J. Benson. A history of Gravesend ... Revised and edited by Robert
Heath Hiscock. Phillimore, 1976. xii, 159p. front., illus, plates,
maps, bibliog.
There is brief mention of the Literary Institute built in 1836 to
house a lending library and reading room, lounge, billiard room and
assembly room. It continued to flourish until the fortunes of
Gravesend as a holiday centre declined. At Penny's Library
established in 1826, visitors and residents foregathered to exchange
gossip and indulge in leisurely reading.

HORSHAM

(2545) A. Windrum. Horsham: an historical survey.

HUNTINGDON

3108 C. Dunn. The book of Huntingdon: a portrait of the town. Chesham,
Bucks, Barracuda Books, 1977. 148p. front., illus, maps, facsims, ports,
bibliog.
Page 67 records the existence of four book clubs in the 1820s. The
Huntingdon Literary and Scientific Institute established in 1842 provided library and reading room facilities in addition to rooms set
aside for billiards, chess, smoking and music. The Archdeaconry Library was built in 1890 to house a large collection of books that came

from Buckden Towers, formerly a palace of the Bishops of Lincoln.

KING'S LYNN

(2546) H. J. Hillen. History of the Borough of King's Lynn.

LEADHILLS, Lanarkshire. READING SOCIETY

3109 P. Jackaman. The company, the common man, and the library: Leadhills
and Wanlockhead.
Lib.Rev. Vol.29 Spring 1980, 27-32.
Examines the nature and organisation of the lead mining industry of
the 18th century in order to discover whether the libraries were
formed as a result of the workers' initiative or the employers'
philanthropy.

LEEDS. LEEDS LIBRARY

(2405) L. S. Godbolt. Sir John Young Walker MacAlister: (1856-1925): a biography.

3110 T. H. Hall. The Leeds Library: an address delivered to the Library
History Group in the Leeds Library on 29 June 1977. Leeds, The Leeds
Library, [n.d.] 15p.
The Library's President outlines its history since its foundation in
1768, with special reference to its librarians, to previous histories
of the institution and to the scope of its collections. He concludes
by describing how in 1976 the Library's future was made financially
secure.

LEIGH, Lancs. LITERARY SOCIETY

(2548) N. Ackers. The history of Leigh Library and its antecedents.

LIVERPOOL. LIVERPOOL LIBRARY

(2405) L. S. Godbolt. Sir John Young Walker MacAlister: (1856-1925): a biography.

3111 J. E. Vaughan. The Liverpool Library: another chapter.
Lib.Hist. 5 (2) 1979, 61-4.
A summary of the local, national and international campaign during
1978-1979 to save Liverpool's Lyceum, built by Thomas Harrison in
1803 to house the Liverpool Library, a newsroom and a coffee room.
The books were sold in 1944.

LIVERPOOL. ST. PAUL'S YOUNG MENS FRIENDLY SOCIETY LIBRARY

(2713) J. E. Vaughan. The former St. Paul's Young Men's Friendly Society Library.

LONDON

3112 V. A. Berch. Notes on some unrecorded circulating libraries of
eighteenth century London.
Factotum 1 (6) 1979, 15-19.
Brief details of the libraries, discovered as a result of scanning
contemporary newspapers, are arranged under proprietor, with a
separate list of unidentified proprietors.

(3040) A. Lejeune and M. Lewis. The gentlemen's clubs of London.

3113 I. Maxted. The London book trades 1775-1800: a preliminary checklist
of members. Folkestone, Dawson, 1977. xxxv, 257p.
Provides information about 4,000 individuals and firms, the term
'book trade' being interpreted widely. Many libraries are mentioned.
Sources are discussed and listed in the introduction.

3114 I. Maxted. The London book trades, 1775-1800: a topographical guide,
including a correction of major errors in the author's 'Preliminary
checklist of members.' Exeter: The Author, 1980. 16p. maps.
This booklet accompanies five microfiche which form an index to
"The London book trades, 1775-1800: a preliminary checklist of
members," above.

(2722) J. Noyce. Radicalism, literacy and a pint of coffee: working people's
coffee houses in London, 1830-c.1836.

LONDON. INFIDEL LIBRARY, Fleet Street

3115 J. Noyce. Richard Carlile and the Infidel Library.
Studies in Labour History No.1 1976, 15-18.
An attempt to reconstruct the subscription library formed by the
freethinking publisher Richard Carlile in 1828. It was associated
with the School for Free Discussion which met every Sunday at his
house in Fleet Street.

LONDON. LONDON INSTITUTION

(2461) T. D. Rogers. Thomas Symonds to William Upcott.

LONDON. LONDON LIBRARY (f.1841)

3116 A. Bell. Intellectual oasis of the Capital: the London Library.
      Country Life 164 (4245) 1978, 1610-2. illus, ports.
      A general outline history.

(2386) S. Gillam. "Genial temper and ready and agreeable speech".

3117 [The London Library]
      Adam International Review 1 (397-400) 1976/77. 95p. illus, plates,
      facsims.
           The whole issue is given over to tributes to the London Library.
           Some are historical. Miron Grindea's 'Lisez, pour vivre!' is a
           lengthy article dealing with the Library's foundation and the
           personalities surrounding it. Stanley Gillan also covers its birth,
           but more briefly, and Michael Higgins discusses the Library's Russian
           manuscripts. Charles Hagberg Wright's 'The soul's dispensary', first
           published in 1922, is reprinted. Other contributors, many of them
           celebrated writers, communicate their affection for the unique
           institution in prose and verse. Their recollections and anecdotes
           are themselves of considerable historic interest.
           Reissued in hardcover as "The London Library" edited by Miron
           Grindea. Ipswich, Boydell Press in association with Adam Inter-
           national Review, 1978.

LONDON. LONDON SOCIETY OF COMPOSITORS

3118 D. Mayall. The Library of the London Society of Compositors, 1855-1896.
      Lib.Hist. 5 (2) 1979, 55-60.
           A library was formed at the Society's headquarters off Fleet Street
           in 1855, with 900 volumes. It represented a desire for self improve-
           ment among this group of skilled artisans, although fiction was in
           greater demand than trade literature. By 1878 there were 7000
           volumes, after which the bookstock and membership declined. The
           reasons for this are examined.

LONDON. ORIENTAL CLUB

(3050) D. Forrest. The Oriental: life story of a West End Club.

(3051) F. M. Innes. Oriental Club: Library.

LONDON REFORM CLUB

(3041) G. Woodbridge. The Reform Club, 1836-1978: a history from the Club's records.

NEWCASTLE UPON TYNE

3119   J. Knott. Newcastle-upon-Tyne newsrooms.
Lib.Hist. 4 (4) 1977, 101-11.

A survey of newsroom facilities in Newcastle from the early 19th
century until the end of the century, when the cheap press and the
provision of public library facilities had resulted in the decline
of the commercial newsrooms. Subscription newsrooms for the middle
classes, mechanics' institutes, working men's clubs, church and
radical institutes are all considered.

NEWCASTLE UPON TYNE. LITERARY AND PHILOSOPHICAL SOCIETY

(3021) R. J. Charleton. Newcastle town.

NORWICH

3120   T. Fawcett. Music circulating libraries in Norwich.
Musical Times Vol.119 July 1978, 594-5.

Details are given of three music circulating libraries in Norwich in
the first third of the 19th century. William Fish the proprietor of
the longest lasting, combined this activity with that of a general
music shop, the hire of musical instruments, and with the teaching of
music. He later established a general circulating library in
addition.

NORWICH. CITY LIBRARY

(3022) D. Stoker. Doctor Collinges and the revival of Norwich City Library.

NORWICH. NORFOLK AND NORWICH LIBRARY

3121   P. Minet. The rise and fall of the subscription library.
Antiquarian Book Monthly Review 5 (10) 1978, 441;
5 (11) 1978, 491

Records the demise of the Norfolk and Norwich Library, apart from the
local collection which is to be endowed by the sale of the rest of
the stock. The 16,000 volumes in question were purchased by the
bookseller Paul Minet himself for resale.

3122   Sotheby and Co. Catalogue of travel and topography [and] Catalogue of
printed books [including] the property of the Norfolk and Norwich Library (in all 249 lots). London, 1 March and 15 March, 1979. 2 vols.
pp.5-21, 5-15.
> Continuation of the sales of this library. All volumes with their
> book-plate.

NOTTINGHAM

3123   S. Dolman. History and social effects of Nottingham's libraries before
1850. Manchester Polytechnic, Department of Library and Information
Studies, 1980. 88p. illus, maps, facsims, bibliog. [Thesis submitted
for B.A. degree. Typescript]
> An investigation into Nottingham's early library provision, including
> subscription and circulating libraries, mechanics' institutes and
> operatives' libraries housed in public houses. The effects on their
> clientele and the local community, e.g. as agents against crime and
> drunkenness is then illustrated.

(2724) J. J. Rowley. Drink and the public house in Nottingham, 1830-1860.

OXFORD

(3001) M. Graham. Public library facilities in Oxford before 1914.

PLYMOUTH. ATHENAEUM

3124   Sotheby Parke Bernet and Co. Catalogue of printed books comprising the
property of the Plymouth Athenaeum ... London, 29 September 1980. 48p.
> Only a small number of miscellaneous 18th and 19th century printed
> books were offered at this sale.

PLYMOUTH. PROPRIETARY LIBRARY

3125   Sotheby and Co. Catalogue of Western Manuscripts (including 'the
Property of the Plymouth Proprietary Library', lots 56-63). Sotheby,
14 December, 1977. n.p.
> Descriptions of nine early manuscripts (13th to 15th centuries) given
> to the Library by J. O. Halliwell-Phillipps (1820-1889), here un-
> compromisingly described by the Sotheby cataloguer as 'book collector
> (and perhaps thief) and hated son-in-law of Sir Thomas Phillipps'.
> Four of the lots contain cuttings from a catalogue probably relating
> to a Rhinelander who collected manuscripts soon after the suppression
> of the monasteries.

SEVENOAKS

(3004) P. Swan. A short history of library services in Sevenoaks 1905-1980.

SWANSEA

(3008) G. Williams. Adoption at Swansea, 1868-1970.

TAUNTON

3126 R. Bush. The book of Taunton: the story of a county town. Chesham,
Bucks, Barracuda Books, 1977. 148p. front., illus, maps, facsims, ports,
bibliog.
On page 104 there are brief details of 18th century reading societies,
the Taunton and Somerset Institution (f.1822), the Literary and
Philosophical Society (f.1893) and the opening of the public library
in 1905.

WANLOCKHEAD, Dumfriesshire. MINERS' LIBRARY

3127 J. C. Crawford. The restoration of the Wanlockhead Miners' Library.
SLA News 1 (146) 1978, 138-40.
Reports on the programme of work undertaken during 1977 and 1978
using the Job Creation Scheme to clean, repair and catalogue the stock
prior to its re-opening on 15th July 1978.

3128 J. C. Crawford. Wanlockhead Miners' Library: a guide book.
Wanlockhead Museum Trust, 1978. [1], 16p. illus.
The library is one of the few surviving examples in Scotland of the
community, or subscription, library. It was founded in 1756 and
flourished until the beginning of the 20th century. In the 1930s the
declining population of the village led to its closure. It was subsequently restored in 1974-8. This booklet gives the history of the
library, outlines the work of restoration and forms a guide to the
library as it is today.

3129 J. C. Crawford. Wanlockhead Museum Trust and the restoration of Wanlockhead Miners' Library.
SLA News 1 (139) 1977, 287-91.
The Trust was formed in July 1974 and took over responsibility for the
Miners' Library soon afterwards. The library building is being
restored to its original condition and the 3,000 volumes are being re-
bound, repaired and reshelved in their original order. It is also
planned to recatalogue the collection.

3130   J. Crawford and S. James. Library's history reflects changing fortunes
        of a miners' village high in the Lowlands.
        Lib.Assn Rec. 80 (10) 1978, 518-9.
            The Library's history, administration, stock and building are des-
            cribed.

(3109) P. Jackaman. The company, the common man, and the library: Leadhills
        and Wanlockhead.

3131   P. Keating. A miners' library.
        T.L.S. Jan.6, 1978, 16-17. illus, facsim.
            Records the history of the Wanlockhead Reading Society from its
            foundation in 1756 to the winding up of the Society's affairs in 1946,
            viewed in the context of the rise and fall of the lead mining com-
            munity. Particular attention is paid to the way in which the Society
            functioned.

        WEST BROMWICH. PEOPLE'S LIBRARY AND READING ROOM

3132   M. Branson. Aristocratic and entrepreneurial paternalism in West Brom-
        wich in the first half of the Nineteenth century.
        West Midland Studies Vol.12 1979, 40-5.
            There are brief details of the People's Library and Reading Room, a
            subscription library founded by George Kenrick, the Unitarian
            industrialist, in 1846. It ceased to operate after his death in 1848,
            but was revived by his brother in 1853, when the books were trans-
            ferred to a local temperance institute.

READING

3133   F. Bell. Reading habits in Middlesbrough.
In: Into unknown England 1866-1913: selections from the social explorers,
edited by Peter Keating. Fontana, 1976, 285-303.

> An extract from Lady Florence Bell's 'At the works' 1907. She
> records, wherever possible in the very wording, the replies made in
> 200 working class houses visited, to questions respecting the reading
> habits of the inmates. She summarises and comments upon the results
> of the enquiry. The role of the public library and two small lending
> libraries connected with ironworks, is also discussed.

3134   G. Boyce and others, editors. Newspaper history from the seventeenth
century to the present day. Constable, 1978. 423p. facsims, ports,
bibliog.

> These essays have little direct relevance, but collectively provide
> considerable information on literacy, newspaper readership and
> popular culture, and occasional references to newspapers in coffee
> houses and public houses.

(2756) B. Capp. Astrology and the popular press: English almanacs 1500-1800.

3135   M. T. Clanchy. From memory to written record: England 1066-1307.
Arnold, 1979. xiii, 300p. facsims.
Rev. J.Lib.Hist. 15 (3) 1980, 339-42 (E. Poole)

> The first part of the book describes the making of records and the
> growth of the use of writing for secular purposes. The second part
> analyses the development of literate ways of thought. There are also
> many references to book ownership, both personal and institutional,
> with particular reference to English kings and to monastic libraries
> and to developments brought about by the Franciscans and Dominicans.

3136   P. Clark. English provincial society from the Reformation to the
Revolution: religion, politics and society in Kent 1500-1640.
Hassocks, Sussex, Harvester Press, 1977. xiii, 504p. maps.

> Primary sources are used as evidence of literacy and book ownership
> during the late 16th and early 17th centuries.

3137 P. Corrigan and V. Gillespie. Class struggle, social literacy and idle time: the provision of public libraries in England. Brighton, Noyce, 1978. 37p. bibliog.

The main theme is the struggle of working people for social literacy from 1790 to the 1850s and understood within the social and political context. Education, libraries and publishing are all considered. Opposition to manifestations of working class social literacy is seen as being of a negative type e.g. fiscal and legislative coercion, or a positive type, e.g. paternalist mechanics' institutes and the public library movement. The accompanying notes and references to contemporary publications and recent studies are wide ranging and most useful.

3138 B. Cottle. Popular reading and our public libraries: the abjured pre-scription.
Lib.Rev. Vol.27 Winter 1978, 222-7.

A somewhat discursive look at changes in reading tastes over the last century, together with the attitudes of public libraries towards their responsibilities in this respect.

3139 D. Cressy. Levels of illiteracy in England 1530-1730.
Historical Journal 20 (1) 1977, 1-23. tables.

The depositions of the Consistory Court of the diocese of Norwich are used to delineate the social dimensions of illiteracy from the Reformation to the early 18th century. In particular, various phases in the fluctuations of illiteracy of different social groups are traced, with their alternating periods of improvement and setback. Illiteracy is also related to changes in educational provision.

3140 D. Cressy. Literacy and the social order: reading and writing in Tudor and Stuart England. Cambridge U.P., 1980. x, 246p. tables, maps, bibliog.

A wide ranging study based on original sources, considering such matters as the measurement of the extent of literacy, the social structure of illiteracy and the acquisition and progress of literacy. Dr. Cressy questions the reliability of probate inventories as a guide to the extent of literacy, and instead puts forward detailed evidence drawn from certain mass public declarations and covenants.

3141 E. L. Eisenstein. The printing press as an agent of change: communications and cultural transformations in early-modern Europe. Cambridge U.P., 1979. 2 vols.

A wide ranging historical investigation of the impact of the advent of printing and its importance as an agent of change. In particular, the relationship between the communications revolution and the Renaissance, the Reformation and the rise of modern science, is examined. Volume 1 includes a survey of current scholarship and volume 2 a bibliographical index to footnotes.

3142 P. Gaskell. Books bought by Whitgift's pupils in the 1570s. Trans. Cambridge Bibl.Soc. 7 (3) 1979, 284-93.
John Whitgift (c.1530-1604) was Master of Trinity College, Cambridge, from 1567 to 1577, and surviving accounts show that he frequently bought books, mainly texts of classics, on behalf of his students.

(2689) B. Heeney. A different kind of gentleman: parish clergy as professional men in early and mid-Victorian England.

3143 G. H. Jenkins. Bywiogrwydd crefyddol a llenyddol Dyffryn Teifi, 1689-1740.
Ceredigion Vol.8 1979, 439-77.
In the Vale of Tywi an impressive band of religious reformers (Anglicans and Dissenters), literary scholars, bards and antiquarians - fired by a burning zeal for saving souls and a proper pride in their country's literary heritage - were responsible for copying, translating, publishing and distributing a wealth of religious, educational and literary books in the Welsh language, this helping to plant the cardinal doctrines of the Reformation, to revivify Welsh culture and to foster the growth of literacy in general.

3144 G. H. Jenkins. Literature, religion and society in Wales 1660-1730. Univ. of Wales Press, 1978. 351p. front.
The final three chapters on authorship, book trade practice and the ubiquity of subscription purchase is the first full treatment of this field in modern Welsh historical writing.

(2767) G. R. Keiser. Lincoln Cathedral Library MS. 91: life and milieu of the scribe.

(2544) I.R.M. Mowat. Literacy, libraries and literature in 18th and 19th century Easter Ross.

3145 V. E. Neuburg. Popular literature: a history and guide from the beginning of printing to the year 1897. Woburn Press, 1977. 302p. illus, facsims.
Rev. J.Librarianship 9 (4) 1977, 323-5 (J. Allred)
T.L.S. 18 Aug.1977, 979 (P. Keating)
Contains several references to literacy, readership and circulating

libraries. Numerous examples of popular literature are cited and the work contains a comprehensive critical bibliography.

3146 D. C. Peck. Government suppression of Elizabethan Catholic books: the case of Leicester's Commonwealth.
Lib.Q. 47 (2) 1977, 163-77.

Provides a case history of the government's response to one book in order to observe those methods in operation, the steps taken to circumvent them, and to attempt to gauge their efficiency. This is seen in the context of the printing, importing, distribution and reading of Catholic books in the reign of Elizabeth.

3147 E. H. Robbins. Children's reading, 1700-1975: some reflections on the effect of price and availability in the formation of taste and preferences. Univ. College, London School of Library, Archive and Information Studies, 1975. [3], 70p. [Thesis submitted for M.A. degree. Typescript]

Nearly one third is devoted to the development of literacy. The price of books is related to income levels. There is little reference to libraries in the consideration of availability.

3148 R. S. Schofield. Dimensions of illiteracy, 1750-1850.
Explorations in Economic History Vol.10 1973, 437-54. tables.
Considers the evidence, especially that of marriage registers, emphasising differences in the literacy rate between different parts of England and Wales and between different parts of individual counties. Progress was very slow and uneven.

3149 M. Spufford. First steps in literacy: the reading and writing experiences of the humblest seventeenth-century spiritual autobiographers.
Social History 4 (3) 1979, 407-35.

Investigates the acquisition of reading and writing skills among boys up to the social level of yeomen, as revealed in Puritan spiritual autobiographies. Such boys were quite likely to learn to read, since reading was taught at an age when they could earn little, whereas writing was commonly taught at an age after the earning lives of the boys had begun.

3150 R. M. Wiles. The relish for reading in provincial England two centuries ago.
In: The widening circle: essays on the circulation of literature in eighteenth-century Europe, edited by Paul J. Korshin. Philadelphia, Univ. of Pennsylvania Press, 1976, 87-115.

Local newspapers are used to provide evidence of the availability of books (including those published in numbers) magazines and newspapers for sale, subscription and loan via subscription and circulating libraries.

3151   C. P. Wormald.   The uses of literacy in Anglo-Saxon England and its neighbours.
Transactions of the Royal Historical Society   Vol.27 1977, 95-114.

A reconsideration of the extent of lay literacy before the Norman Conquest, relating England and Ireland to the Continent. Particular attention is given to the situation inherited by King Alfred, his own policy and its results. Evidence for lay readership and book ownership is provided. Reasons are given why laywomen were surprisingly prominent as the owners, dedicatees and authors of books.

STUDY OF LIBRARY HISTORY

3152   J. Gibbs, compiler. A bibliography of the published writings of N. R. Ker.

In: Medieval scribes, manuscripts and libraries: essays presented to N. R. Ker, edited by M. B. Parkes and Andrew G. Watson. Scolar Press, 1978, 371-9.

3153   S. J. Glogoff. Cannons' Bibliography of Library Economy and its role in the development of bibliographic tools in librarianship.

J.Lib.Hist. 12 (1) 1977, 57-63.

> Includes an analysis of incorrect citations in Cannons. Its influence upon American bibliographical tools is commented upon.

3154   P. A. Hoare. Library history.

In: British librarianship and information science 1971-1975; edited by H. A. Whatley. Lib.Assn, 1977, 332-9.

> A critical survey of some of the most significant contributions to British library history dating from 1971-1975, arranged under types of library and professional activity. Peter Hoare also points out and discusses neglected areas requiring further research.

3155   D. F. Keeling, editor. British library history: bibliography 1973-1976. Lib.Assn, 1979. 200p.

Rev.Lib.Hist. 5 (3) 1980, 85-7 (J. G. Ollé)

> For the previous volume see no.2331.

3156   Library Association Library. FLA theses: abstracts of all theses accepted for the Fellowship of the Library Association from 1964 [edited by] L. J. Taylor. British Library: Lib.Assn Library, 1979. [5], 90p.

> Covers theses accepted up to October 1978. The abstracts are revised and in many cases abridged versions of those which have appeared before in the Lib.Assn Library and information bulletin between 1967 and 1974, and since 1975 in CABLIS: Current awareness for British Library staff.

3157   Library history in archives: West Midlands.

Lib.Hist. 4 (5) 1978, 164-7.

> Brief details of documents relating to the history of libraries acquired by Birmingham Central Public Library and the record offices

of Gloucestershire, Herefordshire, Warwickshire and Worcestershire.

(2397) [Obituary of Raymond Irwin, 1902-1977]

3158   J. G. Ollé. Library history. Bingley, 1979. 114p.
    Rev. J.Lib.Hist. 15 (4) 1980, 478-80 (J. C. Colson)
        Lib.Assn Rec. 82 (4) 1980, 179 (J. Allred)
        Lib.Hist. 5 (4) 1980, 122-4 (P. S. Morrish)
    A general assessment of what has been accomplished in the field of
    library history in Great Britain and the U.S.A. since the historical
    studies of Edward Edwards, with chapters devoted to studies of
    individual libraries and biographical works. Contains useful hints
    for the library history student and researcher, together with sug-
    gestions for assignments and areas requiring further study. There
    are also helpful notes on reference aids and bibliographies.

3159   R. P. Sturges. Do librarians care for their past?
    Lib.Assn Rec. 82 (7) 1980, 317-8.
    Summarises the results of a questionnaire on the provision British
    public libraries are currently making for the preservation and care
    of their own administrative records.

3160   P. J. Taylor, editor. Library and information studies in the United
    Kingdom and Ireland, 1950-1974: an index to theses. Aslib, 1976, viii,
    69p.
    Among these theses accepted for higher degrees, are a number relevant
    to British library history.

3161   I. R. Willison. On the history of libraries and scholarship: a paper
    presented before the Library History Round Table of the American Library
    Association, June 26, 1980. Washington, Library of Congress, 1980. [2],
    26p.
    Considers the convergence between the history of libraries and the
    history of scholarship, with particular reference to the sophisti-
    cation in method and theme of the new historical approach.

AUTHOR INDEX

Corporate authors and the writers of obituaries are excluded.

Crook, A.C., 2609-10
Crosby, B., 2668
Crossley, A., 2551
Crowley, D.A., 2557
Cruickshank, D.W., 2614
Crum, N., 2644
Crump, M.J., 3092

Dale, D.C., 2940
Davey, J., 2481
Davies, A.C., 2372
Davies, H., 2532
Davis, A., 2871
Davis, N., 2449, 2881
Davison, P., 2773
De La Mare, A.C., 2393
De V. White, T., 2348
De Wit, J., 2896
Deacon, M., 2579
Delaissé, L.M.J., 2896
Dennis, B., 2819
Dent, K., 2760
Dewe, M., 2929, 2992
Dibdin, T.F., 2810
Digby, S., 3081-2
Ditmas, E.M.R., 2495
Dixon, E., 3026
Dixon, V., 2614
Dolman, S., 3123
Doughan, D., 3042
Dowd, T.P., 2975
Downing, J., 2471
Doyle, A.I., 2655
Drage, C.L., 2635
Dreyfus, J., 2615
Dumville, D.N., 2685
Dunlop, B.G., 3023
Dunne, C., 3108
Dunne, T., 2970
Durbidge, L.G., 3018

Durkan, J., 2621, 2664, 2834, 2867, 2900

Eames, P., 2531
Edmondston, E., 2571
Edwards, A.C., 2869
Edwards, A.R., 2373
Edwards, A.S.G., 2761
Edwards, J.A., 2572
Edwards, R.J., 2465
Eisenstein, E.L., 3141
Elliott, M., 2987
Ellis, A., 2580, 2930-3
Ellman, R., 2852
Ellwood, M., 2535
Engel, W.F., 2837
English, J.S., 2931
Erskine, A.M., 2670
Evans, R.J.W., 2645
Evans, W.B.L., 2749

Fairthorne, R.A., 2364
Farmer, A.L., 2934
Farnworth, H.A., 2588
Fawcett, T., 3120
Feather, J., 3106
Fenning, H., 2814
Ferguson, J.P., 2701
Filon, S.P.L., 2484
Finch, R.J.A., 2641
Finlayson, C.P., 2862
Fletcher, J.M., 2643, 2657
Fogarty, M., 2726
Follett, D., 3088
Foot, M.M., 2733
Foot, M.R.D., 2429
Ford, W.K., 2897
Forrest, D., 3050
Fothergill, B., 2787
Fox, R.V., 2563

Francis, F.C., 2526
Francis, H., 2717-8
Fraser, D., 2547
Freeman, M.J., 2827
Friedman, J.E., 2694
Friendly, A., 2786
Fuggles, J.F., 2660-1, 2856

Garratt, M., 2935
Garrod, H.W., 2658
Garton, C., 2795
Garton, E., 2702
Gaskell, P., 2612, 3142
Gemmett, R.J., 2774
Gerard, D.E., 2395, 2688, 3017, 3093
Gibbs, J., 3152
Gibson, M., 2667
Gilbert, C., 2762
Gillam, S., 2386
Gillespie, R.A., 2980
Gillespie, V., 3137
Gingell, P.J., 2558
Girouard, M., 2763
Glogoff, S.J., 3153
Godbolt, L.S., 2405, 3066
Gordon, J.E., 2844
Gosset, M., 2352
Goulden, R.J., 3092
Graham, B., 2719
Graham, M., 3001
Gratton, P.D., 2936
Gray, A., 2608
Green, E., 3031
Green, V.H.H., 2656
Grewcock, C.E., 2721
Griffiths, D., 2675
Griffiths, D.F., 2537
Grinke, P., 2866
Guinness, D., 2542
Gunther, A.E., 2734

Hall, A.W., 2628
Hall, R.M.S., 3083
Hall, T., 2399
Hall, T.H., 2890, 3110
Hancock, P.D., 2616
Hardman, P., 2747
Hardy, J., 2806
Hargreaves, E., 2514
Harris, B.E., 2538, 2973
Harris, J., 2633, 2698
Harris, L.J., 2624
Harris, M.H., 2468, 2508, 2524
Harris, P.R., 2735
Harrison, B., 2715
Harrison, J., 2873
Harrison, K.C., 2445, 2452, 2503,
    2527, 2948
Harrison, W., 2592
Harrop, S., 3103
Harthan, J., 2764
Harvey, R.A., 2803
Haslam, D.D., 2504
Haugh, W.S., 2953
Hawes, D.F.W., 2528
Hay, D., 2971
Hayward, H., 2806
Heaney, M., 2646
Heeney, B., 2689
Henchy, P., 2850
Hendry, J.D., 2440
Herbruggen, H.S., 2870
Herrmann, F., 2765
Hewish, J., 3084
Heyes, J.T., 2968
Hibberd, D., 2875
Highfield, J.R.L., 2658
Hillen, H.J., 2546
Hiscock, R.H., 3107
Hixson, J.C., 2913
Hoare, P.A., 3154

Hobbs, M., 2811
Hobson, A.R.A., 2861
Hockey, F., 2736
Hodges, A.R., 2833
Hoggart, R., 2940-1
Holland, D.C.L., 2948, 2953
Hollis, P., 2715
Holt, J.C., 2662
Hood, J.B., 2529
Hooper, W., 2703
Hopkins, J., 3025
Horton, M.C., 2720
Howell, G., 2723
Howley, M., 3011
Hubbard, T., 2421
Hudson, T.P., 2554
Huelin, G., 2631
Hughes, H., 2982
Humphreys, K.W., 2595
Hunt, R.W., 2659, 2684
Hunter, E.J., 2472, 2937
Hunter, M., 2841
Hutton, R.S., 2496

Ijsewijn, J., 2642
Innes, F.M., 3051

Jackaman, P., 2938, 3109
Jackson, W.A., 2776
James, B.Ll., 2624
James, M.R., 2607
James, S., 3130
Jamison, K., 2802
Jannetta, M.J., 3094
Jardine, L., 2766
Jefferson, G., 2565
Jeffreys, A., 2473
Jenkins, G.H., 3143-4
Jesson, A.F., 3032
Johnson, D.A., 2553

Johnson, E.D., 2524
Jones, A., 2695
Jones, B., 2482
Jones, D., 2567
Jones, G., 2445, 2931, 2953
Jones, J.W., 2506
Jones, W.R., 2676

Kaula, P.N., 2507, 2939
Keating, P., 3131, 3145
Keeling, D.F., 2993, 3155
Keiser, G.R., 2767
Kelly, T., 2940-1
Kennedy, J.C., 2512
Ker, N.R., 2530, 2642, 2681, 2849
Ker, S., 2639
Keynes, G., 2812-3, 2833
King, A.H., 2737, 3078, 3095
King, E.M.B., 3029
King-Hele, D., 3104
Kipling, G., 2843
Kirk, J., 2867
Kirkpatrick, B.J., 2801
Knight, R.J.B., 3090
Knott, J., 2525, 2550, 2997-8, 3119
Kornicki, P.F., 2738
Krivatsy, N.H., 2855
Künzle, P., 2681

Ladd, F.J., 2868
Lancaster, J.C., 3049
Larkin, P., 2942
Lavigueur, P., 2989
Lee, B.N., 2768
Lee, J.M., 2392
Lejeune, A., 3040
Lenneberg, H., 2737
Levine, J.M., 2389
Levy, S.L.M., 2943
Lewis, L., 2858

217

Lewis, M., 3040
Lewis, R.H., 2750-1
Lewis, W.J., 2752
Lewis, W.S., 2920
Lister, T.A., 2824
Lloyd, L.J., 2825
Lloyd, M., 2462
Lloyd, T.G., 2606
London, G., 2474
Longbotham, J., 2827
Lowe, R., 2581
Lowe, R.A., 2725
Lowerson, J., 2555
Lowery, R., 2715
Lucas, S.T., 2564
Lunn, A., 2475

McAdams, F., 2436-7, 2486, 2490
McCann, A., 2901
McCarthy, M., 2927, 3017
MacFarlane, J.D., 2944
McKelvie, C., 2851, 3015
MacKenna, R.O., 2596
McKitterick, D.J., 2611, 2773, 2793, 2855
McLean, R., 2861
MacLochlainn, A., 2746
McMullen, H., 2941
Maddison, F., 2860
Maidment, W.R., 2945
Malhan, I.V., 2356
Manley, K.A., 2502, 2647-50
Marrow, J., 2896
Marshall, J.D., 2986
Marshall, M., 2489
Matthews, G.F., 2492
Matthews, N., 3079
Maxim, G.E., 2993
Maxted, I., 2773, 3113-4
Mayall, D., 3118

Mehlman, F., 2769
Merryweather, F.S., 2677
Metzger, P.A., 2810
Miall, A., 2770
Miall, P., 2770
Middleton, J., 2984
Miller, E.J., 2430, 2739, 2771, 2946
Minet, P., 3121
Minto, C.S., 2445
Mirsky, J., 2740
Mitchell, L.J., 2999
Moholy, L., 2497
Mole, A., 2466
Montgomery, A.C., 2467
Moon, N.S., 2573
Moore, J.S., 2772
Moran, J.H., 2559
Morgan, P., 2417, 2526, 2643, 2690
Morland, S.C., 2710
Morris, J., 2651
Morris, R.J.B., 2947-8
Morrish, P.S., 2627, 2819, 2925, 2941, 3158
Mortimer, R., 2708
Morton, L.T., 2513
Mowat, I.R.M., 2544, 2784
Moys, E.M., 2500
Mullett, M., 2707
Munby, A.N.L., 2773-4
Munford, W.A.. 2339, 2342, 2424, 2439, 2444, 2508-9, 2948, 2953
Murison, W.J., 2484, 2976
Murray, K.M.E., 2741
Muthesius, H., 2775
Myers, R., 2354, 2895
Myerscough, J., 2555

Nauta, M.F., 3012
Naylor, B., 2629
Naylor, G., 2612

Neill, S.D., 2468

Neuburg, V.E., 3145

Newman, C.E., 3068-70

Nicholas, R.M., 2630

Nicholson, E., 2716

Nickson, M.A.E., 2905

Nixon, H.M., 2469, 2733, 2776

Noel-Tod, A., 2652

Norris, R., 2833

Norris, R.C., 2669

Noyce, J., 2722, 3115

Nuttall, G.F., 2577

O'Day, R., 2777

O'Sullivan, W., 2530

Olden, A., 2381

Oliver, H., 2903

Ollard, R., 2882

Ollé, J.G., 2375, 2445-7, 2468, 2510, 2940-1, 2948-9, 2989, 3158

Orton, G.I.J., 2950

Orton, I., 3011

Otness, H.M., 3062

Owings, F.N., 2853

Pafford, J.H.P., 2484

Page, R.I., 2878

Paley, M.D., 2791

Palmer, B.I., 2490-1, 2963

Paquet, J., 2642

Pargeter, S., 2817

Parkes, M.B., 2655, 2682, 2684, 2785, 3152

Parr, L.J., 3065

Parry, T., 2442

Partridge, M., 2874

Paton, W.B., 2951

Payne, E.A., 3034

Payne, L.M., 3068-70

Peck, D.C., 3146

Pelling, M., 2860

Pemberton, J.E., 2952-3

Percival, J., 2636

Pfaff, R.W., 2476

Philip, I.G., 2653

Piper, A.J., 2682

Plumb, G., 2514

Plumb, J.H., 2831

Plumb, P.W., 2483, 2511

Poole, E., 3135

Potter, J.M., 2587

Powell, J.S., 2961

Powell, W.R., 2978

Price, D.T.W., 2625

Prichard, R., 2954

Pringle, R.V., 2664

Pritchard, A., 3042

Pritchard, F.C., 2583

Quarrie, P., 2584

Ratcliffe, F.W., 2597

Rayward, W.B., 2392, 2477

Read, E.A., 2666

Reidy, D.V., 2432

Rhodes, D.E., 2604, 2742

Richmond, G., 2800

Ricklefs, M.C., 3080

Rider, A.D., 2525

Robbins, E.H., 3147

Roberts, B.F., 2859

Roberts, N., 2522, 2598-9

Roberts, R.J., 2774, 2892

Robertson, D., 2816

Robertson, E.H., 2709

Robinson, E., 2983

Robson, A.P., 2956

Rogers, B., 2743

Rogers, T.D., 2411, 2461

Rose, J., 3063

Thomas, D.J., 3013

Thompson, G., 3019

Thompson, J., 2468, 2596, 2599-601, 2629

Thompson, L.S., 2678, 2779

Thomson, R.M., 2679-80

Thornton, J.L., 3085

Thornton, P., 2780, 2865

Thrall, A., 2540

Tite, C.G.C., 2805

Tomlin, M., 2865

Townsend, J.A.B., 2638

Trapp, J.B., 2870

Tully, R.I.J., 3085

Turner, C.M., 2958

Turner, H., 3071

Turner, J., 2518, 2613, 2789

Turner, K., 3064

Turner, T., 2918

Tyler, A., 3035

Tyler, W.E., 2437

Urquhart, D.J., 2353, 2468, 2485

Vaughan, A., 2562, 2602

Vaughan, J.E., 2713, 3111

Vavigueur, P., 2926

Vickers, J.E., 3005

Vickery, J.E., 2828

Vidler, A.R., 3037

Voigt, M.J., 2508

Voorhoeve, P., 3080

Vowles, M., 2808

Wainwright, C., 2923

Wainwright, M.D., 3079

Walker, R., 3056

Walkling, G., 2781

Walsh, M.J., 2576

Walters, G., 2854

Watson, A.G., 2682, 2684, 2731, 2785, 3152

Webb, B., 2634

Webb, C.A., 2828

Webb, S., 2634

Webster, C., 2860

Weibel, K., 2959

Wimerskirch, P.J., 2434-5

Weir, M., 2409

Wesencraft, A., 2891

Whatley, H.A., 2966-7, 3154

Wheeler, M.D., 2829

Wheeler, W.G., 2774

Wheldon, H., 2831

White, G.K., 2590

White, T. de V., 2348

Whiteman, P., 2419, 2989

Whitting, C.E.J., 3082

Wiles, R.M., 3150

Wilkie, J., 2931

Wilkinson, J., 2953

Williams, D., 2721

Williams, D.M., 2691-2, 2704-5

Williams, E.G., 3086

Williams, G., 2468, 2855, 3008-10

Williams, P., 2659

Williams, R., 2960

Williams, R.D., 2993

Willis, N.E., 2970

Willison, I.R., 2727, 2744, 3161

Wilson, E.M., 2884

Wilson, L., 2499

Wilson, M.I., 2782

Wilson, R., 2697, 2985

Windrum, A., 2545

Wise, M., 2603

Wood, J.L., 2906

Wood, P.B., 2873

Woodbridge, G., 3041

Wormald, C.P., 3151

SUBJECT INDEX

2476, 2511, 2526-32, 2677, 3135,
3152, 3154-9, 4689, 4940, for
individual libraries see under
names and places
British Lib., London, 2359, 2376,
  2381, 2410-11, 2426-35, 2450,
  2475, 2728-44, 2804-5, 2828, 2830,
  2904-6
British Lib. of Political and
  Economic Science, London, 2633-4,
  2899
British Museum see under British Lib.
British National Bibliography, 2475
British Postgraduate Medical
  Federation, London, 2630
British Scientific Instrument
  Research Association, London, 2383
Britton, Thomas, 2797
Broadwater, Sussex: general, 2554
Brodie family, 2798
Brogan, John, 2355
Bromley: public lib., 2444-6
Brooke family, 2965
Brookes, Joshua, 2893
Brotherton Lib., Leeds, 2626-7
Broxbourne Lib., 2818
Brown, James Duff, 2356
Brown, Lancelot, 2868
Brown, Richard, 3023
Brown, Samuel, 3013
Browne, John 2799
Browne, Sir Richard, 2821
Browne, Sir Thomas, 2800
Browning, Edward Frank, 2357
Bryce, David, 2848
Brynmor Jones Lib., Univ. of Hull,
  2622-3
Buildings, library, 2562, 2601, 2929,
  2989-90, 2992
Burgess, Thomas, 2624

Burton, Sir Richard, 2801
Buxton: circulating lib., 3094

Caesar, Sir Julius, 2776
Caithness: county lib., 2971
Calderdale: public lib., 2456
Callander, Thomas Edward, 2358
Cambridge:
  Corpus Christi College, 2878
  friary libs, 2681
  Jesus College, 2608
  King's College, 2799
  Magdalene College, 2420, 2882-4
  public lib., 2972
  St. John's College, 2609-11
  Trinity College, 2612-3, 2873, 3142
  univ.lib., 2354, 2360, 2411, 2476,
    2607, 2614-5, 2641, 2754, 2766,
    2855
Cambridgeshire: parochial libs, 2693
Campbell, Frank, 2359
Cannons, H.G.T., 3153
Canterbury:
  cathedral lib., 2667
  monastic lib., 2667
  private libs, 2757
Capesthorne Hall, Cheshire, 2807
Cardiganshire: county lib., 2373,
  2752
Carlile, Richard, 3115
Carlisle:
  mechanics' institute, 2719
  working men's reading rooms, 2719
Carmarthenshire:
  general, 2537
  county lib., 2537
  diocesan lib., 2537
  mechanics' institutes, 2537
  miners' institutes, 2537
  parochial libs, 2537

Carnegie United Kingdom Trust, 2409,
  2932, 3013
Carrothers, Edward Norman, 2802
Castle Book Society, Colchester, 2539
Castlemilk, Dumfriesshire, 2848
Castleton, Derbyshire: parochial lib.,
  2694
Castletown, Isle of Man: parochial
  lib., 2701
Cataloguing, 2392, 2470-7, 2676, 2838
Cathedral libs: general, 2666
Cavendish, Henry, 2803
Ceadel, Eric, 2360
Central Lib. for Students, London,
  2484
Chadwick, David, 2995
Charing Cross Hospital Medical School,
  London, 3066
Charlecote Park, Warwickshire, 2863
Chelsea: College of St. Mark and
  St. John, 2568
Cheltenham: public lib., 2378
Cherry Burton, Yorks: reading room,
  2560
Cheshire:
  county lib., 2347, 2973
  subscription libs, 3103
Chester:
  general, 2538, 3086
  abbey lib., 2538
  Archaeological Society, 3086
  cathedral lib., 2538
  mechanics' institute, 2538, 3086
  public lib., 3086
  Society of Natural Science, 3086
Chetham's Lib., Manchester, 3020
Chichester: cathedral lib., 2811
Chippendale, Thomas, 2762
Chippenham: public lib., 2974
Christ Church College, Oxford, 2654,

2799
Circulating libs see under
  Subscription libs
City of London Polytechnic, 3042
City Univ., London, 2569
Clapham, Sussex: general, 2554
Clarke, Desmond John, 2361
Classification, 2392, 2447, 2473,
  2477-9, 2646-7
Cleveland:
  mechanics' institutes, 2720
  public lib., 2720
Clough, Eric Allen, 2362
Clough family, 2903
Clubs, London, 3040
Clydebank: public lib., 2355
Coast guard stations, 3063
Coatbridge: public lib., 2370
Coblans, Herbert, 2363-5
Cockburn, James Watson, 2366
Coke, Sir Robert, 3039
Coke family, 2412
Colchester:
  general, 2539
  Castle Book Society, 2539
  mechanics' institute, 2539
  public lib., 2539
  subscription libs, 2539
Coleridge, Samuel Taylor, 2926
College libs: general, 2563-5
College of Advocates and Doctors of
  Law, London, 3052
College of Librarianship Wales,
  Aberystwyth, 2368, 2373
Collinges, John, 3022
Cook, Florence Elsie, 2367
Cornwall: county lib., 2346
Corpus Christi College, Cambridge,
  2878
Corsham Court, Wilts, 2868

Cottingham, Yorks: reading room, 2560
Cotton, Sir Robert Bruce, 2804-5
Coulsdon and Purley: public lib.,
    2358
Coventry: public lib., 2440, 2444-6
Coxe, Henry Octavius, 2648
Crawford, Alexander William Crawford
    Lindsay, 25th Earl, 2861
Crawford, James Ludovic Lindsay,
    26th Earl, 2861, 3030
Cronshaw, F.E., 2969
Crosby: public lib., 2343
Crouch End: general, 2549
Croydon: public lib., 2358, 2444-7
Cumberland: county lib., 2367
Curzon, Nathaniel, 1st Baron
    Scarsdale, 2806

Darwin, Erasmus, 3104-5
Davenport, Edward Davies, 2807
Davis, Henry, 2733, 2808
Dearden, James Arthur, 2368
Dee, John, 2749
Derby:
    Midland Railway Institute, 2342
    Philosophical Society, 3104-5
Derbyshire: county lib., 2423
Devey, Thomas 2809
Dibdin, Thomas Frognall, 2810
Dickinson, Arscott Sabine Harvey,
    2369
Digby, Sir Kenelm, 2785
Dr. Steevens' Hospital, Dublin, 2927
Dr. Williams' lib., London, 2819-20
Doddridge, Philip, 2577, 2579
Domestic libs see under Private libs
Doncaster:
    general, 2540
    mechanics' institutes, 2540
    public lib., 2540

    subscription lib., 2540
Donne, John, 2811-3
Donnelly, John, 2814
Dorset, John Frederick Sackville,
    3rd Duke, 2897
Douglas, Gavin, 2815
Douglas, James, 2619
Dow, Alexander, 2370
Down:
    general, 2541
    circulating libs, 2541
    monastic libs, 2541
    Repeal reading rooms, 2541
    school libs, 2712
    Sunday school libs, 2712
Drewery, Robert Forrester, 2371
Drummond, David, 3019
Dublin:
    general, 2542-3
    Archbishop Marsh's Lib., 2542,
    3016-7
    Co-operative Reference Lib., 3099
    Dr. Steevens' Hospital, 2927
    Irish Central Lib. for Students,
    2399
    National Lib. of Ireland, 2348,
    2745-6, 2850
    public lib., 2975
    Royal Dublin Society, 2361, 2745-6,
    2850
    St. Columba's College, 2590
Dumbarton: public lib., 2414
Dumfriesshire: county lib., 2408
Dunfermline: public lib., 2976
Durham:
    cathedral lib., 2668-9, 2682
    county lib., 2720
    mechanics' institutes, 2720
    monastic lib., 2682
Dyce, Alexander, 3029

Galashiels:
  general, 2552
  public lib., 2406
Gardiner, Edwin, 2828
Gardner, Frank, 2379
Gaskell, Elizabeth, 2829
Gaskell family, 2829
Gaster, Moses, 2635
Gateshead: public lib., 2997-8
Geological Society of London, 3044
George I, King of Great Britain and
  Ireland, 2855
George III, King of Great Britain and
  Ireland, 2830-1
Gibbon, Edward, 2832-3
Gifford, Andrew, 2573-4
Gisborne, Thomas, 3070
Glamorgan:
  general, 2979
  county lib., 2463, 2979
Glasgow:
  Andersonian Institution, 2566
  public lib., 2351, 2395, 2440,
  2454, 2950, 2980-1
  School of Art, 2755
  univ.lib., 2617-21, 2867
Glazier, George, 2380
Goodson, Richard, 2799
Gosse, Sir Edmund William, 2381
Gravesend:
  public lib., 2439
  subscription libs, 3107
Gray's Inn, London, 3053
Green, James, 2382
Greenhill School, Tenby, 2592
Greenock: public lib., 2355, 2437
Grierson, John, 2834
Grindal, Edward, 2835
Grosvenor Gallery Lib., London, 3100
Guernsey: public lib., 2982

Guildford: school lib., 2595
Guilford, Frederick North, 5th Earl,
  2874

Haig, Douglas, 1st Earl Haig of
  Bemersyde, 2836
Hales, Stephen, 2687
Halifax: public lib., 2456
Halliwell-Phillips, James Orchard,
  2837, 3125
Ham House, Surrey, 2865
Hamilton: public lib., 2454
Hammersmith: public lib., 2992
Hammond, John, 2863
Hampshire: county lib., 2341, 2451
Hanley: mechanics' institute, 2725
Hanover Square Unitarian Chapel,
  Newcastle upon Tyne, 2550
Hanson, Christopher Wharton, 2383
Hare, Henry Thomas, 2992
Hargreaves, Cyril, 2384
Harley, Edward, 2nd Earl of Oxford,
  2838-40
Harries, Edward Rhys, 2385
Harrison, Robert, 2386
Harrison, William, 2574
Harrod's Circulating Lib., Stamford,
  3092
Harvey, Gabriel, 2841
Harvey, William, 2842
Haslam, Daniel Denton, 2387
Hatfield Broad Oak, Essex: parochial
  lib., 2695
Hawarden: St. Deniol's Lib., 3037
Hawick:
  public lib., 2983
  subscription lib., 2983
Haworth, Mary, 2388
Hearne, Thomas, 2389
Heene, Sussex: general, 2554

Lewes, George Henry, 2819-20
Lewis family of Pilgrim's Hall,
Essex, 2858
Lhuyd, Edward, 2859
Librarians: general, 2336-9
for individual librarians see under
names
Librarianship: general, 2464-8
Libraries:
general, 2336, 2468, 2524-5
British Isles: general, 2393, 2465,
2476, 2511, 2526-32, 2677, 3135,
3152, 3154-9, 4689, 4940, for
individual libraries see under
names and places
Library (periodical), 2405
Library architecture, 2562, 2601,
2929, 2989-90, 2992
Library Assistant (periodical), 2453
Library Assistants' Association, 2447
Library Association:
general, 2337-9, 2375, 2387, 2405,
2424-5, 2444-6, 2464, 2502-11,
2528, 2951-2, 2954, 2994
County Libraries Section, 2512
Medical Section, 2513
Reference, Special and Information
Section, 2514
University and Research Section,
2519
Youth Libraries Group, 2515
Library Association Record, 2357
Library buildings: 2562, 2601, 2929,
2989-90, 2992
Library co-operation: general, 2480-3
Library Council (Ireland), 2399
Library education: general, 2424-5,
2465, 2489-91
Library equipment, 2960, 2989
Library furniture, 2531, 2755, 2759,

2762, 2769, 2775, 2780-2, 2865,
2989
Library history, study of, 2397,
3152-60
Library publishing, 2363-5, 2409,
2453, 2522-3
Library Review, 2409
Lichfield:
cathedral lib., 2671
public lib., 2340, 2988
Lightbown, Joseph, 2402
Linacre, Thomas, 2860
Lincoln College, Oxford, 2656
Lincoln's Inn, London, 3055-6
Lindisfarne: monastic lib., 2682
Lindsay, Alwxander William Crawford,
25th Earl of Crawford, 2861
Lindsay, James Ludovic, 26th Earl of
Crawford, 2861, 3030
Literacy, see under Reading
Litill, Clement, 2616, 2862
Liverpool:
Liverpool Lib., 2405, 3111
St. Paul's Young Men's Friendly
Society, 2713
univ.lib., 2628
Llanbadarn Fawr, Dyfed: parochial
lib., 2699
Llanelli: public lib., 2537
Lloyd, William, 2644
Lock, Reginald Northwood, 2403
London:
Architectural Association, 3026
Berridge House, Hampstead, 2571
British and Foreign Bible Society,
3032
British Lib., 2359, 2375, 2410-11,
2426-35, 2450, 2475, 2728-44,
2804-5, 2828, 2830, 2904-6
British Lib. of Political and

2342, 2397
univ.lib., 2629-30
Victoria and Albert Museum, 3028-9
War Office, 2400
Wellcome Historical Medical Lib.,
3071-2
Westbourne Park Institute, 2709
Whitelands College, 2639
Women's Service Lib., 3042
workers' libs, 2722-3
Worshipful Company of Clockmakers,
3046
Wye College, 2640
Longleat House, Wilts., 2916-7
Longmuir, George Watson, 2404
Lord, Lewis C., 3082
Loughborough: Univ. of Technology,
Department of Library and
Information Studies, 2492
Lovett, William, 2723
Lowery, Robert, 2715
Lucy family, 2863
Luton: public lib., 2379
Lyster, Thomas William, 2746

MacAlister, Sir John Young Walker,
2405
Macclesfield: public lib., 2995
McCorkindale, Neil Russell, 2406
McDonald, Francis Noel, 2407
MacKintosh, Charles Rennie, 2755
MacLachlan family of Kilbride, 2864
McLean, Mary, 2408
MacLeod, Robert Duncan, 2409
Madden, Sir Frederick, 2410-2, 2426
Magdalen College, Oxford, 2849
Magdalene College, Cambridge, 2420,
2882-4
Maidstone:
parochial lib., 2700

private libs, 2757
Maitland, John, 1st Duke of
Lauderdale, 2865
Malmesbury, William of, 2679-80
Malvern: public lib., 2417-9
Man, Isle of: parochial libs, 2701
Manchester:
Chetham's Lib., 3020
John Rylands Lib., 2368
public lib., 2368, 2829, 2950
Maria Grey College, Isleworth, 2567
Marine libs: general, 3062-4
Marsh, Narcissus, 2542, 3016-7
Martin, Stanley Walter, 2413
Martin, Tom, 2866
Martin, William McBarron, 2414
Maxwell, Sir William Stirling, 2618
Mechanics' institutes: general, 2634,
2715-6, 3091, 3137
Medical libs, 2405, 2630, 2790, 2844,
2927, 3065-72
Medical Library Association of Great
Britain, 2513
Melville, Andrew, 2867
Merton College, Oxford, 2657-8
Methuen family, 2868
Meyler's Circulating Lib., Bath, 3094
Middlesbrough: general, 3133
Middlesex:
general, 2549
county lib., 2347
Midland Railway Institute, Derby,
2342
Mildmay, Benjamin, Earl Fitzwalter,
2869
Miller, Kennard Desmond, 2415
Miners' institutes:
general, 3091
Wales, 2717-8
Mitchell Lib., Glasgow, 2351, 2395,

general, 3123
Artisans' Lib., 3000
mechanics' institutes, 3123
Medico-Chirurgical Society, 3067
Naturalists' Society, 3000
operatives' libs, 2724, 3123
public lib., 3000
temperance institutions, 2724
univ.lib., 2377
Nurses' libs, 3065

Oldham: Microscopical Society, 3087
Orford, Horace Walpole, 4th Earl,
2919-20
Oriental Club, London, 3050-1
Oriental studies: general, 3079-80
Osborne, Edgar, 2423
Ouseley, Sir Frederick, 2591
Owen, Wilfred, 2875-6
Oxford, Edward Harley, 2nd Earl,
2838-40
Oxford:
general, 2551, 3001
Bodleian Lib., 2389-90, 2393-4,
2449, 2461, 2644-53, 2785, 2856
Christ Church College, 2654, 2799
Institute Lib., 2551
Keble College, 2655
Lincoln College, 2656
Magdalen College, 2849
Merton College, 2657-8
monastic libs, 2682
New College, 2659
Pembroke Hall, 2835
public lib., 3001
Queen's College, 2835
St. John's College, 2660-1
Short's Coffee House, 2551
subscription libs, 2551, 3001
univ. lib., 2641-3, 2652, 2754

Univ. Society of Bibliophiles, 2516
Worcester College, 2922

Paddington: public lib., 2993
Paisley: public lib., 3002
Palmer, Bernard Ira, 2424-5
Panizzi, Sir Anthony, 2426-35, 2728
Parish libs: general, 2687-92
Parker, Frank, 3036
Parker, John, 2877
Parker, Matthew, 2607, 2685, 2878
Parker family, 2878
Parkes, James William, 2880
Parkhurst, John, 2585
Parochial libs: general, 2687-92
Partridge, Eric, 2743
Paston family, 2881
Patent Office Lib., London, 3083-4
Paton, William Bryce, 2436-7
Pembroke Hall, Oxford, 2835
Penzance: Royal Geological Society
of Cornwall, 3045
People's Palace, Stepney, 2398
Pepin, Harold Neville Percival, 2438
Pepys, Samuel, 2882-4
Personal libs: general, 2469, 2516,
2518, 2559, 2704, 2753-82, 2810,
2883, 3024, 3078, 3080, 3085, 3136
Petworth House, Sussex, 2901
Philip, Alexander John, 2439
Phillipps, Sir Thomas, 2593, 2885
Phillips, Thomas, 2624
Phillpotts, Henry, 3036
Pitt, Septimus Albert, 2440
Plymouth:
Athenaeum, 3124
Proprietary Lib., 3125
Pollard, Henry Graham, 2886
Pollen, John Hungerford, 2846
Polytechnic libs: general, 2563, 2565

St. Andrews:
friary lib., 2834
univ.lib., 2663-4
St. Columba's College, nr
Rathfarnham, 2590
St. David's Univ. College, Lampeter,
2624-5
St. Deniol's Lib., Hawarden, 3037
St. George's Chapel, Windsor Castle,
2714
St. John's College, Cambridge, 2609-
11
St. John's College, Oxford, 2660-1
St. Katharine's College, Tottenham,
2571
St. Margaret's Church, King's Lynn,
2546, 2697, 2985
St. Michael's College, Tenbury Wells,
2591
St. Nicholas's Chapel, King's Lynn,
2546, 2697
St. Nicholas's Church, Newcastle
upon Tyne, 2550, 3021
St. Paul's Young Men's Friendly
Society, Liverpool, 2713
Salisbury:
cathedral lib., 2672
circulating lib., 3092
Salt, William, 2553
Saltram, Devon, 2879
Sandhurst: Royal Military Academy,
3074
Savage, Ernest Albert, 2444-6
Sawley, Cambs.: monastic lib., 2685
Sayers, William Charles Berwick, 2447
Scarsdale, Nathaniel Curzon, 1st
Baron, 2806
Schmoller, Hans, 2899
Schmoller, Tanya, 2899
School libs: general, 2580-1

School of Slavonic and East European
Studies, London, 2448
Schurer, Heinz, 2448
Science libs: general, 3085
Science Museum, London, 2352-3,
3088-9
Science Reference Lib., London,
3083-4
Scotland:
general, 2534 for individual
libraries see under names and
places
public libs, 2962
Scottish Central Lib., Edinburgh,
2486-8
Scottish Library Association, 2520
Scrimgeour, Henry, 2900
Seafarers Education Service, 3064
Seamen's libs, 3062-4
Seely, Sir Charles, 2999, 3011
Selkirkshire: general, 2552
Sevenoaks:
public lib., 2401, 3004
subscription libs, 3004
Seymour family, Dukes of Somerset,
2901
Shachar, Yeshayahu, 2902
Shackleton, Robert, 2449
Sharp, Noel, 2450
Sheaf catalogues, 2490
Sheffield:
general, 2561
College of Technology, 2459
public lib., 2396, 2459, 3005
univ.lib., 2665
Univ. of Sheffield Postgraduate
School of Librarianship and
Information Studies, 2493
Sherry, Herbert Maurice, 2451
Shetlands: county lib., 2404